T0369425

GRAPHOTHERAPY
Write to Find Your Truer Self

MARIA MOULTON-BARRETT, M.D.

Order this book online at www.trafford.com
or email orders@trafford.com

Most Trafford titles are also available at major online book retailers.

Print information available on the last page.

ISBN: 978-1-4120-3436-4 (sc)

Trafford rev. 10/28/2019

 www.trafford.com

North America & international
toll-free: 1 888 232 4444 (USA & Canada)
fax: 812 355 4082

Upon this gifted age, in its dark hour,
Rains from the sky a meteoric shower
Of facts... they lie unquestioned, uncombined,
Wisdom enough to leech us of our ill
Is daily spun, but there exists no loom
To weave it into fabric.

Edna St. Vincent Millay, Sonnet #37

CONTENTS

ILLUSTRATIONS

PREFACE

The pages that follow are not written in the spirit of objectivity. Though intensely subjective, they are, I'm convinced, more universally applicable. They spring from the depth of years of lived experience, situated in the deepest part, within my house, somewhere deeper even than between Samuel Beckett's "the sea's froth and the ship's keel." It has been a struggle to induce and then record my free associations in an effort to capture the language of an eluding, laughing, crying, blaspheming, diamond-hard, and all-encompassing unconscious. It emerged at times with childish intonations. Even other people's writing about their own personal pursuit in understanding themselves and their times better, for instance N. Wiener's autobiographical study, yielded 'packets' of sudden recognition.

The process of free-associative writing required pages of

'unveiling.' Freud was right: afterwards one is amazed at the logical sequence in all these digressions. Seemingly unrelated memories arose and eventually allowed the pieces to be assembled into a more acceptable kind of 'sentence.' Many—far too many aspects of life as Carl Jung indicated—which should also have been experienced lie in the lumber-room among dusty memories; but sometimes, too, they are glowing coals under grey ashes. It is better, I think, to let these rejected alternatives come through to us, to make them surface, and acknowledge them as our own. The experiences told here may stir up and awaken such dreams in others.

It has occurred to me that I placed special emphasis on the physical aspect of the love life of middle-aged women. It is a time when so many of us are plagued by physical problems as well as emotional difficulties. If I am expressly attentive to physical details, it is because I believe too little has been said about its touching aspect, the beauty rather than the pathos which underlines sudden bodily transformations. The latter underscore the temporary weaning of certain hormones, and is followed at times by an immense upsurge of sexual appetites characteristic of the post and peri-menopausal stages. Skin impregnated by the spun threads of time, new love encounters can have an exquisitely delicate texture at this stage. With increasingly prolonged and more vigorously lived middle years, we are, I'm certain, in great need of a combination of different approaches.

Other women, more creative and literary than I, like Anais Nin, have written well of the "ever-recurring continuity in their love life." My own new experiences have tended to cause me to look back fearfully. First I was the sickly, emaciated, fourth and last child. Later I was considered the *petite peste* or *petite vipère*, the sharp tongued little viper my mother always urged my three unwilling older sisters to take along with them, until eventually they found a place for me—a far away convent situated on the shores of the cold, green North Sea, the white-edged waves thunderously rolling and breaking on the beach.

The child finally awoke, and tried to swim as fast as the tides. I have found her here—she sounds so ridiculously young coming from me at this stage. But this is just what it is about:

"They say that age makes people children;
I say it merely finds us still true children."
Goethe

The middle years of life's journey are a propitious time to turn inward and "take stock." The effort to understand the meaning of one's past experiences, might lead ultimately, to recognition, to the self-acceptance many of us have consummately reached for.

Our common experience as psychoanalysts, therapists of the mind and soul, healers of crises, comes across as repeatedly the same: "Get in touch with your feelings—don't intellectualize— let's find out what your real feelings are on a gut level" (the latter seems to occur only on a gynecologist's table, or something similar, and not in a psychotherapist's office). I've spent some thirty, forty, fifty years of my working life training, giving—and in some measure thereby receiving—therapy. I have encouraged patients to *free-associate, pursue what one is reminded of*—while keeping the censorship out wherever, whenever possible and feasible; and always, to bring the present of their dreams.

Often during individual therapy, while a patient was free associating with a dream, I have felt that the patient and I were running along the banks of a fast-flowing river. We kept up with its heaving currents, as well as with the counter waves brought on by the swollen seas toward which it sped. Ultimately diving in, we would join beneath the surface. I would eagerly tug them down to even murkier depths. These subterranean explorations lead us to aged rock-like structures. When able to dislodge them we would surface dripping with the clinging muck of old shame, gasping for clean breath, feeling somehow relieved, released in the end. During exceptional moments, we came dizzily close to earthly grace.

Their buried memories have not always haunted me, unlike my own, which continued to pursue me. I was inclined to talk about them too often, unable to send them away to their own house of reality where they belonged. I tried in the past to rid myself of them, but had not succeeded. I talked "around them" to Karen Horney, who had been my teacher. She dealt with the most pressing business on hand and said to me: "Study medicine or you will forever feel incomplete as a psychotherapist." I followed her advice. I left the new world I had loved, and went to study in Geneva, Switzerland. During my six years of training as a physician at the University of Geneva, I underwent a 'classical' didactical analysis with Dr. Charles Baudouin, then a Privat-Docent at the University, and Director of his own International Institute of Pedagogy and Psychotherapy. Pierre Favarger, my biochemistry professor and later a true friend, knew of him, and advocated strongly that I seek therapy with him. Baudouin was a Freudian-Jungian, non-directive, almost mute analyst. Mute, that is, except for offering good dream interpretations, which were to encourage me to explore my own nocturnal creations. He wrote down (I believed) all the material during the thrice-weekly sessions. I wrote my dreams down on the right side of the paper—that was essential, for one as he, who was not only a poet but strongly Jungian—and the left side was kept for that which came from the side of the heart, namely one's free associations which (I thought) he then wrote down. I typed my dreams for him for two solid years. When I did not bring a dream there was mostly silence. At the end of our work together, after two years, he said with good humor: "You can't scoop up the sea by spoonfuls, can you now? We might as well stop here." He returned the two hundred some sheets on which about a hundred dreams had been typed. His only imprimatur consisted of a sequential number in the upper right hand corner to indicate the order in which they followed one another. The left side of the paper was not written on—remained uninhabited…

I was certain he was one of the mutest analysts in Geneva at the time. Years later a brilliant scientist from Geneva, cynical in his outlook, asked me in passing,

"Ah, you knew Baudouin?"

"Do you mean the King of all Belgians, King Baudouin?" I asked in jest.

"No," he answered seriously, "the one who analyzed Kings."

"Well—", I said carefully, surprised by the above revelation, "vaguely—I've eventually read everything he wrote. Why?"

Said the cynic, "I used to think he talked too much… during therapy."

How could any one, I wondered, accuse Baudouin of talking too much? He taught well, and the analytical process ordained by him for me was a most valid one. He was a psycho-synthesist of sorts—an analyst fit for Kings.

This was true then. Now, many years later what is its validity in the light of the newness of experiences, the thousands of lives shared with our patients? How unaffected does one remain? What with the different demands made by life at this stage? Not that many provisions were made for re-examinations, for seeing to it that the initial process of 'a type of growth' by recognition and acceptance of where one tended to fall down, how this learning, this recognition was to be sustained, looked out for. I have read Fritz Perls at work with himself and Barry Stevens, too. I found these Gestalt Therapists' "Top Dog, Under Dog" technique of holding a dialogue with oneself in order to get to a more uninhibited state, inspiring and useful. I felt the best I might achieve in my time-constricted circumstances would be to follow their example and hold a series of self-analytic sessions. I felt in need of it, and patients, one in particular, provided the immediate impetus for it.

Thus the possibility of a specific *graphein* from the Gr. for writing, and *therapeuein*, to treat—more at self-therapy *graphotherapy*—emerged. This led to for instance: "taking stock" meaningfully, before turning to others for therapy of a specifically encountered unresolved problem. This might prove most advantageous, particularly when lengthy displacements (in space!), are not feasible, and could more than defray the expense of the fee for examination and analysis by a trusted and willing therapist. Shattering at times, exhilarating even, are two of the adjectives that come to mind about the work of Graphotherapy. Feedback comes through inner feelings of resolution, and no one knows that moment better than oneself.

Writing is a sharing with the world in which we live. Language is a discipline which by its channeling into readable prose or poetry, imposes its own universal and unavoidable rules. Not a day in my long life has gone by without my having been made aware of the positive outcome for people who have written enquiringly about specifically stressful experiences in their life with the goal of understanding what truthfully occurred. The endeavor of describing according to the preordained rules one follows while writing with as little moral censorship as feasible and its consequential obtainment of relief of anguish, has lead one to speculate about the many creative endeavors of mankind. It would seem likely that many an artist in his/her chosen field, might have survived for as long as some have been able to, despite their emotional difficulties, because they've succeeded in channeling their creativity, their apparitions, visions, sounds, and theorems, into a recognizable language, with its own rules. Though we remember that Lacan assigns to language the role of structuring all social relations between humans, we are still unraveling the art of translating from the language of the Unconscious (primary process) into the language in which we usually live.

The *Graphotherapy* book which follows is of the nature of a self-analysis at a mature point in life. The free association section is preceded by chapters of biography. These introduce the contesting characters. The free association work begins with a dream about a major conflict, namely "The Love for an Elliptical Admirer," which the "Mephistopheles Dream" has evoked. The important relationship with a mathematician named Claude to which it refers remains painfully in need of greater understanding—even resolution as one describes such in analysis. The process whereby past attitudes are analyzed evolves into a learning experience about the NOW. By shedding blame, and shame, and unconsciously held assumptions about the moral behavior of others, a greater responsibility for the subjective self is gradually and finally assumed.

The first free association exercise is followed by a rather daringly candid description of a series of adventurous "Reaching Out to Others" experiences during a particularly vulnerable period when "Grandfather Incest" followed by "Carlos in the House of Yu" make their appearance.

The work done in this Graphotherapy book is based on Karen Horney's theories which evolved from Freudian premises about the etiology of neuroses. Horney's and Jung's assumptions about the moral, and religious strivings of the unconscious, surprisingly imposed themselves within the context of this work. I was often reminded of the stress that Sandor Ferenzci placed on the changes which occur in one's state of mind during one's analysis, and by extension during any psychotherapy; an approach which as far as I know none of Freud's other early associates were that cognizant of.

I used Gestalt therapy techniques in order also to arrive at a better feeling contact with the subjective self. I placed myself—as any analyzand does—on the postmortem slab for examination and diagnosis. I learned a lot and hope this might prove to be a good method of teaching self-analysis through Graphotherapy. Learning through example is what I always sought in the writings of others. Greater, honest self-expressiveness in writing has become acceptable for men and now for women too, hopefully leading in the end to better ways of applying preventive therapy.

AN INTRODUCTION: WHO AM I?

In Flemish Antwerp, in Belgium, there is a small group of people who devote their not inconsiderable skill and passion to the country's renowned diamond industry. They are involved in the business of cutting, sorting, and setting diamonds; much of the work is meant for locally-designed jewelry. A few concern themselves mainly with diamonds meant for industries located in distant corners of the world. Most of those involved in the selling and buying are called diamond brokers. They pass their precious and scintillating merchandise to one another on the basis of a promise—on one's honor—to abide by one's word. In such a manner, for a mere handshake, a throw of the hand, accompanied by the ritualistic pronouncement of "Mazel en Bruhe," which literally means good luck and may this exchange be blessed, millions of dollars' worth of merchandise pass from one person to another. This takes place in the form of a crackling, though silky, parchment-like paper, a small rectangle lined with a barely perceptible, bluish cotton layer. When filled, this specially folded small wrap is called by the chosen members of the diamond trade "a packet."

Legend has it that the name Antwerp is derived from the phrase "Hand Werpen," which means "to throw the hand." This is based on the story of a mythological Roman giant, Druon Antigonus, who supposedly cut off the hands of those mariners who sailed past his castle without paying tolls, and threw them in the Scheldt, the wide river which connects with the important harbor of Antwerp by extensive locks. The river traverses the city which sprawls on its east bank, with its many spiraling slate-roofed cathedrals silhouetted against luminous grey skies. Antwerp is only fifty-five miles away from the North Sea and its famed North winds which carry the pungent scent of seaweed. They also carry the clavichord harmonies which strike hourly on the carillons of Antwerp's oldest cathedral, into the fabric of children's windswept, chiming dreams in these parts of the Flanders lowlands.

By the time we reach the fall season of our life, we carry certain treasured packets with us against all odds. This is what my mother carried alone, during WWII right from under the noses of the thugs, the thieves, the murderers who wanted what belonged to her alone. They were cherished burdens to her, and she carried them sewn to the linings of intimate undergarments she wore over the softly cascading folds of her aging and silken skin. They were packets of preciously retained wealth, symbolizing the fullness of her past and the richness of our own personal history. She said she must carry these multifaceted treasures for the sake of our future, as well as for her own. Although burdened by their weight, she fled, as though programmed by her genetic history's imperatives. Now, I too carry some of these same burdens, a few of the packets symbolically sewn to my own intimate apparel. At times I have found them cumbersome, and I attempted to forget they were there. They got in my way, especially when I was young and I wished I could place them, as my parents did, in their respectable safes, and respond to the demands on hand in the jewelry store of my own life.

I like running my own practice. Just as my father gloried in his diamond expertise, his secret love of colored stones and very old paintings, so I take pride now in what I have learned. It has taken a long time to come to fruition. Now that I am almost at the age he was when he died, I only take on and work with the patients I believe I can help. My mother reproached him for a similar tendency: "Be an opportunist—look out for yourself— *Carpe Diem*—Your family comes first!" Her agonized reproaches I now hear for myself. I took as long as forty years to let her go on her own, and ultimately to realize I had earned her respect. She was a fighting mountain of a woman, remonstrative, half-maddened by life especially during WWII. Much later, when she died—she was nearly eighty—I finally accepted the truth others had long known. For in the heart beneath her smooth breasts, she treasured only one of her four daughters as a memorable and true ruby. I, certainly, wasn't the one.

SECTION ONE
Memoirs

CHAPTER 1

Clara

A lesson learned in middle adulthood, and a theory or an idea can be more deeply and more gratefully felt than earlier in life. When Harry S. Searles lectured us one summer and touchingly defended his original conviction that patients and therapists are innately therapeutic to one another, this was such a lesson learned. The child in his dependency was described by him as therapeutic to the mother who needs to nurture; at the same time, her desire to love is therapeutic to the child's ever-wanting receptivity. Patients in their dependency are therapeutic to the therapist. The healer needs to heal, nurture, console. We feel that the situation demands us to play mother, father, or some other significant person—and the patient usually lets us.

We play silent witness, or loving presence, in therapeutic response to them. With how many dreams do they present us— a present, an offering—in order to please our own unconscious needs of omnipotence, our need to be their healers? This is less complicated than it sounds. When one's analyst is, say a Jungian, one has Jungian dreams. Were he or she to be mainly Freudian, incestuous cravings will come to the fore more often than with a neo-Freudian therapist. As a result of Searles' hypothesis, I recognized that some of my patients had been inclined recently to delve into my personal life and that this might stem as much from a response to their therapeutic attempts towards me as to themselves.

One such, Clara, infiltrated my past. Did I encourage this? She learned from inscriptions in books she borrowed from me that I had once deeply loved a man named Claude. His picture hung in my office, and, curiously enough, the first time she came to see me she asked if this were my father. She wanted to know all about him and me. Whenever feasible I spoke the truth. She insisted my present knew too much void. I could have dismissed her need to know me better as a simple avoidance technique, a way of not coming to grips with her own problems, but I preferred Searles' explanation.

How was one to react to Clara, this often dying, beautiful swan of 23 years? She was after all, barely surviving not yet reborn—consumed by what was provisionally diagnosed as a not necessarily fatal lung disease. It required chemotherapy and frequent irradiations with dreadful aftermaths. At those times she asked to come to my office which was located near the hospital where she was given treatments.

Clara. Waiting. Longing, lonely warm summer nights. The moon reflecting on the blue still water in our backyard pool. Silver fringed black clouds speed by at night, pulsed by southern winds; they remind one the sea is less than two hundred miles away.

My fifteen year old son has left for Anchorage today. He was with me only fourteen days. He looks suddenly like a tall oriental prince with enormous, velvety warm brown eyes. His back is as straight as his English grandfather's. He has large hands with long fingers as my father's were. They are those of a fine jeweler's grandson. A reflective, rather absent-minded smile is forever on his lips. His skin, dark from the sun, has the matte texture of flower petals. His cheeks have the powdered blush of peaches. His chest still has ripples of female curviness. A haze, a softness, envelops him: his is an ephemeral, sudden beauty, like young trees in bloom in the early spring. We were surrounded by gardens where pink and purple dog-wood trees were bursting with flowers; the sweet scent of honeysuckle, springing up around the nooks of doors and garden walls overtook us. The two weeks he spent home fled by faster than an hour. When he left I felt I must light candles and cover the furniture, the house seemed that abandoned. My daughter too was gone for the summer. But the void filled itself with demands from patients, and Clara had come that afternoon for an hour on an emergency call, so others had to wait and appointments had to be adjusted.

The last patient left around ten that evening. I roamed about the house picking up after whatever the boy might have forgotten. It was midnight. The doorbell rang. Hearing an imploring female voice I opened the door but was astonished to see it was Clara who had left my office a few hours ago. She entered the hallway; she literally flew in, and I felt the flutter of wings that came from the ethereal silk of her flowing dress, as she uttered little shrieks. Her inarticulate cries, long delicate claws on my face made my hair stand up with fear. The house suddenly echoed with her high-pitched voice. As she calmed down finally, she became like a lost babe abandoned on my doorstep. As she fluttered past me, I could smell vapors of heavy liquor—pure gin Martinis for sure. And what else? I took her extended hand and led her into the office. I felt dizzy with the mere scent of alcohol that filled the air immediately. I begged her to tell me what had gone wrong. There were little inarticulate sounds, a struggle, and finally: "I just had to come—I just have to be with you, near you. Let me kiss you, please, please... " She'd obviously gone off the beam.

"My God! You want mothering, Clara! Come, I love you too, as a daughter, my son. Let me make you some tea... Too many Martinis... "

Dearest Clara,—it's wonderful to feel needed, desired—especially tonight. I dashed to the kitchen. If she changed her mind and became brutal, I preferred it to be in the kitchen for some reason. She joined me and she began to cry.

Clara, how will I ever tell you how tempting a very young woman you are? How warmly attractive—but not to me, not ever, love... That late night, pathetically forlorn, Clara and I dueled with words, with gestures, with feelings. She pushed a few chairs around, spoke her mind boldly and said she wanted to come up to my bedroom with me. I spoke words I regretted as soon as I heard them. "If I'd known you'd go into all this acting out... I would have refused to take you on... "

She was hurt. I reached for her hands and touched her silky long blond hair, her ever so clever head, and held her large face between my hands, my eyes meeting the green studded pools of hers, reassuringly. I held her delightfully feminine hands. They felt consolingly warm and soft against my calloused palms. I fed her and watched her eagerly drink the ritualistic tea. Her tears, her soft hands uncannily evoked the absence of my daughter.

In the beginning of her therapy she said I reminded her of a

European aunt on her mother's side she'd found helpful in her growing years. While in Manhattan she had a rather successful career as a model in view of her good height and finely boned body. She also had exquisite features and looked exotic with a middle European type of panache. For long months while in the city, she felt cold and feverish all the time. Her friends laughed at her as she walked around in furs in Manhattan's sweltering July heat. Finally she was diagnosed here in town with cancer of the lung's nymph nodes, probably not immediately fatal. Following threats of suicide and too much involvement with her "savior" internist she was referred to me.

The therapeutic interaction between us was intense from the beginning. Transference was highly positive and her internal medicine specialist in oncology must have sighed with relief. She was groping for an identity that was more acceptable to her. The wretched illness kept cropping up, and we were back to the fearful, dependent young woman who wanted a strong and consoling hand to hold hers. I thought she ought to take time off from some of her studies and get back to writing. She was creative in the literary sense. But Death itself became an intimate companion to our interactions. And then there was great hope again when for the second, or was it the third time, she'd overcome what had seemed a hopeless struggle.

During Clara's midnight session it was hard to retract the hurtful words she heard me say. After an hour, she drove off to return to her young husband who anxiously waited for her at their new apartment. A few days later she said it had made her feel enormously good (though she was heavily inebriated and under the influence) to have been able to approach me assertively. She felt "she'd been up to a man's approach". (I thought that was nothing to gloat over.) We resumed work together where we left off. Still, this was the last of the acting out behavior she did with me. Was I ever ambivalent with her about wanting her for a friend instead of a patient? Yes, and no. In view of the nature of her physical illness, I opened up, no doubt, more than I usually would, but not to the point where she wanted to take me. Why not? Isn't heterosexuality, to the extreme exclusion of other modalities, a culturally biased impoverishment of possible experiences? That might be so. But if one does not stir from within in response to another's want, why call it negation of the senses?

You cannot be a healer wanting for yourself with your patients, for you'll hurt them in the end. To enter into "incestuous relationships" with patients (for such I consider they would be) cannot possibly help the situation. Were I to consider the practice of indulging in this type of self-serving parenting, I could not escape the knowledge that such was possibly one of the great difficulties experienced from the beginning by a hyper-vulnerable individual. Touching is good. I agree. Beyond immediacy it is the heart that must be touched. After nearly a half century in practice, your nose says so—Follow it.

Not too long after our midnight interaction, Clara sent me a letter which moved me deeply, for one of the lines referred to what she really felt about our interactions:

"… You are afraid. Afraid to feel. Afraid to connect… Distances… never to be transgressed if one remains the doctor and the other the patient… I don't care what you do with your life. That is your business. But be honest about it. Don't rationalize. Do you think because you are a Doctor and 50 that you know everything there is to know and ergo your Life should be over? *He was often visited by attacks of devastating remorse, Because his casual cynical present was the original future of those past Days.* [Sartre: The Age of Reason].

… You are not dead yet."
'You know not how to love, you know not how in vain I love you so, you know not how to love, you know not how and you shall never know… ' [Sartre]

She perceived an "empty nest syndrome" which she thought I remedied by holding on strongly to the past, and that I indulged cynically in casual sex adventures. In my estimation this was not entirely correct. Nevertheless, her attempts at filling what she perceived to be a void within me led to the strange acting out behavior on her part. I found this coming from her, as a patient, sufficiently threatening to induce careful self-scrutiny. I have often reminded myself of the fact that ambulatory patients, however screwed up they might otherwise be, are functioning as ordinary beings a good deal of the time. Patients are innately therapeutic to the therapist, Harry Searles had said that summer, and Clara precipitated that long overdue self-analysis. I have remained forever lovingly indebted to her compelling person.

CHAPTER 2

Dix Ans Avant—Geneva Revisited

At that time, surprisingly, I experienced a new and strong love. It seemed astounding that it should blossom within a few months into inexpressible, unsurpassed fulfillment. The experience of a new tone of feeling, a certain lasting pleasurable emotion, intense, equal to delight, was a revelation. Ultimately, at the very peak of that stage, I felt whole for the first time; it seemed that all the pieces fit together.

When I met this younger man, I had been alone for some eight months. Circumstances had come about which equaled being a separated wife again. We became acquainted accidentally; we had adjoining seats on an airplane flying out of the area in north-western New York to which my family and I had moved the previous year. We were to continue together, fortuitously, on a similar airline via New York to the South of France. He spoke French fluently and with great clarity, and much to my pleasure,

I found music in his English intonations. The gentleness in his manner almost made one wonder if he were, perhaps, rather effeminate. He had silky, flaxen hair, strands of which fell attractively over his dark-rimmed glasses. He appeared rather unassuming physically. Because of his extreme fairness and light blue eyes, he reminded me of a Swiss resident physician whom I had worked for and lived with during the last part of my medical studies at Geneva University. I thought of Switzerland a great deal when I met this kind stranger, for I was to revisit there following a short holiday in France. I was to visit new people in old surroundings—or perhaps the opposite? My first impression of his unassuming physique and manner was what the French call *un bien brâve homme*. His two children, who were approximately the same age as mine, and his wife, all of Welsh nationality, were at home in England, I discovered, though the family resided on the South coast of France at the time. He had been in America only a few days, and his car was waiting at the airport in Nice. When we landed in Nice itself, he offered to drive us to our flat, some distance away at Juan-les-Pins. In the 3rd floor apartment—my sister's delightful summer residence, which he seemed to enjoy—he lingered on, excitedly. It appeared that he stayed just a short while longer than expected. The children and I were also loath to see this youthful and helpful travel companion of some hours leave us. We invited him to visit us if he should return to America. He had been in that section of New York as a science consultant, and was employed at the time by an American electronics manufacturing firm. (I myself was employed by the Children's Division of one of New York State's Hospitals). He was obliged to travel a lot and was to leave again within a few days, and since we, too, were only passing by, we would not be able to get the families together.

An impression lingers—the difference in attitude on the part of the men towards me as a woman in this new near middle-age stage while in Juan-les-Pins. Compared to the previous times I had been able to spend a few days there—a mere 'few years' earlier—like ten years or five years perhaps?—I sensed the change. At first I attributed it to the fact that my husband had previously visited us here. This time I was walking about mostly with the children, or else roaming the crowded streets alone, especially with the art galleries open until two in the morning, I could not help but take note. During the daytime some men would pass us by on the promenade and utter audibly: *Les beaux enfants! La jolie petite!* They complimented me on the good looks of the children, of my little girl this time around. I remember a young photographer in particular who came up to me one late evening, and asked "*Seule?*" Alone? I smiled, flattered, expecting to be asked out for a coffee, as had happened in the recent past—five years or so earlier. Instead, he asked "If you're interested, I can do things for you." What made me flee was the leering look in his eyes, defiant, angry, unloving. He certainly wasn't offering me photographs but I did not know what exactly he meant for me to buy from him. But then when an old hairdresser whispered, not to be heard by his assistants, the exact same words I began to wonder in truth what had happened to me. As usual I attributed their change in attitude to my not being the nymphetted creature I still aspired to become! I thought I evidently looked lonely, and that they could sense this. I felt ashamed. Did I perhaps look much the *cocotte*—the floozy? Had the three Ks taken their toll, certainly at least "Kinder and Kúche"?[1] Regarding the first K, I could only thank fate for having made them singularly open, and contented seeming children. Regarding the second K, from the day we settled in, mornings they might fetch breakfast of

---

[1] *Kinder, Kuche, Kinder*—the three German domestic virtues of children, kitchen, and church.

fresh buns and eggs by themselves, frequenting the shops along the promenade bordering our apartment house. My six-year-old son would hurriedly set the table on the veranda under a brightly colored parasol, while my eight-year-old daughter came to tell me of the latest adventures encountered during their shopping. After we consumed a leisurely cooked breakfast and cleaned up hurriedly we scurried to the beach, where they spent much time with new found friends. These were two delightfully mannered American children of their own ages, polyglots, as they resided in Geneva. Their tall, blonde, good-looking mother was having a calm affair with a heavy-tongued, sturdily built Schweitzer Bürger, who would not let her out of his sight. He was a school teacher in Geneva and taught languages. As is usual with native polyglots, he spoke no language well. When the American children's father appeared on the scene, lying next to us on the beach in the place usually occupied by the Schweitzer Bürger, no one appeared to take notice. The Swiss fellow simply did not show up again. Nor was his disappearance alluded to during conversations between the regulars like me, who met daily at the same beach and were assigned a paying mattress to lie on. I watched her sadness. Her husband, unusually fine featured, was quite attractive, but a strange haziness, like a mist, surrounded his gestures, his posture. There was a hesitance about him, an incompleteness, such as one might detect around an identical twin, (although he claimed he was not one). The boy had gone, but I could not sense the man in him.

We had had a marvelously recuperative time at Juan-les-Pins—it was not as crowded then as it has since become. From there, I returned to the birthplace of Calvin and Calvinism. While to the rest of Switzerland Geneva signifies inexplicably, a kind of New York City—a town of light and of light morals, constantly overrun by foreigners—to me it has always been a place of narrow, rather humorless application. As a student there, a decade earlier, my thoughts had often gone back to the Free University of Brussels in Belgium, where idealism and freedom of political thought formed an exciting part of a student's life. (It had been a shock to find, on admission to Geneva University, that one was required to sign a document to the effect that one would abstain from all political activity.) With my children, I was now taken around the bio-chemistry laboratories and the new bio-chemistry research institute by Professor Pierre Favarger. Despite the professor's kind welcome and his obvious amusement at playing the guide to a former pupil, I quickly fell victim again to that feeling of awe which I had labored under as a student here. Even during the warm vacation month of August the empty laboratories retained that cold, forbidding look I remembered so well. The spirit of the university lay heavy here, a spirit of ageless and untouchable traditions, whose incarnation was the unseen, unreachable University Administration Board. No, here at least things did not change.

I imagined that the large number of students who would be starting in September would still be considered persons of no importance, and that the main preoccupation of the university would still be to decimate their ranks by a cruel sequence of eliminatory examinations—the mortality rate would be about fifty per cent. (I would remember that much, as I nearly left them my own life at the examinations which followed the first two years of studies). At the time of my admission, Swiss nationals were in the minority, outnumbered by far by the Americans, most of whom were World War II veterans. The collective noun for them was 'The Savages,' as distinct from 'The Oriental Princes' for the Arab and Israeli students. For the few of us foreigners who spoke French—usually better-sounding than what the Swiss themselves spoke—and for many fine Americans, doors were cautiously, but then widely opened. Friendships of lasting quality developed. Friendships which would shape destinies.

A new admissions policy which favored foreign students from the underdeveloped countries had now played havoc with the American students, who had to emigrate to countries like Mexico and Italy. Their adjustment in those countries was less happy. The Swiss felt they were not obligated any longer to pay for the education of America's future physicians. I could understand this, but felt sad for the boys and girls from the U.S.A. They had been happy here in my days, and their studies had prepared them well for their future medical development. I also felt they had become humanized by their prolonged exile in Switzerland. Some had come as boys, gaudily dressed, too loud-voiced, and rather ill-mannered. They left happily as well-spoken, bilingual, informed men. On the Swiss scale I stood somewhere between the half American "Savage" and the "Oriental Princess". There was not much I could do about it, especially as for six years I had hidden my status of divorcée student.

I was allowed to work at the University Psychiatric Hospital from early on in my medical studies. The hospital then had a population of between 600 and 800 beds, with some additional space in the Neurological Service of the University Cantonal (county) Hospital in town. The psychiatric hospital, innocently called *La Clinique Bel-Air*, was situated on the Swiss side of the 3,300 foot high Salève Mountains, on the outskirts of Geneva, and about five minutes by car from the French border. Getting to the hospital was a hard struggle for a student who lived in town and was usually penniless. I remember the windswept and hungry mornings, the snowbound ground over which I hurried to catch the 7 o'clock train, and the heavy fog that rolled over each mountain toward its neighbor. The fog of Geneva winter mornings… it made us greet each other with "good-evening" when we met in the cafés following the first morning classes. On arrival, I would squeeze along with four or five others into the office of Dr. Mutrux, who ten years later was still Associate Director. Dr. Mutrux was always extremely kind to me; it was only later that I learned of the bets he had placed with his colleagues that I would very quickly throw up Geneva, return to America, get a Ph.D. in psychology, practice lay-analysis, and make a fortune (as he supposed every one over there did).

The purpose of our morning gathering was the weekly diagnostic session with Professor F. Morel. Before being privileged to attend these meetings, it had been made clear to me what heresies I must avoid if my presence was to be tolerated. This was 1950-1953: Trained as I had been during my pre-medical years by the Gestalt Psychology School in New York, and then in psychoanalysis by Karen Horney and Raymond de Saussure, I freely wielded interpretations based on neurotic conflicts. *Neurotic conflicts? Why? Where?* The Professor's unlined, youthful face, (though he was nearly sixty years old), registered surprise and acute displeasure. And would Mademoiselle have the kindness to indicate to him where in the Brain Substance such conflicts could be localized, which set of neurons would be included which he and his neuro-physiologists could examine through their microscopes, following the death of the patient? This was almost too much to bear, it was clear. It was bad enough, he was obviously thinking, that I was a woman, and therefore a disturbing influence on his male patients, but much worse, my head was full of this unscientific nonsense. He was known as a misogynist. There I was, my teeth chattering after my polar trek, shy, ashamed of my own thoughts, never asked to give my opinion. No wonder that, in the many sessions I attended with the Professor and his assistants, not once did I open my mouth. I felt grateful for small blessings, for at least he called me Mademoiselle, unlike our impressive professor of pathology, Dr.Ruthishouser, who would question the veracity of the appellation whenever given the opportunity to do so in a male-dominated crowd.

I never quite learned how and what Professor F. Morel felt about another man. One case only remains outstanding in my mind: his use of the German term "Beziehungswahn" to describe ideas of reference. He spoke of this kind of folly with a passion. I remember when he diagnosed a rather young-looking man who seemed most unhappy with the thoughts about his wife's supposed deception: her imaginary lover was placing some ill-defined poison in his house by a hidden underground road which led to his garbage bin. When one of the foreign assistants—who like myself was inclined toward heresy—namely psychoanalysis—described the sexual habits of this patient as part of his background history—among others that his wife performed fellatio with him—a dead silence fell. I was carried away by the prevailing atmosphere allusive to what I believed suddenly transpired as a perversion (why else mention it?) I felt self-conscious for the first time of being the only woman in the room. Uncomfortable, I rustled in my seat, overcome by shame as if I had confessed aloud just then to a love for exotic sex every night of the week. The professor was obviously displeased with the information, which he regarded as useless—or was he? Not one word was spoken later of possible antecedent tensions in the man.

On the other hand, Professor Morel's lectures were quite

clear and beyond the range of textbooks, especially with respect to the more demonstrable and physically founded illnesses of the mind. A disease of the skull which affects the brain's functions was named after him when he identified it as the Syndrome of Morel-Morgani. That was rather good in view of the fact that the professor was nearly forty years old when he switched from a religious order and began his studies of medicine. I will always maintain that some rumors about him which circulated among us when we were students were not totally unfounded, namely, that patients seemed to Professor Morel to be future slides to be scrutinized for ultimate signs under the microscope. It was said that he therefore paid special attention to the diet of his establishment, as a thin person's brain slides were difficult to stain and thus to study. Whatever was said among us at the time, in 1952, he did give the order to get rid of the camisoles (straight jackets) at Bel-Air. When he died in 1959, Professor J.d'Ajuriaguerra, a Basque exile from France, was named in his place. The order given by him was to destroy the camisoles— things were to change indeed. A psychiatric client, an old *habitué* of Bel-Air, became truly human and of primary interest to someone at last. Perhaps for the first time in Geneva's history human dignity entered Bel-Air, and this with an all-pervasive strength. From what we saw on our return visit, things must have followed a steadily improving course. The bars had been taken off the windows, and relatives and visitors had lost some of the awe which the clinic had inspired in them for years. The press came to see things the new Professor's way. Radio and television broadcasted a series of discussions on mental health which were recorded at the clinic. On the night of the first television showing, the new Professor was heard to say to his assistants in his deeply Spanish accented French, "Let's go and see if we look like conmen or artists." It was four years after the arrival of the new director when we sauntered around with Dr. Mutrux, and we saw two new buildings and remarkable changes within the old ones. The large lawns, so stern looking in the past, bloomed with flowers, and the entire hospital, which is beautifully situated near the Alp and Jura mountain chain, seemed now a most pleasant temporary abode for the ill. The new wards were large and sunny and comprised at most thirty patients. They were entirely open, with enormous bay windows running the full length of the three sides. A heavy and rather steep concrete staircase, covered with red vinyl tile, ran from the fourth side of each ward to an enormous square room, where numerous forms of occupational therapy were carried on simultaneously. We were told that many of the prominent American women living in Geneva came voluntarily to work with the patients in these activities. This was greatly appreciated. The large bay windows were totally of glass… Unbreakable glass? I wondered. Dr. Mutrux smiled at the question and told me that so far no-one had even tried to break them. I muttered, half aloud, half to myself, "and would it not have been worth it, even if someone had tried?" Worth it for the unspeakable joy of feeling free and unhampered, a feeling denied to hundreds of inmates over the years… would it not have been worth it?

Much of Professor d'Ajuriaguerra's success with the people of Geneva was due I believe, to his rather unassuming, extremely witty and lively personality. Above all, in every one of his ideas and decisions he was impregnated by an enormous respect for the needs and feelings of his fellow men. Another important element was his deeply artistic temperament, so often found, but not always recognized among scientists. His love of sculpture and painting remained with him throughout his challenging travails as Asylum Director, and he convinced local artists to exhibit their works on a permanent basis in the gardens of Bel-Air. His complete success with the people of Geneva was no doubt due above all to his ability to convey to them his personal, most fundamental belief that without liberty life is not worth living. On the afternoon of our re-visit we met personally with him and his vivacious Corsican wife.

Two weeks later, in August of that year following our return to America, I met the Professor again, but this time in New York City, where I was able to reciprocate his hospitality. As I had promised his wife, I drove him to the hospitals he wanted to see here. As we climbed, at the mere touch of a finger, to the fortieth floor of the New York Hilton in the elevator, someone asked him if he had ever gone so high. "Only in the Alps… " he answered in a whisper. On parting in Switzerland his wife had nervously implored, *"Occupez-vous de mon mari."* (Do take care of my husband). I kept my word to her, but in the U.S.A. this encounter rapidly took on shades of the French farce *Occupez-vous d'Amélie*. You can no doubt guess who was eventually taking care of whom. I felt most impressed by his sharp, clear delineations in any given situation that involved human interactions. I found it astounding that when he was psycho-analyzed he could never remember anything, absolutely nothing, which preceded his twelfth year, and never had since. I believe he was my senior by more than a decade, and I felt flattered when his "aloneness" in the metropolis caused him to cling fondly to me. He was quite openly fascinated by women in general, and part of his life pivoted playfully around this interest. His fond kindness towards me I received gratefully. In his presence I felt womanly again. Have I said he was a Spaniard from the Basque country? His advice to me regarding the personal problems I occasionally mentioned to him: the work at the hospital with the incarcerated children? *C'est un travail à longue échéance…* A work in progress for years. I felt regretfully that I did not have that much time. In regard to my marriage? "Impossible situation—you must get out of it at once!" He might have been a matador who had just killed a bull readying to bow to public acclaim. He was most emphatic in this short pronouncement. "But then," I asked on the verge of panic, "how would leaving their father affect our children?" With a great smile he said, "What's the difference? He was never there!"

My advice to him? "Learn to count in English!" He refused. He had arrived in New York City with hundreds of single bills folded in his right pocket. Whatever change he received he placed in his left pocket. He refused to be distracted by what he called "useless information" of the kind that made one have to learn to count foreign currency! He asked only one non-technical question during his stay, "How old are you?"

"Guess," I suggested. He pinched—too hard I felt—the skin under the fold of the upper arm and said seemingly with smiling expertise "By the texture of the skin not a day over twenty-five." I laughingly admitted to being as old as Happy Rockefeller, who was much in the news at the time.

One day while walking the streets of Manhattan, we turned a corner near Fifth Avenue. I remember then seeing the face of Martin Luther King for the first time. We had chanced upon a televised broadcast of him at a large Washington gathering through a shop window. I watched his face and felt drawn by a magnetic field and was overcome by sympathy for him. I burst out crying. I barely knew of him then, but was stirred by ancient memories in response to King's potently dignified deportment. The quiet, contained anger, symbolized by the way in which he communicated his admirable determination to reach out for change. I felt touched as if by an atavistic remembrance—my mother's people, the miracle rabbis pursued by centuries of hate. The hurt in the determination. I remembered the agony I had seen in the eyes of the abandoned people during WWII in their internment camps in the Bordeaux region of France. I had not thought of these faces until I saw them again through King's expression. Unable to stop crying I held on painfully to the professor's arm. I shook him and cried out, "God, they are going to have to fight—there is no other way!" The Professor was quiet and watched me quizzically. I believe I was as one taken by a fright. I think it was the first time in adulthood that something different of this nature was happening inside of me. I began to realize that with the onset of menopause the equilibrating mechanisms were markedly slowed up.

I left him in the care of another woman professional who was to travel with him to a meeting in California. He said to me in parting, more in a statement than a question,

"*Y'a un nouveau coco.* There's a new guy on the scene?"

Yes, there was, for on my return home from New York, following on the heels of the Professor's departure, three months earlier, the kind and unassuming Welsh scientist who had driven us from the airport in Nice to my sister Fanny's apartment in Juan-les-Pins had, to my great surprise, indeed come to call on us.

On the Way to Sayre, Pa., watercolor

CHAPTER 3

Indian Summer

He was to remain for a few days in our area, and at first visited only occasionally. When his work required a longer, yet indeterminate stay, he came on weekends. When I was on duty at the hospital, he frequently remained in town to be helpful. My housekeeper at the time was Mrs. Elizabeth Thomas, a kindly, well-spoken, heavily bespectacled, middle-aged American woman. Though emaciated looking, she was actually quite sturdy and took pride in her physical well-being—appearances to the contrary. Married to a blind man, they managed together to raise eight children from various marriages. I owe her my job, for though my husband was unemployed at the time, I was unable to go to work in my new position (where I was needed), unless seconded by dependable help. The powers at the hospital scrambled through the New York State Employment Office, and this was how Mrs. Thomas came to us. I also owe her my prolonged peace of mind. While she worked for us she said it would influence the children too strongly were she to tell them about her religious beliefs, so she never did.

Unless urged, she rarely commented on our new visitor 'from abroad'. Was she somewhat attached to my husband, Henry? Although she feared his outbursts of temper, she said she liked him. I suspect she really appreciated the culinary expertise he taught her.

Our new acquaintance's visits became predictably regular. My nine-year-old daughter would listen for hours on end with him to an English recording of Alice in Wonderland that he had found for her. He had brought my seven-year-old son a small microscope, and together they looked at slides; we listened to music whenever he came. True to his reputation as a Welshman, he was extremely musical, and showed an extraordinarily well versed appreciation for fine music. His enthusiasm communicated itself to us irresistibly. The classics became appealing again. Before he came, I was too preoccupied to listen. This was odd in view of the fact that music permeated every nook of my childhood. As when with Claude, now renowned in special science quarters as a genius in applied mathematics, and whom I had once known intimately, music once again became an integral part of life. Melodious harmony, serenity reigned, when he was with the children in the house. I often asked him to stay for dinner. At times the four of us ate out and would then attend a show. I began to introduce him to a few close friends. Retained continuously by his work in our town for over two months, he brooded more and more, I thought. Increasingly he lost himself in the records he listened to at our house. Once when I picked him up early on a Sunday morning at his motel room, I found him sitting reading on his already made bed, the room immaculate. He said his mother, now widowed, did outside housekeeping work like Mrs. Thomas, and he disliked overburdening the room maid. He said the help had commented on his neat habits: "They found me rather strange, and asked where I was from. The woman said this morning I couldn't possibly be from these parts. People are inclined to leave a mess behind them… The woman was Irish herself," he said with smiles, but his light blue eyes showed a serious determination.

He was sturdily built, and not tall, with a loose, fleshy belly. In movement he became gracious, airy, harmonious. His clothes, though usually of the casual kind, appeared an impediment to his delightfully fluid shape. It was silly, but at times I worried about leaving him alone with my son for an entire day… then once I saw him play and run excitedly with my small daughter, and this, too, I came to wonder about… When they ran together, my daughter and he, their eyes glowed with fun and excitement. He looked both flushed and so alive… sexual abstinence can play nasty tricks on one's perception of healthy interactions.

My husband had been gone for eight months. From the scanty correspondence between us at the time, it did not appear that he had any plans to return to New York. When I thought of him, I felt drained and was unable, during the previous weeks in Europe, to go with the children to see him in Egypt. He had been promoted to chief pilot and chief of operations for the Egyptian National Airline. Then I was told by an Englishman (who was supposed to be a friend to both of us) that he was transporting arms and ammunitions, and among other things this displeased me. I could not understand why, for the first time in our ten-year marriage, he occasionally sent almost adequate funds to contribute his half share of the upkeep of our children and home. I exchanged views about this with my new friend, who apparently was brooding over his own long absence from his family. To my surprise he said, "I have come to dislike him thoroughly. I consider him despicable!" On another occasion he commented, "The English aristocracy and vested country squires are, unbeknown to most, a rather unintellectual, pretty dull, uninformed group of people. Their main concerns are food and game."

"Food for certain!" I exclaimed in recognition, while he continued, "Really, they want to live a comfortable, unburdened life. They pretty much want to be left alone. The good things in life to them do not comprise music, books." I had not realized this until he spoke of it. Certain difficulties I had had in the past in my marriage to Henry came into relief and seemed more understandable to me.

Gradually he told me more about his wife. For one thing, she was quite a bit taller than he was. He said she had put on too much weight lately. She was a few years older than he, but not quite as many as I, and had been a strikingly capable woman before they moved to France. He wondered with pain: "Why does she always cry? Why is she so unhappy?" He meant to speak about the tearful discontent with which she met him almost daily. Her utter disorder, the disarray around their house, he could not understand. He at least tried to make some sense out of her frustrations. Sometimes I perceived ill-disguised personal hurt; he felt unable to make her happy. Through him I could not help sympathizing with her and finding her likable. I thought her wise to resist the uprooting. I volunteered happy medical advice for her and his two girls, and these long distance, "in absentia" consultations appeared helpful and to make him smile gladly. For some reason, though, he had not mentioned us to them.

His world appeared so different from mine! I learned that earlier he had been the youngest instructor in mathematics at a famous English University. He was the son of a Welsh proletarian, possibly mining, family, and he spoke mainly about getting his education and always having to help his older, more sports-oriented, brother with his studies. "I did it mainly to please her," that is, his mother, "to see her happier… " He was promoted through a series of scholarships and hard application. His gift for mathematics was obvious early in life; he still bore a mark on his forehead of a forceps used at delivery. (An out of the ordinary birth, which appears not unusual in prodigy children.)

When he spoke of his mother, he described her as one who always worked—"always doing, helping—no end to it… " He clearly felt much tenderness for her, while he expressed little affection for his father. He said with convincing sadness when he spoke of them, "I told him, everyone likes being taken out!" His father retorted defensively that she didn't care ever to go out. His own wife and children had become unhealthy. They were unhappy with their temporary residence on the south coast of France (though he insisted it was lavishly furnished by the Persian pundit who owned it), and she wanted to return to England. He simply loved that sunny section of France, but detested the French public schools which his girls attended. He said, "I really find them too arduous and demanding on young children." He said with rancor "they have to carry some five or six heavy texts with them daily." He felt it was hopelessly silly. "Small delicate girls, heavily burdened each day… " He really didn't like it at all. "I realize," he said "it will become necessary

49

to leave the continent one of these days. My wife really doesn't like it there at all… " He smiled sadly looking away in the distance, toward Europe.

He had said earlier he saw little reason to worry her uselessly about his frequent visits to us. Indeed, I thought, he never once made a gesture which indicated that he cared for me as a woman. Between the work and the children I perceived him as but a helpful messenger from Europe really. I thought of him as an inspired and inspiring addition to our family. I found him a delight to speak with, to listen to. I was thankful when he was quiet and played his records for I was often beside myself with too much to look after. He made few demands on my time—if any. It was always at the most propitious moment when he would suggest an outing. I enjoyed talking to him about Claude, the other mathematician, whose work he knew and admired. In truth, he often reminded me of Claude by the clear and rational manner in which he advanced his thought.

When he told me, many months into his prolonged stay, during an illumined fall evening that year, that he had developed too great an attachment to me, it took me by surprise. That night, as was customary after the children were asleep, we went for a walk high above the hospital grounds. It was a luminous, starry night. We watched the gentle flow of the river and the glitter of lights from the city's angular structures beneath us. From the height, on a windy hill, my heart always went out to a gentle curve made by the river as it ribbons and cascades to enter the center of town, meeting the calm broad flow of another stream. I wanted him to see the curving, bending encounter of the two rivers united beneath the darkly laced arm of a steel bridge in the distance.

When I turned to him, I saw him smile, though he seemed

self-absorbed, pensive and disturbed. He spoke suddenly, hesitantly. I was struck by the unfamiliar tone of voice in which he said, "I have thought for weeks about how I would tell you this... " His words stumbled over each other. He seemed very agitated and said in a whisper, "I believe I really care for you!" I frowned, shook my head, and smiled dumbly. He meant to describe his feelings in a certain unpresuming way, with a speech prepared for the occasion, and now, "I find to my confusion I'm unable to say anything... " He seemed markedly excited and said almost inaudibly, "I also wondered, would I dare to kiss you?" We stood still at a distance from one another. I believed I felt amused by his touching utterances. Then I felt stirred and suddenly worried. I felt increasingly uneasy, even oppressed. I kept quiet and thought I should go home. It seemed to me we walked down from the hill very quickly as I muttered to the effect of "you know, you've been gone from your family for a long time... " I was unprepared to consider that I too might be openly available and responsive. That first time, in the wake of his inspired approach, as we descended from high above the hospital grounds, he warned, "I have not been with anyone except for my wife... " But he behaved in a manner that led me to believe he knew the ways of women quite well. When we returned home, to the house on the hill of the hospital, we finally touched timidly in the dark of the hallway and kissed. Soon after, I found myself in his arms, moaning and joyous with shared desire for him. That very evening, as he made love to me, I invited him to join me upstairs in my bedroom; I vaguely realized, as though I were suddenly possessed, that I had gone up to change, and returned to him in the living room wearing merely a nightgown. It was a lovely new French gown of starched cotton, white with pale blue flowers. My gown—a robe, an offering to spring time! I caught the look of excited amazement in his bright blue eyes, the strange pleasure in the manner his head turned toward me as I came down the stairs to meet him. Did I presume, did I know intuitively that he would want me in ways that would please us to that extent?

My newfound love knew a lot about women, much less about himself and his own wants. Together, he became a revelation to us. Together, we became an unendingly desirous playful mystery to both. From the point of view of stages in one's life, I reached a peak, and remained nestled there for over a year. There was a previously unheard of beauty in the brilliance of the foliage that fall. Scintillating autumnal high mountain colors extolled the indigo imbued Indian Summer glory of the gently curved hills that surround our town. That fall, those evenings, what heart rending, tender moments we spent together!

Unknown to us at the time, we were both, I believe, in desperate want of a new stance in life. For some twelve years we had mainly known work and duty, duty and work, unremittingly. The summer I met him on the way to France was the first time in twelve years I had been able to take a vacation that lasted more than a few days. We were weighted heavily with everything we had learned in some twenty-five years of schooling; the momentum of carving our way into the resisting outside world with the material and practical application of our acquired skills had consumed us both. At the same time we had become "over-adult" parents — We had, I certainly had to keep in step with a younger and more resilient group of freer parents. I believe all of the foregoing had similarly disoriented both of us. We were in dire need of respite, of distance; we hungered for reevaluation. To my mind *les jours sans lendemain sont faits pour les jeunes* — it has a more agreeable sound in French, and means only that the days without tomorrow are meant for the young . . .

He often wondered aloud why I worked so hard. (Henry had called me lazy when I complained.) I told him that he traveled too much and that it hurt him and his family. I thought he must learn to be enjoyed simply for what he was. He ventured the opinion that I should let go some of the additional work I did at a clinic some nights. I thought he should change managers if the one he had was unable to appreciate his obvious genius in his field. I felt he should write, teach again some day. He convinced me that in educating the children, "one only gets what one pays for." He wondered sadly if he could be happy if he had to live in America. He thought, "There are so few great things here... " I found his preoccupations sadly sobering, but felt relieved at not having to make any decisions myself. I believe that together we began, as though in darkness, as though we had been blindfolded in the past, to search gropingly for our own particular futures. I did not envision a prolonged future when I would always be able to be with him. I did not think either of a future where we could no longer exchange the smallest particles of our lives when apart. I spoke of my renewed hope to enter private practice, where I could at last see some cases through and assume full responsibility for treatment. He felt I must be encouraged to do this, and could find no valid reason for my hesitance. Together we looked at an apartment I could move into. I supervised both his and his distant family's diet. There was an improvement in his complaints of chronic indigestion. Without semblance of interference, we helped each other overcome old fears. I faced the present with decreasing anxiety, for a hopeful future was contained therein. Once a week I ran to our Main Street Woolworth's to get our horoscopes. They were bought there for five pennies each from two public weighing scales, a round, cellophane-wrapped, mysterious-looking scroll, like that of the ten commandments inserted in a holder on the doors of our houses when I was a child in Antwerp. We would wait for a moment of quiet and peace, and while we sat together on the hammock in the garden behind our house on the hill, I would read him the latest edicts about our future.

I discovered later that our State Hospital director used to watch with binoculars from his house—the castle—perched above ours. I had gone personally to him to ask for a few trees to obtain privacy, as I felt that some few hundred people with nothing better to do could look down from their barricaded windows into our garden and rooms. I explained to the director that I loved to sunbathe, and felt that this was inappropriate in full view of people who were sweltering in closed wards. His comments "You don't want to hide behind trees—I won't have anything to look at then. After all, you as a psychoanalyst must understand this—I too want to fill the time with something good—I like looking." No, I did not see his point at all! I found the thought of his binoculars and alcohol-soaked system distasteful, and installed new shades on our bedroom windows.

As I communicated the certainty of our future to my mathematician on our hammock, he was amused by the scene we offered. He thought it was rather unusually ludicrous for two people with our combined schooling and experience to be credulous of this sort of thing. Though he listened intently, he laughingly felt obliged to dismiss our habit as a bankruptcy in our ratiocinating powers. To me, it was fitting—it resounded somehow with the unknown, unexplored element of newness we were pursuing. The unexpected had happened, and I felt I must guard myself against the premonition of disaster. I did not consciously realize at the time the strength of his loyalties to his personal history, which he had spent a lifetime to uphold and cherish. He was completely integrated into his own culture and society. I recall one of his early Cambridge University memories. It was late at night and he heard a fellow instructor come up the stairs, probably somewhat drunk, singing exuberantly in utter disregard of every one else: "One enchanted evening. When you least expect it… " and he wondered, would he ever be able to let himself go like this? Once, I wore a precious piece of jewelry, a bracelet of diamonds from our pre-WWII store in Ostend, Belgium. Seemingly quixotically, my mother had insisted on giving it to me. I realize now she was preparing for death, and before she sailed to Europe she was allocating her precious packets to her children. I told him about it, wondering why she had urged me to take this beautiful but highly valuable piece. When I wore it to dinner with him in New York, he asked me "Would you be offended if I were to ask you about what this is worth?" I wondered and then speaking as a person of the trade, replied, "To a merchant—which means not counting the 'façon' (craftsmanship)—quite a few thousand. In a store about double, I guess… "

"That's amazing, isn't it?" he exclaimed, as if sadly stunned.

"Guess it is… why?"

"Before I knew you, it just would not occur to me that people would want to spend their money like this. Think of the average person's earnings where I came from."

"This sort of thing," I said uneasily, defensively, "is an excellent investment, so I am told. I don't consider it mine really. It goes to the children; I hope I won't ever have to sell it."

I felt he would probably never shed the oppression of class consciousness. At the time I thought it was a weakness, just as with my husband Henry, who was caught rigidly within a self-righteous prison and walked about with the narrow blinkers imposed by his own aspired-to upper class consciousness. Later I came to think it was this man's strength in the end. He knew very clearly from where he stemmed and he knew where he wanted to be. He had a choice, upward bound. Because of his native gifts of mathematics and intelligence, he had cornered a distinct advantage over the rest of mankind. And yet still, at times, I perceived oppression from within. There was a reticence, a need clearly to define matters class wise before he chose certain moves, while I would consider them unimportant, and pass them over laughingly.

He seemed fascinated and attracted by the lighthearted refinements (gifts from Europe) I surrounded myself with at the time. He saw me move as an outsider by choice. When he questioned me about this, I could only say: "I'm all right, as long as they leave me alone and don't try to include me in any system, or class consciousness. I detest constraints from the outside, I have enough of my own. I wouldn't mind if I never did another day's work, except for private practice. My own practice, that is—Must give this a try; if I don't, I think I'll die… "

I thought I succeeded in making him more carefree, for together we laughed a lot. When he decided to stay with me, it was truly right from the very first night. With him, by him, I came to realize the happiness one may find in mature love. We did not pretend to fill each other's dreams. I thought we engulfed each other's aspirations simply by being. With him, for the first time in my life, I was able to be myself. He seemed eager to absorb my past and live the present fully when we were together. In the end, by knowing him, I felt mysteriously redeemed. I felt he had indefinably recaptured the betrayed past for me—by loving me the way he did—by my loving him the way I did. I was made healthy and whole—almost—for he gave me a taste of the ultimate delight which left a soaring hunger for completion.

Fritz Perls wrote once:

"… each of us has male and female substance… the pure male man and the pure female woman are rare… in many neuroses, and many psychoses as well, I saw the male and female substances in severe conflict; in the genius I see the opposites integrated … "

I felt that his was such a personality—He was the best integrated scientific genius I'd known! I was not in love with him. I loved and liked him. Must one have reached forty or so, be on a first stage menopausal high, to know such excited peace and creative reciprocity? In this newfound love, I considered the most prized possession of our time together to be his letters to me. My husband found most of them, and sent them to his wife. She then made him choose between the two of us, and all that this signified. A choice, he once wrote before the debacle occurred, that he would have to make over again every hour of his waking life.

A few months ago, I removed a drawer of a chest in my bedroom to look for a piece of lost jewelry. Glued to the resin that had dribbled down the wood of the wall of the chest, I found a love letter written by him a few weeks before events overtook us.

"It was wonderful wonderful wonderful being with you again—full of perfect moments to add to the many others I have stored in my memory… Your friend Robert considers it to be a simply physical affair. However it seems to me that our experiences together and the joy I derive from them permeate through my whole being and life so that in no way am I the same as before I met you. In any case I find myself out of sympathy with the purely intellectual. It seems to me

that the world is too full of intellect—too full of words—
and lacking in tenderness. To me, to have found someone
like you is to have found the wisest wisdom of all.
I continue to think often of the photo album of your Geneva
days. To have seen you as you were in those days has touched
me profoundly... In pondering on the fact that 'America'
meant 'Maria' to me, I came across the facts that the first
name contains the second and that '*amer*' is the French for
'bitter' and that is one of the meanings of your name...
Swimming now holds few terrors for me so I swim out quite
far—impossible a year ago.
You are very close to me... "

To recall him, as I read him and wrote about him, to have
felt the delight of his presence again for a few days, made me
excited. I wanted to sing, to run, to laugh. While I write, I am
staying on the grounds of Cornell University. From the window
in my room I see a broad expanse of cloudy but luminous sky.
Low hills, still covered at this time of late fall with multicolored
brilliance. The shimmering waters of Cayuga Lake can be seen
from the Olin Library situated on a high hill. The library room
where I have usually been at work is a large, window-encased
conference room, into which sunlight streams unimpaired from
one of three directions at different hours of the day. It is on
the highest, the seventh floor, and I can look over much of this
lovely campus. I see the small lighthouse on this side of the lake.
The structures, the specifically named halls, surrounding us are
made of beautiful stone; some halls are very old for this country.
The building, whose roof keeps gnawing at me for attention
while I read, is made of fantastic looking blue slate. Its azure,
sky reflecting surface, the neo-gothic architectural structure,
surmounted by its glistening surface, reminds me of Belgium, of

Brugge in particular, and also of the Free University of Brussels. I think Cambridge, where he spent so many years, and of which he had fond memories, cannot be that different. The students here are very serious; they often work intently. They scurry about. Many are strikingly good-looking and appear much involved with their studies. Some have stayed on in this room till midnight, as I often do. These are mainly pre-medical and pre-veterinary school students. Girls and boys, and I think of him as I write this. I realize I have prolonged my evocation of him, for I hate to let him go just yet.

He would not see me when I tried to reach him, as I fled to the south coast of France with our children, to be away from my husband who had become dispossessed of his senses. I have seen him but once again, in passing, here in America. We talked. I had let myself go quite a bit.. I was too heavy and looked it. There was little hope in anything. We talked almost unhindered. He mentioned, as if in passing, that he knew I was alone in the struggle that ensued during my separation from my husband. He abstained from contacts, but could not have done otherwise. He said he was sorry my mother had died just then, the way she did. I expressed my guilt, for mysteriously I had not disposed of his letters, so that they would have been out of Henry's reach. He then told me, which was astounding to me, that he could have prevented his wife from seeing them. He felt impelled not to intercept the packet containing many of his letters, (which my husband had sent by registered mail), for it was addressed to her, his wife. With his unique excited amazement, he said he would always care... I believed him. During our last and chance meeting we avoided lighting the fire in the hearth. To have been able to bring him here while I wrote about him, on these lovely grounds... I am loath to have to let him go... When

I return to my practice-home tomorrow I will find him again for a few hours.. I hope to locate the ending section to the only letter I still have of his. I am glad I was able to resurrect part of the published article of "Geneva Revisited" which he edited. A spiritual sorcerer, a troubadour, he enlivened what he touched with an exciting, perfection-aspiring, melodious voice. You see, as in the past, now ten years later, he can still enchant my mornings…

"et j'ai le mal d'amour et j'ai
le mal de toi… "
Barbara

CHAPTER 4

The End of a Marriage—
"Il a voulu que je me quitte"

A t the end of fall that year when the heavy snows came,
I still corresponded happily with my newfound love.
Although I was but rarely able to see him the future appeared
auspiciously bright and new. I no longer felt alone. But then
I was suddenly thrown into a new set of circumstances: I was
married again. Seriously ill, Henry, my husband returned
unexpectedly from his position in Egypt. I had lost the
opportunity for divorce while he was still healthy and away.
The letter I had written to him in Egypt a mere few weeks
earlier, which clearly stated my intention to divorce him,
had been returned; it came back mysteriously unopened,
via Torquay, England, which he had given as his forwarding
address while he worked for the National Egyptian Air Line.

He had always insisted on keeping his private affairs to himself...

The fact that this letter was returned, and that he did not open it upon his own return, gave me an uncanny feeling that catastrophe was to follow. Five months later when Henry was considered fully and officially recovered, I built up enough courage to ask him again for a divorce. I also made it known that I would resign my positions at the hospital and at the mental health clinic. Both institutions were at the time barely good substitutes for optimal therapy; the pay barely sufficed to keep us afloat, and the hours were by far too long.

Henry considered it "most unreasonable" to leave the security of home and board at the hospital. I tried to explain to him that they were vying for cheap doctors, not good medicine. I felt my debt to society was repaid and it was time to move on—To no avail. The battles between us began again. He kept wondering aloud why I wanted to leave him. He stressed there was no reason on earth that was sufficient for us to victimize our children by subjecting them to the advertised agony of "The Broken Home."

"What, dear child, is wrong with you?" he argued, although only a year or so older than I. Until I meant to leave, he had found me by far easier to live with, he said, and since his unplanned return it had been "heaven." Then why did I want to break this up? Other pilots' wives, he argued, were able to take their husbands' absence. Why couldn't I? (The two pilots' wives I had closely befriended in California, where I had moved to be near him for a year—where as soon as I arrived he was posted back to N.Y.—had since been hospitalized for emotional difficulties.) The same English friend of the family who had earlier informed me of Henry's alleged pro-Egyptian work, struck the final *coup de grâce*. He had met the Welsh mathematician and told Henry about him. Someone broke into my office and under shelves of medicine found their way to his letters... These Henry sent off to his wife in France. Thereupon I was left alone; of that Henry made certain. Still, he was willing to make a clean slate of the past, as he expressed it. "We could start over again". HE was willing to forgive and forget...

As for his being willing "to forgive and forget," I retorted he hadn't exactly behaved like a schoolboy while away, either. I wavered. I wanted signed promises through the courts this time; he must take a more equal share in the financial responsibilities, and there was to be equality all around. He wouldn't—he couldn't. He would resume his old postures of "It's no better than being a prostitute, demanding all that money... " Meaning? He'd fight as though his life depended on it over paying for gas! ... After all, he reminded me, it was my car, not his... though he had to steer, for he would not stand for "ruddy aggressive American females who drive their big cars with meek husbands in tow. I wouldn't be caught dead being driven by a woman, especially my wife!" he would explode. I always suspected he was right in demanding we share fairly in the upkeep of the children: *"Les putains—les vraies—sont celles qui se font payer pas avant—mais après,"* as Jacques Brel sang in his poetic realism. But when he demanded I carry the entire burden of the household, the matter became more complicated, for I was simultaneously being told: "You must know your place as a woman... " at which contradictory assignments I finally exploded with bewilderment, and resolved once and for all that I'd been pushed beyond myself and must move on. In an outburst of systematized compulsion, he oddly undertook the task of what I considered an attempt to erase my past; he destroyed all the photographs he could find. Pictures from my student days in

Geneva, black friends shown in the hug of camaraderie—he tore. Gauche but delicate drawings I did of Claude aeons earlier—he tore. Previously kept letters and remembrances, vintage years of first discoveries; I had clung to them during many an uprooting. Through them I had found continuity, a semblance of unity that tied the past to the present. He expedited Claude's letters and pictures off to his wife, too. He called them. He called on every unsuspecting colleague in our medical community. He even called on my patients… His purpose: through a process of intimidation, to dissuade, to awaken me to reality. His battle cry: "I'll break you in yet." My mother's verdict at that stage: "You can't live with Henry—No woman could. But you can't leave him either because of the children; You've made your bed and now… "

I did not in the least consider how deeply wounded Henry was from within. He was precipitated into an anguished world of reawakened childhood conflicts: rejection, vulnerability, and above all helplessness. It tore him asunder. He was convinced beyond all reason that he was losing his children. His offensive vengefulness led to outbursts of violence. I dealt only with personal wounds, those inflicted mainly by what I perceived as an erasure, a shattering blow to my past. In addition to the above, the near destruction of our material future reawakened within me a world of previously repressed hostility towards him. Torn by ambivalence, I even felt I must kill him or myself. When we moved from the hospital to the apartment chosen with love, and to my long awaited private practice, he felt he must move in with us. I literally fought against this tooth and nail. My argument: "I'm paying the rent—ergo, it's my flat." His posture: "They're my children… " The insufferably slow courts prolonged the agony for everyone concerned. Henry was advised to make an attempt to woo his wife back. He did so with knives in the night and by locking me into closets, while patients waited for me across the street in my new office. My young son fetched help for me. My daughter wisely refused to witness the goings-on. I saw them suffer in their love for him, especially my daughter. My son still seemed totally undivided, and stood by me. I knew these events were traumatizing to them. There was no way left but to flee for a while at the earliest opportunity. For a while I was destroyed... except for the children, it seemed useless to continue the chronically sickening struggle. Henry's father had died the previous year, and I appealed to his mother. From the harbor-hugging confines of Torquay in England she responded at once: "No man worth his salt gives up without a fight." Vivat Regina!

Had he not been made to feel so frantically dispossessed of his rigid defenses... had he not attributed all his woes to another, a younger man, whom he absurdly considered far beneath him socially... had he not been reminded by what was happening to him of his days in the RAF... (He was twenty years old then, shot down on his last mission over Germany as a bomber pilot, taken prisoner for two years, to land eventually in a concentration camp... One of the few to whom so many owed so much). Had he not felt so trapped by his terrorizing anger. Had I only been able to pardon him all the "money" I had continually advanced him: All the "money" I was certain he owed me from the past. After the many years in service at State Hospitals I left the house on the hill without a spoon to our name.

The end came quite suddenly when within the matter of a few hours he was forced out of the house by court order. In a last effort to dissuade me from leaving the hospital, the administration, in fear of my setting a precedent for future physicians, and in terms very similar to my husband's, painted a disconcerting picture of the threat of bankruptcy, prison, and disgrace to our name. The

Assistant Director, a Dr. Young, whom I thought was a wise old man, told me in parting: "I might as well warn you; your patients will be Jewish women and they are very neurotic, but they don't pay. Don't say I haven't warned you... You may still reconsider... " I decided then and there he was as mad as the others. For in reality what was there to reconsider? I was to be the first psychoanalyst to practice in town, the first woman to practice privately and full time. By simple word of mouth the calls for appointments were so numerous that all the hospital's telephone lines were tied up even before I got to my own office. If only I could have let Henry off the hook scot-free (which he asked me to do), he might have signed separation papers, given me a divorce, as partners in parting... As it was, I was to spend the next two years trying to locate him between Honolulu, Wake Island, and the Unknown. Thousands of dollars were paid to attorneys before I obtained support money from Henry for the children, namely $15.00 per week for each child; Still, I urged them to visit him wherever he was. Six years and many attorneys later, by the grace of a court in Delaware, child support was increased to $30.00 per week per child... Henry has remained highly esteemed as an airline pilot, and has never been unemployed from the time he left our area. Financially successful, he has climbed steadily on the priority list of his company. My professional work, while the children grew, amounted to less than that of half a person, for when I was married and a mother, I was mostly alone. When I was divorced I was just as alone, if not more so...

The fact was the relationship with my last love could never be resumed. But when Henry left me free, work became totally absorbing as I was able to enter into a partnership with most of the people who consulted me. The more you have experienced yourself, the better equipped you become to see others through their own upheavals. The incisive wounds of mutual deceptions, the scarred pain of an unusual past served well to undo the binding sufferings of others. Long experience became the most trustworthy ally. Not suffering as the mathematician Henri de Poincarré said is to be viewed as a negative ideal.

Friends wondered what impelled me to make such a drastic break all at once, with position as well as with marital ties. A well-meaning colleague, a Dr Gerald Ansell, a fine and popular gynecologist originally from England, who helped me to establish myself with the older members of our medical community, advocated wisdom, respite. He pleaded for restraint on my part. His advice was indeed wise, but I could not heed it. I observe others who seem to be undergoing similar heartbreaking experiences. This has now become a frequent, almost grievously familiar pattern. They stand precariously on the brink of their middle years. The past is lost, or looms unacceptable. A last convulsive effort is made to regain a feeling of anticipation—of last sprung hope in a self-willed direction of one's future. Men leave their contemporary wives, their confused, drug-impelled children. They abandon previously secure positions—all in one sharp, divisive sweep. The women leave, in a final attempt to regain victory over themselves in their condition, a perennial fight in pursuit of self-esteem. In an upsurge of excitability, of vitality, they run with the intoxicating scent of last hope.

From my own observations, the break with the past at this middle point in our life is usually shatteringly abrupt and complete. It has none of the laboriously planned quality of earlier times, during our reproductive, cyclical years. The sudden divisiveness in women at the middle point is more reminiscent of adolescence, when young people may leave their parent's home forever to flee in a frenzy towards the irresistible future's unknown. I believe the hormonal upheavals that rack our organism at this time run in functional parallelism with our emotional conduct, and incite us toward 'acting out' behavior in response to heightened tension and conflict.

As Barry Stevens, the lone goddess of Gestalt therapy might have seen it, Henry was perhaps an all right kind of a guy, but he was not right for me, ever, nor I for him. If only he had not been so strikingly attractive… But then as my mother had warned me from the beginning: "Handsome men—They are for other women… Not for you to marry." The fundamental trend I am trying to pin down here: when I married Henry, I was an adult, previously divorced, experienced woman. With him, though, the very fiber of my daily life was one of loneliness, a prolonged waiting, accompanied by an inexplicable longing. An unconscious mechanism then entered into play, in such a manner that these consciously felt discomforts became more familiar. Instead of suffering through the actual separation of Henry leaving repeatedly for long periods of time to fly as a civilian pilot to war-infested areas of the world—this longing became disembodied , possibly also because of his lack of responsiveness to our situation. At first it became an unfulfilled longing for an absent love. When I sent our two children to their grandparents in Torquay, England, while I prepared for the New York State Medical Board Examinations, it became a guilt festering longing; a waiting, a want. A separation for at least three months seemed essential to our family. Neither Henry's work, nor his contributed income towards us was dependable. Everyone, of course, needed looking after, and this demanded at least one reliable salary. Without a state license, my own position as a physician in New York State, or elsewhere in the U.S. was in jeopardy. My son was then barely two years old, and was, I thought, increasingly neglected and poorly looked after.

When his grandfather became chronically ill, his grandmother minded the additional bother entailed by two small children, and despite my long distance pleas with money to enable her to hire help, the children were placed in what I considered to be a second rate boarding school, euphemistically called "Auntie Nancy's" in Peighton, near their home. These months of separation may, rather must, always mean too much to one as young as my son was at the time. I well recall the end of my fifth and last day of the written medical examinations at the Armory in New York City. I obtained a ride back to Long Island that night with a colleague who had gone through this five day ordeal three times within a five year span. In a fit of sudden relief I told him and his wife that I didn't see which of the tests I failed—ergo, "I must have passed the series once and for all!" They looked at me for a minute with great pity followed by alarm in their eyes as they advised me to "take it very easy for awhile!" I meant to leave for England to see the children the next day, and succeeded in this despite a bad fall on the ice at the hospital the night before leaving. When I met Henry in Great Britain, he insisted at once that the children were better off in England where they could obtain what he called "a proper upbringing for a lady and gentleman." My joyous excitement faded rapidly: In vain I pleaded that the "gentleman" was less than three years old, the "lady" barely five! He thought my laments were ridiculous. Though our boy looked in poor shape, and would not—understandably to me—speak to either of us at first, Henry insisted it was because he had a bad cold; he also blamed the miserable heating system and the cold English weather. He made it clear he found me irritatingly hyper-emotive, strongly lacking in forethought, and unmindful of the children's well-being. I insisted they return at once with us to our home in America. We then quarreled openly as we never had before. His parents remained carefully uninvolved in our disputes. Henry pointed out repeatedly that as their father it was his duty to insist on their having a "proper upbringing," which to him meant their remaining in England. "He simply takes it to be his duty to rule," said Elizabeth Barrett of her father. As he, Henry wanted "to make happy according to his own views of the propriety of happiness… he takes it to be his duty to rule like kings of Christendom by divine right."

We left the children in England and spent a few miserable, interminable days with my family at a North Sea resort in Belgium, where we were invited to celebrate the New Year with them. We traveled by way of Antwerp, my first home. He did not know the city at all. I wanted to show him the oldest diamond center, the "Fortunia," erected with the aid of my father for the benefit of his Dutch compatriots. I suggested we walk through the handsome historical building. He said there was no time for this sort of thing, and insisted on going to a famous tourist haunt for a copious Flemish seafood meal. He was restless, and kept on the telephone with his Airplane Company in London. He was told there was neither work just then, nor any urgency for his return.

He denied feeling bad for the children. I felt their absence, their hurt, and knew that an irreparable betrayal had taken place. While with Henry in Antwerp I felt acutely the absence of an ally, a companion, a friend, a father to our children. I became depressed and unable to sleep. I believe our union as a couple broke irrevocably, at that point while in Antwerp, forcibly away from the children. He then flew for three months to what was then the Belgian Congo, on a sub-contract to the United Nations during the uprisings which ensued during that country's first bid for independence.

While Henry and the children were away, I lived on the grounds of the State Hospital at Central Islip. I was assigned to be in charge of six hundred female patients considered a maximum security risk. The woman physician who had preceded me in that capacity was eventually fired. I believe not only because of her racism, but mainly because her attitude rightfully provoked letters of complaint on the part of patients' relatives. These reached the headquarters of the New York State Department of Mental Hygiene and the people in charge of the hospital were obliged by law to investigate and report back to Albany. I thought she disliked the work, not to mention the patients involved, and she made this quite obvious. The most humane co-workers who stayed on endlessly were a few odd souls, who were employed as nurses, or aides. An unshakable compassion consumed them. One man, dark skinned, deep and quiet voiced, a Dr Correoso, who was to be my supervisor for a short while, allowed me to witness daily the most touching humanity I would ever observe—the gentle manner in which he spoke with and about children in trouble left me shaken by his moral integrity. Rooted in mercy, he was truly an Albert Schweitzer-like character whose reverence for life awed me. I am told he was promoted to the highest position. This is remarkable in view of the fact that most psychiatric state hospital directors in New York consistently appeared to be persons unsuitable to be physicians functioning on their own. My contribution there, in another large unit, was to do what could best be described as "black-market" psychiatry, by instituting group therapy with whoever was willing to follow me; also by distributing the first birth control pills to young patients incarcerated during years for sexual acting out. I found a good reason—for I wanted to see if the young epileptic patients, some of whom were also inclined to act out their frustrations pre-menstrually, would have fewer seizures if placed on the pill. I mentioned the seizure-free group as research control patients. Eventually, I was called onto the carpet for this. I gradually shrank away from commitment to individual patients. I viewed the demands made on us by our self-serving administrators as essentially reducible to those of cheap doctoring. I felt badly for the patients who were there—and badly for myself. Our common denominator: for whatever reason, varying from illness' unreason to a compulsion to become imprisoned within the realm of helplessness, we all felt incarcerated on the Central Islip State Hospital grounds.

I lived from day to day with a central preoccupation: the harm that was being done to our children by this prolonged separation. It took another three months to find out that I had passed the Medical Boards on first attempt. Motivated as I was who would not have? I had to threaten divorce by an attorney before I was able to receive assurance that the children would come back. Henry's father, although a most honorable man, while conceding that the children were rather urgently in need of being parented, still would not surrender them to me without his son's permission. As a young man, during WW I, he had been disowned by his family for joining the R.A.F. to be a pilot. This occupation was considered by his own mostly absent father "unsuited for a gentleman!" I thought he must therefore have an intrepid spirit and be an individualist, unbounded by local conventions. I felt I had treated his son well and could not understand his position. I had helped Henry in every manner when he was unemployed. He had indeed had a difficult time being transplanted to America from England. When he found full time employment and finally promised to pay for his share of the expenses incurred for the upkeep of the household, I was rarely able to hold him to any agreement made about our finances. He was compulsively manipulative with me about this. I perceived his attitude as a rejection of me as a woman. What hospital friends laughingly referred to as his free ride, to him it probably meant being loved unconditionally. When he felt received in this manner, he would tell me, "I worship you... " This astounded me, as he often treated me like dirt beneath his feet.

This wretched feeling of being unloved by him and overly manipulated became as pervasive as a cancer, and eventually rendered me incapable of receiving from him what he could best offer to the relationship which was a tremendously developed sensuality. He had a quality of strong earthiness in matters of nature, to which (compared to me), he related with grace and marked ease. In intimacy he abounded in innovativeness. His physique was imposing, superb really. He was usually described as suave, and people found him mild mannered and really charming in a quiet sort of a way. When with the children, he seemed to forget his obsessive composure and could be loving, especially when not short tempered under the influence of copious daily drinks of Scotch.

I remember meeting him during this period in a hotel room in New York City, where he was to stay for less than a day en route to Africa. I had not seen him or the children for three months, since the time of our unhappy trip to Belgium. I had spent the preceding weekend at the home of the now married Claude. When Henry took me in his arms, and I felt his warmth and the touch of his fine skin, the muscles in my face twitched, lips trembled, I heaved with dry sobs, then the tears came... Henry seemed most embarrassed for me and ran to the window, searching his uniform pockets clumsily to find his handkerchief. This he handed me with one hand from behind his back, while the other tugged hard on the curtains to seal them closed more hermetically than they already were. With me in the hotel bedroom he double checked the Venetian blinds again, and drew on the curtains to the point where one rod fell loose off the wall. He cursed: "Bloody Gerry built... " He checked the door, which he opened and then bolted again. "These people will damn well never mind their own business." I had forgotten with whom I was dealing. I had forgotten the embalming, entombing rituals of bedrooms which preceded love-making... the handkerchief carrying his manly and lightly scented aroma made me swoon. With the curtain rod dangling, sunlight struck against the carpet, and he switched off the electric lights. We were in a private world at last. When confronted with his manliness, suddenly I did not know whom I was hungrily feeling. My small, perfect son? Claude? The longing overwhelmed me so that I was seized with panic. I heard myself as a stranger cry out to Henry, "I'm fed up! I just can't take this any longer; I so long for the children... I hate the house! I hate the work... " He was rather shocked by my confusion and my tears, and drawing me slowly toward him, said, "Come now, gently now, pull yourself together... Do you think I like doing what I have to do?"

When we returned to the room after we had been out for a while he advised, "After all, you only live once. Enjoy yourself while you can. I won't be here tomorrow. Why don't you make the most of it?"

The United Nations planes he flew in the Congo at the time were being shot at by what he called "the bully boys." When I left him to return to the hospital, I felt we were both either mentally disturbed or natural idiots... We were without funds; both of us had survived a war against many odds, and what the hell were we doing still living as though it had continued forever? What was he doing flying in formation to land in the Congo in the year 1961, while I was locked up in a loony bin separated from my children?

A month later he came to see me for a weekend, still adamant about keeping the children in England. He never called ahead. I saw lights in the distance, and heard a car driving up our isolated hospital roadway. I was sitting quietly at the dinner table with Leroy, an older friend I had not seen for many years. He had paid for the last stage of my stay in Geneva, while I waited to publish my medical thesis, for which he had lent me the money. He had moved to Vienna, Austria, where he now resided. I had run into him in New York, and at my insistence he had come to pay me a short visit, and to see that I had used his help well. I felt truly grateful to him, and tried to persuade him to eventually let me repay him He said he felt repaid, for he thought the work I did was humane.

Henry burst in on us, and soon became abusive. Were it not for the circumstances of Leroy's visit, the scene might have appeared quite farcical. There was stunning Henry, tall and stiff, half smiling while swearing under his breath and examining the bedrooms. Leroy was in an awful hurry to leave—he was even tearfully apologetic in the end. I insisted on at least taking him to the station. On parting he said what most men said, "Henry is certainly a very good looking man… " When I returned home to the hospital Henry tried to make up for his mistake. "After all, try to understand. I've had a long and difficult flight… " He suggested we go out for dinner and forget the whole silly incident. Before we ever got to eat, I became heavily inebriated in the restaurant, then sick. On the way home I wanted to know when our children could come home;. Henry became his abusive, unpredictably explosive self again. This occurred often after a flight. I ran out of the car near a highway, loudly returning insult for insult. When he picked me up again, I kept very quiet. Then, again as a stranger with him, I heard myself whisper loud enough for him to hear, "A woman, Claude's wife, is living my life in Cambridge, Massachusetts, and she has my children too… " For a fraction of a moment he seemed taken aback, touched, hurt. His blue eyes flashed. His arms stiffened against the wheel. Then he said, quite soberly, "That is not true, that is not so—that is not what you want… " I believe I had gone slightly mad—to say the least—with loneliness. The prolonged waiting and longing had become so old and deep, it racked the present, allowing the most familiar first woman's stirrings to erupt.

I was living alone at the Central Islip State Hospital at this time, in one wing of a broken-down house which dated back to 1870, and which had forty empty, toxically-smelling rooms separating me from the other wing, which was occupied by a lone, widowed accountant. The latter had shot a patient one night, mistaking him for a burglar. He complained about having had to clean up the whole bloody mess by himself, as the hospital's police would not help him. (The time he told me this was the only occasion in two years that we met.) My own wing consisted of some twelve enormously high-ceilinged, initially quite barren-looking rooms; our rent amounted to $27.00 per month, which was truly minimal, even for 1961.

While feeling abandoned and alone there, the nature of my longing became intricately confused in me. The greatest part of the time, I brooded about my three year old. Every payday I bought the children clothes; a chronic stream of packages was received by their disgruntled grandparents. By then they were complaining about anything either Henry or I did or failed to do. For the first time I learned of John Bowlby's theories about the ill effects of early separations in children. From Bowlby's implied pleas for good mothering, to René Spitz' and Anna Freud's war-time revelations about the pathological aftermaths of separations in early childhood, I derived such guilt that remains forever with me in my relations with my son. I believe that I will never again feel that I have done right by him. What residue now weighs in him from this agonized period? What about her—my daughter? She never allowed me to forget. I reminded her of this apologetically too often.

Psychologically, the emptiness prolonged beyond tolerance struck deeply and emerged in consciousness with a longing for my first love, the mathematician Claude. I began to feel his absence as strongly as when I was first totally separated from him. The void he left reawakened and became identified with the absence of my vulnerable, chronically cold, helpless, abandoned son. I needed to call Claude on the phone. Taking my courage in hand I went to see the now much-married Claude. Despite the tremendous happiness at seeing him—I had so loved in my youth—it was understandably an upsetting experience for everyone concerned.

SECTION TWO
Biography

Claude and Maria 1942

CHAPTER 5

Claude—An Elliptical Admirer

When Claude and I first met, we were lodgers in the same rooming house at 51 West 11th Street, in what at that time was called the "Bohemian Village" of New York City. I had arrived in America the previous year, alone and an immigrant from war-torn Europe, following the German invasion of Belgium and most of France.

My entire immediate family was still in Europe. I had an inheritance fund in my name in a bank in this country. It consisted of partial payments, after the death of my father, of my share of his wealth, but in trust of my mother. In her absence I signed a request in her name to increase the otherwise insufficient monthly allowance she had allocated to me when she sent me tearfully on my way from occupied Paris to America. Soon after my arrival, the Manufacturers Trust Co. of America, where my inheritance had been deposited, asked me to come down to its headquarters on Wall Street. A soft-spoken, well-groomed representative explained nicely that it was felt that the note they had received was not signed by my mother. He stressed repeatedly how dark I was for a citizen of Belgium; he wanted to know my intentions, and then proceeded to find a clause (though Belgian funds were officially frozen) whereby I could be allocated larger sums for my education. Slowly, I transferred all the money to my own name and managed on it at a reasonable rate for over four years.

I lived in a second floor apartment with my closest friend Evie, whom I had met at the Royal Atheneum in Antwerp, in the equivalent of ninth grade of high school. When she came to America, a refugee from the war, as I, she left her parents, who were all but glad to see me on the scene again. Together we moved into the flat she had found. She liked it because it had a piano, a fireplace, and much light from a courtyard where small trees quivered noisily in the wind. It was early summer—we were both almost eighteen years old. The young black couple who lived in the basement apartment and who cleaned the house, insisted that we meet a fellow who lived above us. He was described by Freddy, who did most of the couple's janitorial work, as a terribly lonely and sad young man. Freddy would then roll his eyes towards heaven to show us how sad this man was. He added enticingly that the above neighbor was smart as the devil, and in common with the two of us, he liked books. He appealed to our sympathy. I only knew at the time that the man from upstairs made a horrendous racket by the repercussions through our thin ceilings like animalistic bangs instead of music. This eventually interfered with my studies, for though I kept late hours, the sounds far outlasted them. When I complained time and again about this to Freddy, (who by then had become our dance instructor, in exchange for my typing lessons to his wife,) it was to no avail. As we did not speak English too well, he would gesticulate in sadness, and direct his gaze upward to indicate we would have to contact our neighbor ourselves.

Eventually I went to see him about the noise. It was, I remember, mainly for Evie's sake, for unlike me she worked regular hours as an assistant to an older man, the editor of "France-Amérique," New York's only French newspaper. I studied, and this mainly at night, while attending all sorts of colleges, till I eventually settled on the *Ecole Libre des Hautes Etudes* (the Sorbonne University in Exile). The School was located around our corner on West 12th Street, and many of the classes were taught at the New School for Social Research. We were eventually to be granted the equivalent of an American M.A. degree through our *Licence ès Lettres* diplomas, which were signed in print by the venerable General Charles de Gaulle.

Claude found a solution to the noise—he placed a heavy mat beneath his large music console. He promised to be more quiet in his love for jazz music, on the condition that we see each other again. When he tried to explain to me what he did, in the simplest English he thought I understood, for the longest time I mistook him for a bookkeeper, an accountant, as my father's assistant in his store had been. Our neighbor always had a pencil in his shirt's pocket. At first he did indeed inspire one's sympathy, for he was extremely thin, and had a prominent Adam's apple. He was pale, and longilinear to the extreme. He had very dark hair, as dark as I believed an American Indian's hair would be. It was straight, and fell attractively in recalcitrant strands over his forehead—he would flip them back like a schoolboy. I was plump, tanned, and sturdy in appearance. He did indeed seem much alone, and did not hide it. I then obtained the impression of him as being someone exceptionally keen and intense. This was no doubt due to large, jade green eyes, which had an unusual sheen. I noticed this, for with them he followed with strange attention what I said in my broken English replete with French and Flemish interjections, as though he were lip-reading to understand me. He had exceptionally sharp features; a long and unusual nose came to an abrupt stop far from his mouth. He laughed in small explosions as though he were coughing, and had never quite learned how to be merry. He had me seated facing him during this very first encounter. This much I remember. I felt embarrassed and sat in profile on the edge of the deep armchair, with its broken springs as ours were on the floor below. I felt uncomfortable in my minimal Belgian tennis shorts, breasts erect and high to the point of choking.

At that time he was employed by a Research Laboratory, not as a bookkeeper, as I had first thought, but as one of their most promising young applied mathematicians. I learned early that he had no patience with matters pertaining to the soul. He considered philosophy, which was my main interest at the time, "certainly not a science!" This meant he viewed the field as "totally useless!" He objected to the fact that Logic, Symbolic Logic, should be considered a branch of philosophy, because he respected logic and it also made sense "operationally" to him. I was mainly interested in Bergson's intuitive approaches, and found revelations in the philosophy of contemporary Hindus like Tagore and Krishnamurti. These approaches made him shudder. He said emphatically that psychology as a field put men to shame—not to mention women, who were rarely intelligent and usually unaccomplished. His true avocation, really a religion at the time, was Science—Mathematics he considered its most perfect form. Its closest disciple, Applied Mathematics, he considered an immediate descendant of the divine.

Neither of us did any cooking, and we often found ourselves eating together on 8th Street. Then he would talk to me about an electrical brain machine that would outdo man's own brain. Most of the time I thought him maddeningly crazy about this; human language applied to machines irked me then. I did not mind eating with him in public, but could not swallow a bite when we were alone, seated across from one another. It seemed so intimate, and I would not open my mouth when he looked up at me. In restaurants he usually filled napkins with strange symbols, while I would try to describe an event in English. He told me, I thought sincerely, that he was not in the least interested in what was happening with the war in Europe. He said he was most unhappy at having to do the piddling work related to it, none of which interested him in the least. He would then return from work to his flat and work until all hours of the night, playing his wretched antique machine through our ceiling, and elaborate on his favored ideas, no doubt initiated earlier in the evening on the paper napkins of our 8th Street restaurant.

All he appeared to require was a clean sheet of paper and his ubiquitous drawing pencil. He had a habit of throwing the latter into the air and recapturing it after it had formed an ellipsoid curve. It was a graceful gesture, one which he performed repeatedly, especially while he was trying to explain a certain point to me. His entire head would follow the up-and-down path of the pencil. Neither his gestures nor his gait were of the usual variety. When I became more knowledgeable about child psychiatry and neurology, I often wondered what made him so uniquely different from most other people. As he worked on his favorite projects throughout the night, he had difficulty getting up on time in the morning. He often went to work afternoons instead of at the appointed time, and would then express guilt toward his employers. He did not seem to fear being drafted were he to lose his position, which he described as classified. He admired the engineers he worked with, especially his immediate superior, and he felt bad about disliking so intensely the projects he was asked to participate in. This all occurred during the first years I knew him (1941-1943), and I did not pay him as much attention at first as I would later when he became my whole life. I do not believe that he considered me too seriously in the beginning either. We just happened to see a lot of each other. Was it at that time, during the guiltily stolen hours from work at the research laboratories, that he continued to work on certain theories which eventually brought him great fame and recognition in the field of applied mathematics? Possibly, for not unlike former mentor Norbert Wiener, he was to become a living legend. The field in which he travailed during those stolen hours became redefined by him.

We would see each other at least twice a week, and upon leaving he would say "Au revoir, see you sometime" or "see you soon." Though I much wanted to, I never once asked "when?" As a properly brought up girl from Antwerp, I never made the first move. Eventually he held this against me, finding me too extreme in this respect, as in many others. After a small quarrel about ideology as usual, he told me once defensively that he had been a chosen pupil of Vanever Busch, and was awarded the highest scholarship available at the time at MIT. He truly won the U.S. National Prize in Engineering when he was barely twenty-two years old. I asked him for a copy of the newspaper article he showed me in which this was mentioned, and in which a photograph of him appeared. I thought of sending it to my mother. By this time she had fled from occupied France to Cuba.

I did not do so. I had unearthed the facts that he just about ran away from home when his father died, when he was fifteen or sixteen years old. His mother was of German descent, and taught German in the high school of a small town in Northern Michigan, where he was born and raised. When I asked him why he had left her, he replied that she was not nice to him after his father died. "She kept giving me all the burned cookies, while her guests got all the scrumptious ones she baked. I got sick of. it." So he went to live with an uncle, whom he left to be on his own. He only saw his mother once again. I had known him for three or four years by then. He went to visit her in a hospital in Chicago, where his only sibling was living; she too was a mathematician. His mother had been operated on for a goiter condition and died shortly after. (I realize the extraordinary sheen to his jade green eyes might have been due to a familial thyroid condition. He said that there was much goiter in that part of Michigan.) It appeared that he never forgave his mother, nor did he allow himself to care for her again. He inherited her car, but I do not believe he ever used it. I was much interested in the fact that he knew how to fly a plane. He expressed annoyance and surprise at my explicitly emotional interest, so I withheld from him my deepest desire to get to fly in order to liberate those in Europe I so worried about.

I saw him increasingly often at the end of that first year, and eventually began to wait eagerly for him to call on me. For a short while, I believe, we formed a threesome with Evie, and I felt torn between them. As long as Claude and I did not become too intimate, I was able to love them both almost equally. Despite suspicions to the contrary on Claude's part,

Evie and I simply had an adolescent infatuation with each other, without there ever having been amorous eruptions of physical closeness. I believe my "crush" on her, which had lasted from the time I was fourteen years old, was probably stronger than the tender and protective feelings she had towards me. She was a very slender, and small breasted but curvaceous girl, delicately boned, with long smooth brown hair which was always in place. She was impeccably dressed, and the neatest young thing alive. I had naturally curly, completely unruly dark brown hair. My breasts were inordinately large and high. The boys in the street would whistle when I ran by, and workmen once called after me, "Hey there, pretty muscle" (or was it Mamselle?)—whatever—it upset me for the rest of the day. I never wore make-up then, and as I had good legs, I often preferred shorts with a simple chemise. I definitely preferred all things masculine, and expressed great rebellion against attitudes required of the women in my family. At times I longed for soft, flowing clothes; at others, I insisted on denying my femininity. I was quite preoccupied with all of this—much more than I feel like getting hold of right here. I lived hourly with a hesitance, a dichotomy between wanting to appear more serious, which to me meant masculine, and a desire to be pretty. On certain days these inner conflicts became insufferable, and for some reason this manifested itself by my fussing for hours with my unruly curls. The latter, worn in long full ringlets when I was a child, had made me the center of attention at school in Antwerp, where the majority of the girls in my school were tow-headed and armed with practicality wore their hair short and straight. My gifts in poetry recitation, mental calculus and composition brought less recognition than this mass of stupid dark ringlets, which on my mother's insistence I wore for school for some eight years.

I believe Evie and I were almost equally repressed in the sexual area. I had received "kissing instruction" from my young brother-in-law Charles, who was a student at the University of Brussels before the war broke out, and whom I had grown to like enormously. My experience had gone no further. While we roamed the North Sea dunes, a cousin on my mother's side, Armand Nr. 1 often tried to instruct me in nudism. By the time I was twelve he convinced me that it was advocated by what he quoted as the holiest of religious texts, the Torah, in which he was well versed. I believed him to the letter, but would not remove my pants. Actually, Evie epitomized the manners of a European middle-class *jeune fille bien rangée*—a well brought up young lady. I was far more rebellious, adventuresome, and less stable in my habits and temperament. For a while I thought Claude preferred her to me. They both had certain of the feline qualities that strongly attracted me, including the elongated muscle structure of the natively slender, something I had had myself until I was twelve years old. Evie's graceful, fine movements I found elegant. There was a boyish, staccato rhythm to everything Claude did. Both had green, cat-like eyes, which invited pursuit. When I thought she might like him too, I became tense and preoccupied, and fled into the study of philosophy and literature for longer and longer hours at night. It was then that I began to think of becoming a writer. Claude encouraged me in this. He often read poetry to me, mainly from T.S. Eliot, whom I could follow. I could not well understand many of the others we read together. French had not been his forte, and despite his outstanding brilliance as a student, it almost grounded him during his Ph.D. examinations at MIT. I translated André Gide for him, and read to him from my Dutch poet hero, Guido

Geselle. I learned to appreciate the "unpredictable, irrational" improvisations in the jazz music he was so fond of, and began to love to listen to his blues singers, especially Teddy Grace. Eventually he compromised by appreciating Brahms.

At one point Professor Claude Lévi-Strauss, the anthropologist, moved into our boarding house. Both Evie and I followed the courses he taught at the nearby *Ecole Libre des Hautes Etudes*. I got to know him better, for like him I worked for a while for the Office of War Information. He, Robert Franc (who had been the chief male singer at the Opera of Paris, who then became a painter), and André Breton, the Dadaist, did the first and most important morning broadcast in French to the underground radio stations in Europe. Early one morning after night work at the Office of War Information, Professor Lévi-Strauss and I found ourselves in the same taxi on our way home. From West 57th Street to 11th Street we had time to talk. He was very much alone and despised his work at the Office of War Information. His humorous comment about the content of the broadcasts: "A good thing we have to give it so early in the morning, when most of us are still totally befuddled in our heads. In this manner it's less insulting to human intelligence." Years later in kind response to a request for a certificate on behalf of Evie's further studies he felt obliged to delegate the moral responsibility for the veracity of his statements to me, in view of his dwindling memory, which he said had by then become non-existent except for immediate work concerns. He nevertheless found it appropriate to remind me of a "kiss in the taxi—that time… " of which I for one had not kept the slightest memory trace.

The two Claudes finally met on the front step of our house one late summer evening. I found them there, the younger mathematician, head resting on folded arms, strumming as he did usually with his fingers, to accompany a sudden hum of a plaintive blues tune. He was looking down from the highest step, closest to the house. The older most pensive, head and shoulders erect, abstracted, looking away in the distance, seated closest to his part of the adjacent section of the house on the lowest step. They sat there, a few feet from one another... two sphinxes... untouchables to each other. I do not believe they exchanged five words during the many hours they sat outside to get some cool air till I introduced them to one another at which time they decided it was time to turn in.

At my philosophy finals, Professor Levi-Strauss saved me from utter disaster at the orals by setting the three other eminences questioning me to battle among themselves. I ran home from the experience humiliated, certain that I had failed. As usual when in difficulty, I ran straight home to my own Claude. His memorable remark when he saw me inconsolable despite his strong efforts to reassure me.

> *"It doesn't really matter, don't you see? After
> all, you're pretty and all that."*

This last comment really undid me, for I was thrown back into the footsteps of my sisters, with whom, in my mind and soul, I could not ever compete on those terms, nor did I want to.

News from my family had ceased; Europe was in ever greater turmoil. This was an incessant concern to me, one which, mysteriously, was not communicated to Claude. He once asked me to go out with him, and when I refused because I had promised to give a typing lesson to the very young wife of Freddy, the house janitor, he made an uncomplimentary remark about black people. He said he even doubted that the two were married, and that their child was probably out of wedlock. He said I was spending too much time with them, and that it was a waste. I had never heard him speak so insensitively of others, and it made me afraid. I never brought up the subject of my people's religion with him. Did I fear he did not care, as he did not care about what was happening in Europe? Did I fear he would reject me?

He did consider me quite a mystery, indeed, for he wondered what I lived on. He was suspicious of my relationship with Evie; homosexuality predominated in the section of the Village where we were living. Possibly too, he was preoccupied with his own frustrations, for by the end of 1942 he must have been sworn to extreme secrecy for the kind of work that went on at the Research Laboratories. And he was no doubt nursing his own secret injuries. His wife of less than one year had left him just before he came to New York, when we first met. Apparently she had been an extremely wealthy heiress, was really clever, the best in her English class, and a good student at Radcliffe College when Claude was a graduate student at nearby MIT. Though he was awarded a very generous fellowship at Princeton University, he told me she would accept small gifts from her relatives, such as furs and jewels. The value of any one of these might almost exceed his annual salary! He wanted her to live on what he proudly offered her—this created conflicts to the point where she simply left one day and never returned. Soon after that she married a Hollywood screen writer. I learned of this accidentally, two years into our relationship. He said they had had to get married for they believed she was pregnant, which then turned out to be not so afterward. When I occasionally cleaned his apartment, I always found the same dust-covered official looking papers on the same spot at his writing table, which he never used. One of the two documents asked for a signature to a separation paper; the other, to a divorce. I do not believe he ever signed either—he may even have left them on the same table when he moved out of the apartment years later.

When did it become clear that he and I were to be together, and Evie the third one in this relationship, the outsider? I cannot know. I do remember, though, that when he kissed me, that very first time, one warm summer night on the roof of our brownstone house, I felt the coolest, gentlest, sweetest lips that ever touched me. I felt transfigured. Thank heavens for the language difficulties between us at the time, for he followed our embraces with much hard swallowing, his Adam's apple pointed and dancing up and down, and then said abruptly, "let's go to bed!" I did not understand what he meant, and exquisitely sensitive, he did not insist. A pretty confused youngster, I was repressed and naive to an unimaginable degree. (This in spite of the fact that when fifteen years old I had witnessed one of my sister's abortions on her kitchen table, performed by two able physicians.) Eventually Claude's passionate kisses had me believing for some time that I was pregnant. (I was not yet menstruating regularly, and the event, when it did occur, was painful and accompanied by acute migraine headaches.) In addition, I believed I had caught a shameful and dreadful disease from him, like syphilis. When he called on me unannounced I would hide the books I had hoarded on the subject. He realized what I was doing, and confronted me with my confusion. At age twenty six he found it laughable that at age nineteen I could still be so "mixed up" when nothing had happened. I stressed I did not believe "nothing happened." As a result of this, I would not see him for weeks. When I entered his flat again, the attraction overwhelmed me, and we were friends again. For months on end, sometimes nightly, we loved each other intimately. Still—I refused to take off my clothes. When I finally gave in to our mutual passion, I believe it was mainly out of guilt for having refused him so often. A love ensued that marked me forever. He became the strong, affectionate father I had lost, perhaps never had. He became a powerful, patient mentor of my thoughts. He became my entire family. He became all I had. Though gentle in his manner, even timid, he spoke in an abrupt, deep-throated voice. At times his approach was tactlessly direct. His prolonged periods of gloom and silence would rack me with self-blame, for he would invariably end psychological withdrawal by saying reproachfully, "Baby, you're awfully quiet at times... " Intuitively I perceived that total subjugation to him was an implicit imperative in exchange for total harmony.

My irrepressible physical want of him was accompanied at all times by guilt at what I had brought about. He complained bitterly about this, for it must have been a tiresome game he was made to play. It appeared that I demanded total reconquering on a monthly basis. Eventually I began to deny, first to Evie, then even to myself, that it had ever happened—that is, that I had given him "my final favor." I once overheard him "jiving" over records with his colleague and friend at the time, Barney Oliver. They snickered like adolescent boys over a girl's "cherry." I found it far from *drôle*. I remained for an amazingly long time in a state best described by the French as *demi-vierge*—indicating a mental state of insufficient devirgination. I thought the subject pretty horrendous. I took as long as a week to realize that the lovely pink stain that marked one side, my side, of his stale bed sheets, had been made by me. What contortions of mind, of body! What pink-blooded, sweet, laurel-leaf shaped, gentle marking!

What utter stupidity in my shattering shame that led me to ever-deepening depths of denial! Gradually a state of psychological disaster ensued. I began to deny the existence of groups of objects related to him and my passion for him. The guilt originated with what I perceived as my mother's total disapproval of what I had done. I went as far as to deny to myself and to others that I was my mother's daughter. The mythomaniacal trend began to pervade interactions with newly found friends. I hovered on being extremely schizy and became a strict vegetarian from a desire for purification.

I never spoke to him about my rather unique religious-cultural heritage. By not speaking to him about this it implied denial. I tested this out on myself in order not to trip over the silence. I remembered well he would not be acceptable to my mother as a member of our chosen sect—who wasn't my mother any longer and about whose whereabouts I worried day and night. Such was the tone of the beginning of our life together. Despite this, I never cease to take delight at all he taught me, also at how he eventually learned to give of himself in this relationship. When I introduced him to the many men I met, he was at times most recalcitrant in communicating with them. At times he confronted them in his flat like the green-eyed cat he could be. His expression was usually one of a hissing snarl. At times, suddenly agitated, he would become sarcastically witty. Friends who came to see us would exclaim, "Now here's a man's man!" At times, I too became painfully jealous of the women about whose beauty he would occasionally comment when I urged him sufficiently to. I realized I must avoid these confrontations, for I found the sharpness of the pain unbearable. Though I brought this jealousy on myself by my testiness, it made me flee again from him for days. Always asking, "Do you find this girl pretty? Don't you like this woman's silky hair? Don't you prefer blondes?," he once exclaimed spontaneously after a Bastille Day Street dance (in the French Quarter of New York) to which I dragged him, "Now that was a pretty girl!" Little did he know what a time we were in for as a result of this... sleepless night for me . . . interrogations . . . unending comparisons between women... I detested myself for what I considered a "lack of seriousness" but compulsively kept on trying to obtain the reassurance that he preferred me. Little did I remember I provoked the remark, for I left him stranded, with a minimal command of French, and danced most of the night with Robert Franc, whose wife of that time created a loud scene, for she mistook me for his Puerto-Rican mistress.

Throughout this period Claude, paternal, mature, and logical most of the time, had the bright idea of introducing me to people who were practiced in the field of psychology by saying, "You see, she's been through all these bad happenings during the war in Belgium and France, and look how balanced, healthy and happy she is!" I cringed from within. He called me his ray of sunshine. I guess I sang a lot, especially when near him. In my relationship with him I resumed the role I had always played at home, that of "the King's Fool": that had been Dr. Baudouin's analysis of my position in the family. This had previously brought recognition and attention. I loved to play, joke, dance and enjoyed athletics. In the Village people took note, for we were obviously lovers. Our markedly contrasting body structures caught the attention of the artists, many of whom lived in the section where we swam in the late summer afternoons. He was taller, Lincolnesque—I, plump, my arms always clinging around his waist. He said I was "the only good thing in his life" at the time. Patiently he helped me with school work, and seemed surprised that I knew how to think about certain subjects in a way that pleased him. He eventually found me the most intelligent girl he had known. His comment sent me to heaven for awhile. He stated nevertheless that he abhorred what he called my "irrationality." He tried by every means at his disposal to correct this in me. I remained as recalcitrant as my unruly hair that he seemed to love to stroke for long periods, pausing at every "unpredictable" curve of it. I perceived that unknowingly my emotivity was part of the attraction he felt for me, though not without anger. When away from him, I became almost a replica of him, repeating his very words and ideas, which were extreme for the time. The ideas he had about machines that could out-think and surpass man's innate fallibility, compared to theoretical, more perfect creations, clung to me. Though I fought with him about some of the nomenclature he so easily wielded, which to me seemed debasing to life, when away from him I parroted his positions with everyone else.

When I swam in the waters of Havana, Cuba (where I had gone to visit my mother, who had finally managed to escape from Europe), I relived every minute spent in intimacy with him. Once, while alone in the large swimming pool at the Hotel National, I looked up and found a man staring at me most intently from one of the high balconies. I shamefully realized that I was not doing this merely for the exercise. Claude once said earnestly, as thou disappointed, that "pragmatically, women's hips are not functional." Was this an allusion to my utter passivity, to the fact that I could not follow his inflamed loins and their graceful frenzy of motion? My passion never followed his concurrently. I only loved the play, the closeness, and feeling all of him. It never went any further than that between us.

In the late summer of 1942, two years after I had last seen my mother, the first question she asked me when we saw each other in Havana was, as I expected, was I still... was this wretched virginity intact... had I been a good girl... I neither said yes nor did I say no. The by then unfamiliar sounds and intonations of her voice, the Latin tempo, the strangely pounding Cuban Spanish, the unceasing agitation, the tormented encounters with her I had so loved—all this finally precipitated a response of psychological flight and I withdrew. I locked myself away in my hotel room for days on end, drinking a lot of *Cuba Libres*. I would not eat, and did not respond to her knocks on the door. I had brought along my easel and paints, and created a rather prophetic picture of Claude. In it he held up a long finger, à la Abraham Lincoln, whom he strongly resembled. The finger was portrayed as an elongated chimney which ended with a smoke stack, reminiscent of a futuristic inverted rocket. I do not believe I had ever seen a rocket then. This symbolized a pretty phallic object—obviously, as I remember it now. On his right shoulder rested a weighty book, which showed a ONE written on the spine of its hard, deep red binding.

After I returned to New York from Cuba, I did not go to see him for a week. Every night I waited for him to call on me. I thought that if I pondered sufficiently and longed strongly enough for him, eventually he would feel these vibrations and come my way. Finally I went to our old brownstone house on 11th Street where he still lived. I wanted to have a look on the telephone message pad near the entrance hall, just to see... Suddenly he emerged from nowhere and handed me an unsealed envelope, saying, "See, Maria, I wrote you a letter. I was going to send it to you while you were away... Where have you been all this time?" The letter was dated a month previously. I believe I moved back into the house with another girl, for Evie had been fetched by her parents under threat of having us arrested. I don't remember why I did not see Claude for almost a month. Then for a reason beyond my control, I was to meet with him again late one evening, in what was to be our most memorable man-woman encounter. A Belgian girl, to whom I had become related in Antwerp, ran away from her strict, disciplinarian, and mad parents. She had gone to hide in Claude's flat when she did not find me in. In the minds of my contemporaries from Antwerp, Claude and I epitomized the emancipated, free-thinking, free-loving couple. What irony! I did not know she was in his flat until her parents called on me to implore my help in getting her to return home. When I expressed sincere surprise at their surmise, that I would have any power to do so, they said she had told them she had received assistance from a very close male friend of mine. I suddenly realized whom they meant. When they left, I went to listen at his door. I heard her voice, and found her inside wearing a man's suit and fedora hat, which Claude had lent her to flee the house. When she left in a crying uproar, I found myself suddenly in the quiet of his familiar flat, alone with him. Unable to move, I stood near the door. I was overcome with the sweet sharp breath of his scent. My head swam in it. I stood about twelve or fifteen feet from him. With his back turned to me I watched him bend deeply over his noisy, antique, eternal music console, changing a record. When he unbent and turned around, calling my name questioningly, we both felt impelled at the same instant towards each other. I do not remember taking more than a single giant step, or rather leap, towards him—or he in my direction. We touched, embraced. I felt a shock, an electrifying spark, a heaving wave which carried me while I felt the earth move away beneath me. When I came to I saw him, breathless, overcome, deadly pale. He was trembling against me and I swayed with him. We held on to each other for we staggered and thought we would fall. He exclaimed, "Jeez, goodness, baby! Did you feel that? It was like electricity… like that!" and he snapped his fingers hard. How could we leave each other then? I have often wondered if such strong sensations have come his way again with others. This terrifying, though sublime sensation of being possessed, as though in total union with the very earth, has never overcome me again. Perhaps the closest would have been giving birth and the weeks after in union with a newly created life. It is likely that we were biologically optimally suited for each other. It was most unfortunate that he did not esteem women in general; he illustrated his belief in their innate inferiority by citing the absence of women mathematicians and physicists in history. Events would disprove him. He was only twenty-five years old when I first knew him, but he was no doubt one of the two or three most natively gifted and intelligent men I have ever known. From the point of view of emotional development, I see both of us at that time as having suffered through a similar hurtful loss in our childhood, at about the same time. In our own way, we were inexperienced, and arrested at a much earlier stage than our intellectual development warranted. I certainly was.

* * *

Racked by loneliness, while still married to Henry and our children were away in England, and I became impelled to go to see Claude again, he received me that first time with his wife and children in their large house situated near the edge of a serenely flowing lake-like river. I was asked to stay overnight. We all slept poorly. I still felt part of my own last marriage. I did not yet know the results of my New York State Board Medical Examinations, and was still studying for them in case I would have to take them over again, as others told me was likely. I spent the greatest part of the night awake in this commodious, well-lived-in home with its fine looking concert piano for his wife's classical music preference in playing, and helter—skelter furnishings. There were mountains of books that lined the walls up to the very high ceilings, and innumerable electronic gadgets that were both gigantic and functional. I remember an electronically-operated ladder that took you from one end of an enormous bookcase to the other. There was also an original creation of his wife's: a 'child-proof' seating gadget that allowed you to ride, child in arm, all the way down to the river's edge and back up to the house. I remember, too, an antique player piano that Claude operated vigorously, pumping its ancient pedals. The music fed into it by early programming cards did not, I thought, justify the enormous expense of energy on his part. Throughout the night I read Merck Manuel's chapter on heart diseases—of all things—over and over, without knowing quite well what I was reading. In the morning, following breakfast, while we sat in the sun on the veranda, Claude rocked himself in his hammock. In answer to my questions he complained about the work involved in teaching for one semester per year. He asked me what appeared at first to be the casual sort of thing one asked about an old girl-friend's newer husband. I described Henry's insistence that appearance be maintained at all times, of his utter conviction that "a proper" appearance was the most important aspect of people. I said this laughingly, and was surprised when Claude asked in earnest, "Doesn't this lead to some pretty bad conflicts between you?" His wife wanted to see a photograph of our family, and on viewing a recent snapshot of Henry and the children, she exclaimed, "My! Henry is handsome!" Claude looked at her quizzically at that. At first I thought her kind, and found her soft, feminine, and very sensitive. Her gestures were smooth, graceful; she was vivacious. She was beautifully built, i.e., very slender, delicately boned, and, for a girl that slender, quite ample-breasted. Facially, as my first husband Robert Berryman had told me, indeed we looked remarkably alike. She certainly had a better figure than I could ever hope to attain, since I was short wasted, yet long-legged. I told myself consolingly I possibly looked more appealing just then. She seemed highly overwrought during my visit, and was kept very busy with the care of their newborn baby girl She employed no one to assist her with the household chores, although Claude was well known by then and probably quite wealthy. The older of his two boys resembled him closely and seemed extremely keen. I told his wife how much resemblance I found between the boy and Claude as I had known him. She expressed her wonder that both boys' heads had looked identical immediately after birth—"exactly of the same mold," and replicas of Claude. She said time and again, perplexed, yet admiringly, how similar they were to each other and to Claude, whereupon I stressed humorously that they were, after all, most probably from the same genetic mold. Only later did I realize that unconsciously she perceived these boys as entirely Claude's.

During that first ill-inspired visit, near the edge of the Mystic River, the old house stood perched on a large stretch of rising ground. Its enormous windows stared, unshielded and cold. Claude watched me as I tenderly held his baby daughter. He looked at me attentively, then looked just as analytically at his wife. Without concealment he looked for my darkened front tooth, which by then was nicely capped. He looked too for the familiar spur on my nose, which had been crushed by another blow. Without the slightest attempt to disguise his feelings, it was clear what he thought as I held his lovable baby girl. His posture proudly seemed to say: "This could have been yours... " I was happy with the children I had; they were more fine-featured than his. True, I would have loved his too. When we were alone on his small boat dock near the water's edge, he asked me why I had twice married men who were airline pilots at the time. This common denominator had never occurred to me before. He had obviously made a better choice; his wife was a mathematician of sorts. She knew him when they both worked at the research labs. She married by all appearances the boy of her dreams. His work was not a secret to her. There was an essential harmony which reigned in this home. People would come, his wife said, friends of Claude, and stay for months. Still, better this way than to see no one, she said, considering Claude's reclusive ways. I thought I didn't quite remember him being that way at all really ... He just had his long pensive days, when the cigarette butts would accumulate in the unlit hearth, but then we would go and dance in Harlem ... The entire household spun around him without question.

While we drifted alone in his row boat on the Mystic River, many large windows at bay, reflecting sunlight, our toes touched. He was staring fixedly at me. I trembled and kept my eyes lowered. I felt his attractiveness, his mystifying appeal as I had years ago ... We ran along the banks of the Mystic River and he took me far into the thickly tree-shaded areas. I kept distant from him. I felt so ashamed of my feelings, so guilt ridden with the conviction that I had abandoned the things dearest on earth to me: him, and now my tiny son.

* * *

Years earlier when we were close, Claude had come for dinner one night to my new flat near Columbia University and Riverside Drive. His mother had died by then. He was neatly dressed and wore a tie, coat, and overcoat. I had rarely seen him so well clothed, and he looked remarkably well in his Sunday best. He occasionally smoked a pipe then. I found him truly and amazingly handsome. I also found him different, calmer, suddenly more mature looking. He seemed contented, liked the dinner, did not press for sex, and we were amicably close. That night I dreamed:

Claude was seated, as on a stage. The chair he sat on was simple, old fashioned, and made of solid wood. It had long legs and a curved back in the shape of a double arch, one inside the other, about 15 cm apart, no arms. The chair stood on a high, dark, lacquered turntable. He would appear suddenly clothed as Mephistopheles, evil-looking as the devil, a hissing expression to his mouth, his darkened eyes narrowed to a slit. He was stretched out in a partially reclined position, leaning easily on an elbow. I felt a nameless dread. The turntable kept turning, and he would appear neatly dressed, sweet looking as earlier that same evening, a young man in his Sunday best. The turntable kept whirling slowly, to my terrible fright, to show up that dark-clothed devilish man again. His reappearance made my blood run cold. His scorn, with satanic ice-coldness, was aimed at me. The unspeakable terror I felt, responded to the reclined figure's simultaneously amused indifference. I felt sick with horror on awakening. I have never discovered where this picture of the young, elongated, half reclining demon stemmed from. Did Freddy's fancy that Claude was "smart as the devil" become a fact to me? This relationship was never to end for me.

SECTION THREE

Free Associations and Reaching Out

CHAPTER 6

Free Association One: Mephistopheles Dream

I can't get hold of this. What if Claude were the Bad Guy? Isn't that possible? What if he were the demoniacal Mephistopheles? A thin, piercingly green eyed spouting Dragon who lurched in my dream to destroy me by his evil gaze? Eyes are schizy sort of things to see around. It's usually the moral judgmental eye. The eye of a storm. A mind's eye. An eye for an eye—eyes of the soul. I loved his eyes; they were full of wittiness. I never associated with the dream before, but I told it to Claude. He said the dream related to my ambivalent feelings about him. He'd had the advantage of quite a bit of analysis by then. He added with his coughing laughter, "I feel that way too—sometimes". He said this as though apologetically.

What relevant data in dictionaries? Mephistopheles: Faust's familiar spirit.

Various etymologies:

Hebrew: MEMPHIS—TOPHEL (destroyer—liar). Greek: MEPHOS PHIGEIN—not loving light... from Lucifigum... wandering in darkness, a mysterious kind of demon... dark through and through, malicious, restless, stormy.

Goethe's Mephistopheles: "A part of that same might which wills the evil course and furthers right."

Finally befooled, resembling in this the comic devil or poor devil...

Can't get hold of this Fritz Perls, don't like the Fritz. Too German? Still? Fritz. Had a cousin on my father's side whose nickname was Fritz. He might still for all I know, be alive in Gheel, Belgium. Family lore has it (probably wrong, for based on my oldest sister Sara's roaming imagination.) She told me he tried to slash his wrists—no—even chop them off! It supposedly happened when he was about twenty years old and was preparing for a career as a concert pianist. They interned him in Gheel where he remained to live out his life. Gheel is a world in miniature, an ancient village occupied and governed entirely by those the rest of the people have declared insane. A few physicians share the life with them. It was believed my mother had managed somehow to cut off all ties with the family on my father's side. As I knew so little of them anyhow, I wish I didn't know even that much—especially about Fritz, that is. Rumors had it that most of my father's people had left Holland at the turn of the century to emigrate to America and England. Those that remained were considered converts, mystics of one heretical sort or another, or children of mixed marriages. Later I gathered they were essentially Dutch in their "Weltanshau."

Many of them had fine and dark curly hair and a *café-au-lait* complexion. I say this for eventually I knew two of my father's brothers, also one of his sisters. The latter was his elder, and we knew her vaguely only by the name of Mme. Sayette. I also knew this aunt by sight. She, too, owned a jewelry store, though hers was small and unimportant. I do not remember anyone ever pointing her out to me, but I knew she was my Aunt Sayette. Did I stop at any time to view the array of precious ornaments on display in her shop's window? Not while she was around. I do remember her curly hair, though... a repressed smile, intensely investigative eyes... a dark, dainty, small-boned, lean woman coming toward me... none of this necessarily inviting. As a result of the unbelievably close relationships that existed between my mother and all her sisters and brothers, my father's total alienation from his own family strikes me as odd. He was described as the most easy going fellow and also as having been one of the best looking men of the entire family. I knew him as a rather timid, quiet man—what happened there? He died so early? I was conceived because my mother lent her douching horn to her youngest sister, whom we called Auntie Antoinette. Oddly enough, both sisters were delivered of a child within 26 days. My cousin Armand No. 1 came first. Obviously my mother had lent Auntie A. her douching horn too late for him, and too soon for me for I was born in the same hospital room in Antwerp, 26 days after his birth on the 26th of May.

On my mother's side everyone lived in adoration and glorification of her father: The Saint. He who kept giving his clothes away, who gave everything away: In the streets, in the singing, dancing, praying, joyous temples. Shoes and all. He always seemed able to meet a poorer religious man more needy than himself. He must indeed have been an inspired sort of a deeply religious man—that much I believe. I also know that as a result of my father's standing in the community, my father was the one who did the most giving to assist the enormous family on my mother's side. They trickled in, unit by unit, to our flourishing seaport town of Antwerp, home of Rubens, Van Dyke, Vermeers, Ruysdaehl, Henri Conscience the poet, and also of the diamond-cutting wheel and of my father and his diamond store. My father liked and venerated the old Saintly boy. The affection between the holy man and the uninitiated was genuine and mutual. Why then didn't my father get on with his own sister who also lived in Antwerp? I believe all the blame was assigned as usual to my mother's character—she was considered rather eccentric.

If my father was that easy going, why then did he just look in on my mother in that same hospital room where I was born? He's said to have peeked in and asked, "What is it this time? A boy or a girl?" When told a girl—I was his fourth—he slammed the door shut. He sent his bookkeeper Mr. Miller, (renamed Ghandi by my sisters in view of his extreme thinness) to the Court House to inscribe my name in the official registration book. I was entered as Maria Deborah. After whom? The episode as told to me might have been the reason for my apology to Henry on the birth of our first child… "I'm so sorry Henry—It's a girl… " He said—music to my ears—"On the contrary, that's wonderful!" Well, he at least had a poetess of renown and originality in his transmitted genes to look forward to. My father's mother was supposedly very fair, and was said to have been a descendant of a King Abbas and to have worn diamonds for buttons. When she was 70 years old she is said to have hid my father in a closet, for she did not want her caller to know that her second youngest was a grown man.

When I came to America I eventually met my father's oldest brother, my uncle Adolf. He was a thin, wiry man with an upturned broad nose and deep set, dark, almond-shaped eyes, high cheek bones and a dark complexion. He was a kind and highly sociable man, garrulous and out-spoken, quite unlike my father. He had emigrated to America from Holland at the turn of the century. He apparently made a fortune which he then lost through the stock market crash. He, and then one of his two grown sons—all of them jewelers—wanted me to come and live with them in Brooklyn. In the end I decided against it. I had grown to love my independence and was almost comfortable in my solitude. Then Evie had come. What is it that I'm inching my way to? I didn't think I cared at all about what preceded. I'd remembered that one of my unknown American cousins became an actress in Hollywood and was said by her family to have mysteriously disappeared. How? It has kept me wondering with unease.

The suicide attempt—is that it? Yes—in Geneva. I was just thinking I would not tell the children about Fritz. Too horribly contagious… I heard a lot about him when I was about 12 or 13, and envisaged a tall youth, a sort of inspired and victimized young man (as said, an accomplished pianist—trying to chop off both hands), the blood streaming… there, I've got hold of it now. My mother said he had a love disappointment. She said his sister never married, for she would not leave her aggrieved mother alone…

The Saint had beautiful, large, kindly blue eyes. He was very fair and soft spoken, though very lively-looking in his advanced age on the few occasions I met him. He was a wispy, lightly passing spirit of a man, small and thin. I met his wife—my maternal grandmother—only once or twice. She was tall and impressed me as being finicky, fidgety. I remember a lot of hand wringing and sighing. That is how I remember her, as a reproach. A horny, spiky, prickly reproach. She admonished me to become a nicer girl—to whom? Had the Saint died then, and was that why she sighed so? My cousin Armand No. 1 told me last year something that might have clued me in much earlier. He said, "She didn't like girls, only boys. Didn't you know that?"

Is that where it started? My mother had no use for boys; the only man she venerated unquestioningly was her Saintly Father. What the hell did this man do for his children, some 10 of them? He allowed my mother (who was considered one of his favorite daughters) to go to work when she was (she said) six (yes, she said six!) years old in the deep snows of Poland, shoeless at that! Filled with love for this man she marched off in the bleak early mornings she said, it was five o'clock in the morning—to do work on sewing machines in a local factory. He stayed home to study and pray and glorify the good Lord. Goodness! She certainly knew how to sew! She said the older women stole from her because she was faster than they were and they didn't want her to hasten the accustomed pace. Could she have meant twelve years old at least? Could she have meant 8 a.m.? Then she got rheumatic fever—I believe that must have been what she meant. She said she swelled up overnight to double her size and was "filled with water". As a result of this she remained housebound for some three or four years. Who then went out to work for the Saint and his continued progeny? Well, she stayed for some four years in her cot in daily contact with him, during which time he tried to teach her and give her instructions, just as he taught his sons all the wisdom of the miserable and inspired rabbis. (That was a bad slip I made back there typing—I had written "miserable" instead of "miracle".)

They may have been well off at one time, as she claimed. He was said to have been the best student at the seminary school in the town of Keltze and was considered most advanced in theology. A result of this was that he was offered in marriage the religious community's best endowed girl, in terms of money and physique. She came along with a tannery, I believe it was, unless it was a distillery. Some natural calamity destroyed this source of income. Still, they kept producing progeny for they loved each other and such was proscribed. What was it that I read about this just the other day? In N.Wiener's book *Ex Prodigy*, he says:

"The Jewish family structure is not irrelevant to the Jewish tradition of learning. At all times, the young learned man, and especially the rabbi, (in my case Saint A.), whether or not he had an ounce of practical judgment," (Hurrah! someone else said it!) "was always a match for the daughter of the rich merchant. Biologically this led to a situation in sharp contrast to that of the Christians of earlier times. The Western Christian learned man was absorbed in the church, and whether he had children or not, he was certainly not supposed to have them, and actually tended to be less fertile than the community around him. On the other hand, the Jewish scholar was very often in a position to have a large family. Thus the biological habits of the Christians tended to breed out of the race whatever hereditary qualities make for learning, whereas the biological habits of the Jews tended to breed these qualities in... It would scarcely be respectable to claim to be the descendant of a medieval monk—the only type of intellectual then existing in Western Christendom."

On my father's side we descended from Sephardic (Spanish-Portuguese—perhaps even Persian regal leaders, but with the passage of time we have not been able to place the King (Abbas) from whom my paternal family claimed we were genetically descended. It's coming together now: The ruddy suicidal attempt by wrist slashing (like the other Fritz) when I was in Geneva. I found out at the same time that Claude had married, that I had been failed in Histology, and that my funds would be cut off by my three brothers in law who had helped. Sara and Paula, two of my three sisters felt they couldn't help. Failing histology meant taking the entire bloody series of orals over again, i.e. anatomy, physiology, and bio-chemistry with Prof. Favarger, that bumbling, over kind, exceptionally good looking new and younger professor, who insisted on being helpful with his English that none of the American students understood but were too embarrassed to tell him so. Also that horrible histology over again. The official condemnation: They said they found my yellow dress (quickly store bought with food money in order to look clean and neat during a hot spell, that morning in Geneva) that it had too wide and revealing a décolleté. The dress was too unbecoming for a future physician. (No doubt they were also thinking of my curly hair and dark skin, not to mention my happy-go-lucky attitude, but mainly my mania with imitating the histology prof's locally accented little voice which sang about the tiny cells he pointed to.) Truth also: I'd never seen one of the slides they came up with. For the first time I felt I had lost everything. I had lost both Claude, and also the reason for which I lost him (leaving him in New York and going to Geneva to study medicine). I wrote a letter about the injustice committed against me by the Histology Prof. Bujard to Prof. Favarger, the helpful, new biochemistry Prof. Shades of cousin Fritz. The professor and others burst into my room early in the morning. Favarger had saved me from disaster. He had received the backing of the famous Prof. Rutishauser, of all people. The University's Board of Regents discovered there had indeed been "fowl play"! I was given a special session of examinations which went smoothly.

U.D.[1]: That was a lot of stuff to cover when one is down and out.

T.D.[2]: Well, don't whine… it took courage not to throw in the towel.

U.D.: Actually I have never given up when the going gets tough.

A few weeks after all that commotion I was called on to go to the hospital to visit with one Bruno from Israel, who had made a similar gesture, under the impact of one of Bujard's failing spells. Bruno had been a double agent for his government at one time, and his nerves were shattered. It was good thinking on the part of the Swiss medics, as I was able to assist Bruno out of his depression. He emerged from his cell at the hospital in no time. It was clever of them to have thought that the one who came out of hell could best help the one who was in a similar hole. That was in 1949, long before R. D. Laing's apocalyptic days.

I ran into Claude and his new wife a few months later, in the streets of Paris while they were on a sort of honeymoon. It was evening, the Place de L'Opéra. I was buying flowers for a Dutch cousin (with the Abbas connection) when I looked up and saw Claude and his new wife. They invited me out for dinner. She was pretty, sweet, talkative, and unreserved compared to him. He seemed rather angry toward me and remained distant at first… He seemed much disturbed by not knowing French and said he felt highly frustrated because of the language gap, as though he were tripped up time and again and no one seemed willing or able to speak English in Paris at the time. I wanted to pay for my share of the dinner and she protested and reassured me that all of this was paid for by "the company." He sort of told her half

[1] Under Dog=U.D.
[2] Top Dog=T.D.

playfully not to say this… Was this a secret again?

I had sobered up considerably by then. I was 25 years old. Still can't get hold of this… Karen Horney is gone. My analyst Baudouin is dead. Claude's analyst is gone. What if Claudeke were sometimes the Lucifer attired, thin, evil, green-glancing dragon? He who lurched into my dream to destroy me by evil gaze. A few years ago I chanced upon a book written by one of his co-genii, N. Wiener. (Again?) Well, in this book, *The Human Use of Human Machines*, my gaze fell upon a passing remark which set me afire with recognition of Claude. In the likes of him, Mephistopheles lurked… Frightened I thought of Claude as I did years ago in my dream of him.

T.D.: Am I projecting my own folly of guilt on him again? Is it truly my own demon I feared finding in him? Even so, I must resolve this and learn to live at peace with both extremes.

U.D.: There is still such a bitter aftertaste which lingers on endlessly.

Post Claude—Dropping lines at dinner table. Sssso… excited this p.m. No doubt possible now. When I drink coffee, my heart hurts. Add the injury of the nicotine content even of a "True" cigarette. Don't inhale! Damn it! Swear to it! C'mon, for Mama's sake! She swore by everything holy that my father died because of his smoking. I began at fourteen yet and reading my sister Fanny's entire ruddy library. It was located on the right side, 3rd section of the Louis XVI Salon buffet set, and was kept under lock and key. She walked with the keys around her waist, jangling them playfully in her pink nudity. Breasts upstanding, with dark pink nipples surrounded by goose flesh. Both nipples looked provocatively and in defiance at me, saying, "I have the keys—you don't!" She usually sang and swayed her hips à la Mae West. I felt put down by her upturned chin, the ugliness of pink, grown nudity. My hate, my envy, my pain. Pauleque, my darker sister and closer to me in age, was already totally developed; I, just four years younger, was completely left out of their games. There were so many delightful men at the house to see the girls all the time, but not one ever for me till they were all gone and I was left alone with my mother.

For how long did I stay the PISSERINEQUE, as they called me? I was closely attached to my oldest sister, Sara. At night—as though a continuation of her body—two lenses, concave-convex, fitting into one another with moist hues to glue us to one another... It felt so warm, so secure. I would not get up, it seems, and often wet... Oddly, I still cannot to this day remember where the bathroom in that large house was. The four of us slept on the fourth and top storey of the house. My parents were on the second floor, I believe. I do remember smoke one evening as I returned from school. My father had experimented with chemicals and they said the new bathroom caught on fire. So we did have a bathroom on our upper floor, but was there a toilet to go with it? I just cannot remember. But I do remember chamber pots, large white ceramic ones, very heavy; pretty full in the morning and not bad smelling at all. Female urine of young girls, rarely mine up there. What about the spot on your "derrière" they laughed at and pointed to? What a big joke it was to them! I screamed with terror as on demand—what a clown!—and it only made them laugh more. It took a long time to know it was a birth mark. I became afraid the fellows might think I did not wipe myself properly, and as a result I became compulsively clean around that area. Also because of Dr. Jadassohn, our dermatology Prof. (Not the father, who was from Basel or Bern and won a Nobel Prize in Medicine for the work he did on pigmented nevi and the treatment by hypnosis on plantar warts; it was his son who taught us.) He said: "I don't care v'at they say... no one on earth can be without some B—p—a—tz eel oo zz—(Bacillus) Coli around the A n n o o ss" (Anus)! There were not that many of us who kept coming to his German-accented lectures daily. I was interested in finding out about my mother's affliction with Vitiligo. Also I liked dermatology. Looking at skin, not unlike looking at diamonds in platinum settings. Due to early exposure my senses in that respect were well developed—though not in histology years before. There too I attended regularly but at once disliked the teaching method (or absence thereof.) What with the small minded teacher and his enormous and nasty woman assistant!

"Mouton" (a co-student, Swiss, of my year) was naturally at the dermatology course almost daily. As most of the Swiss, especially the German-Swiss, she was one of the clearly studious ones. I found her one day, in the waiting room of Dr. Baudouin, my analyst. We barely acknowledged each other's presence. Panic—Right place? Right time? Found out she too was in therapy. It somehow gave us a feeling of more intimate acquaintance, though we rarely if ever spoke to each other. They called her "Mouton" because of her tight blond natural curly hair. What the hell did these cold Switzers call me? Who knows? You know! All because I was the only girl in class that first year with a brassiere, a very pointed one at that like they wore in the States. While out with my closest Swiss girl friend on a night out at a night club I met a Dr M. who directed the surgical emergency clinic next door. My God! That man who had invited himself to my flat tried three times in a row with me—right inside (How did I protect myself???) and he stayed, and stayed, and stayed. Ice and ice and ice—*C'est vrais,* I remember him saying, "It is true, you are difficult to please... " Was that my reputation? Now why would my daughter at age eighteen want to place his picture (found in one of my surviving albums) on her night table? What does she perceive of this man who prided himself on his potency as a young man. He has a beard in the picture, and was photographed in a surgical gown while serving in the Red Cross in an Arabian Country. Well what about Prof. JADASSOHN—son?

"Well," said he, "you might be the most immaculate person on earth, but there will always be some B.coli around the anus, whether you balloon yourself inside-out with enemas three times a day or not. THERE WILL ALWAYS BE B. COLI around." So... I never, never, never let them do it there—they might go back front and *voilà*: I'm stuck with colibacillosis! Didn't we see a lot of that in Switzerland? You must wipe from the front to the back, one way. It's a one way street.

Thinking of primal scenes...

Thinking of going to work in the nearest town at 5 a.m. during our exodus during WWII. What was that town called? Nearly two hours by train from Prunla? It must have been Bordeaux. I went to work in a factory to sew army tents for the Boches—The Germans. With the factory workers I went around at noon-time to hospitals, visiting sick girls. I went around crying like "`a fountain', i.e. a familiar song of the time:

> *Elle pleurait comme une Madeleine,*
> *Elle pleurait, pleurait, pleurait,*
> *Elle pleurait comme une fontaine,*
> *Toutes les larmes de son corp y passaient*
> *Oh la la,la la quel cafard!*
> *Oh la la,la la quel cafard!*

The truth! I was way too sad sewing on things I didn't feel right about. THEY SAW I WAS TOO REFINED! Where did that idea come from?) They sent me to the book-keeping department. They might have found out I knew shorthand in four languages; though I only knew two, I got diplomas in four languages (for business correspondence). The girls in the office were very dainty and pretty and there was lots of laughter and intrigues between the young chiefs and the girls. I felt uncertain at first because of the slowed pace with figures. They said *quatre-vingt-seize* in France, instead of *nonante-six* as the Belgians do. I loved, just loved GEOMETRY, and was the best in the class, till a new and at first dumb seeming girl with a gift in mathematics overtook me (without the slightest apparent effort).

The main point? With my first earnings during the war I bought my sister Pauleque a bottle of perfume. It was a favorite, "Molyneux No 5", which Nathan Milstein, the concert violinist wore the evening he stayed to take me out while he remained overnight in Ostend. Sara and her husband Fred said "nothing doing", and Paula and Charles her young husband spent the evening with him instead. I went to say hello to him some ten years later when he played in Geneva. I told him I was studying medicine; he still looked as handsome as ever and as before truly seemed to approve of me. When he left he said, "Au revoir, Docteur... " How well this sounded in his heavily accented, perfumed Russian voice... What did I buy my mother with those earnings? I have no idea. Something with the scent of Mayflower (Muguet) which she loved? She was supporting the lot of us and was worried. In the village of Prunla the villagers, the old women, talked a lot about Charles, my brother-in-law. What was a strapping young man like him doing around while all their young men were gone? Why wasn't he fighting the Boches? He was an only son, and in addition to his need to flee from these uncomprehending people, he felt he must look after his parents. So he and Pauleque went back and we were never to see him again. They went back into occupied Antwerp and I stayed alone with my mother in Bordeaux. I took some of the contents of a few of the precious packets, and took my loot to the men in the French internment camps for foreign nationals so they might buy off their jailers and run off and go back to their homes. I mistakenly thought it was safe to go home... Some of the other young girls originally from Antwerp and met in Bordeaux at the time, left so to speak voluntarily, to go to the 'labor camps' for they would not abandon their elderly parents. They went to their death. Bordeaux was increasingly occupied by the Germans. Mornings I went to the University to listen to the philosophy lectures; instead, as it was nearing summer vacation time, all I heard was a young woman in high heels and short white socks being grilled in philosophy. These examinations were open to the public. I myself was grilled in the history of philosophy many years later at the *École Libre des Hautes Études*. There were Profs. Lévi-Strauss, Mirkine-Gutzewitz (who had dared to call my friend Evie *une bonne petite bourgeoise*, Raymond de Saussure, the analyst, Gurwitch, who for an entire semester lectured to eight students, including me, at the New School for Social Research, where some of our courses were held till the *École Libre* got its own building across the street on West 12th Street. He lectured straight to my exploding size 38 brassiere tips, while I felt paralysingly choked up most of the time. Given to anxiety attacks about my heavy top I tried to fit into the smallest brassiere size possible for me, which cut right into the under-flesh. Once, pre-menstrually, in Claude's flat I almost cried with the pain of it, and overcome, I suddenly got up and simply opened the snaps beneath my blouse—I felt such relief I told him about it and became good humored, friendly, and babbly again. He was most amused and exclaimed "Ha! Anxiety is a function of chest compression... "

Stinking Gurwitch, going from one breast to the other in class without any self-consciousness, always drooling while he spoke, rarely wiping the spittle from the corners of his thin lips... It greatly embarrassed me. I bought eyeglasses which enlarged the print. They could find nothing wrong with my eyesight, but that way I felt I could hide. Nothing really worked, for whichever corner of the room I chose to hide in, his gaze followed over his own glasses. In addition he marked my paper on the sociology exam with a low grade, when through his lechery he was responsible for what I had been unable to pick up in his classroom.

At the examinations, during the orals thanks to Lévi-Strauss' help...

T.D.: You're dying to go over this again and put Claude in the wrong... What if when you thought you had failed and were behaving like a real baby he did try to bolster your morale by calling you a pretty baby and telling you not to worry, for your looks could see you through in life... ? What's so terrible about that?

U.D.: If I reacted so strongly, obviously I was ambivalent about this, as about almost everything else pertaining to being a whole being, a woman.

I was summoned to Washington when my frantic efforts to bring my family to America demanded the buying of affidavits and an appearance before some mysterious body of men set up by the attorney I hired. They reproached me by saying I had made no effort to become more Americanized; the friends I had mentioned were respectable people from Antwerp met in New York. I could not name Claude, for I thought they would reproach me with having loose morals, nor any of the people associated with us.

"Have you ever heard of a girl named Mata Hari?" they asked.

"Mati Hara?" I couldn't understand what they said in the first place. "No, I haven't."

The silly, mentally obstructed men! They made me feel criminally wrong somehow. In reality I had dealt with a group of ex-refugees who criminally stole money from new immigrants by selling not necessarily valid papers at a very substantial sum… One of them—the one I bought the three affidavits from, (one for Paula and Charles, one for Mama, one for Sara and Fred) a Mr. Rosenzweig—had been highly recommended by my mother before I left Europe. A dear friend she called him, and she placed a hand dramatically near her heart. The crook! In 1941, I paid him $2,400 for three affidavits. The latter were kindly handed out free of charge by an elderly sympathetic philanthropist who tried to save and extricate all the desperate to leave Europeans he could. When I called on him in person he was scandalized. An old man in a wheel chair, he could do nothing to prosecute Rosenzweig for fear of invalidating the numerous affidavits handed out in his name in the past. I believe he got someone to quietly get in touch with Rosenzweig to have him desist from what he was doing. My family was not helped in the least by all this. It became too late to get Charles out, and I do not even know if he would have left his parents.

St. Exupéry, Antoine de… "Vol de nuit", "The little Prince". I too have written a book. A short one entitled, "Dialogues between Krishnamurti and Zarathustra", and later on one called "The Havana Pages". They published one of its poems, "The Guagua", in the paper of the New School, I think it was. A woman reporter might have been told before she interviewed me, "Handle that one gently... " (At the New School they might have considered me "brittle"). She was an artist of sorts... I found her most seductive with a teased hairdo as I'd never seen before and a deeply cut dress with her ample bosom in evidence. I became my usual dumbstruck self, unable all over again to express myself in English. How easy it was at that time to shrink into a cocoon, wrapped up inside, as unravelable as a tightly wound spool of angora wool.

Fritz Perls has published and done!!! Barry Stevens has published, and what hasn't she done!!! They are well known! What the hell have I ever done? Being so often in the presence of "the great ones," having read giants, gives one the illusion one too can take liberties. Max Wertheimer, and Wolfgang Koehler, those good teachers with the bad German accents who taught Gestalt Psychology. Did Fritz Perls ever as much as mention them in his last important autobiographical book? Koehler looked like an uptight prick; Max Wertheimer looked like Einstein, but more lively and less kind. What about their constant attacks on psychoanalysis? I was getting well versed in the latter discipline with the help of Dr. R. de Saussure's teachings across the street, and from Karen Horney, and her daughter, and her disciple Ivimy, who gave their classes one story above the classroom where the Gestaltists taught at the New School. Did Fritz ever mention them in his book "In and Out of the Garbage Pail?" You'd think he invented the term Gestalt Psychology... I may write too, freely! That is the message. To celebrate the "Go ahead" read some Becket! I'm too tuned up, wound-up. (If only I did not have to copy these notes... If only there were a small typewriter as there is a small pocket calculator—how very handy that would be—it should be feasible!) Who wants to sit in a public café and dictate into a recording machine… They'll think I'm some old world reporter and move from me… I stopped for a brandy on my way from the supermarket on College Avenue. I felt it would be better than a Valium tablet… Thinking of following a cure re the smoking when this work is done. A behavior modification approach in a pleasant and undemanding group setting is probably best for smoke-weaning therapy in my case.

I am O.K. too, and not just because I know that Fritz lied—sometimes for his own aggrandizement. I am convinced I helped to send Claude on his way to discovery… that's the worst of all! Why? While I bought flowers near La Place de L'Opera that time, I looked up and saw them cross the avenue—that was the first time I saw her. She would have done that job better than I possibly… Probably…

T.D.: BREAK HIM LOOSE!

U.D.: That is a lie—she could not have—Dr. Abraham K., his analyst, knew it. He said I was just right for him and that I came along at the right moment to inspire him and pull him out of his despair!

T.D.: The first part of the last sentence is possibly fantasy… for how did I inspire him?

U.D.: Well, I humanized him! I taught him all about André Gide, about Nietzche, and Bergson, and Dostoevski.

T.D.: How did that help him?

U.D.: Didn't Gide say 2 plus 2 is beautiful, but 2 plus two makes 5, that is sublime?

T.D.: Claude knew of Riemann's mathematical system long before you heard of it.

U.D.: I held him adoringly, night after night. I loved him—that is what did him good and he became a man.

T.D.: What about the Dr. Abraham K. he went to see because you pushed him so?

U.D.: What? Dr Abraham K. learned a lot of mathematics—that's what Claude said.

T.D.: Also, funnily enough, that Dr Abraham K. "was beginning to think more scientifically toward the end."

U.D.: What about his anxiety at public meetings and the discomfort with teaching? What did his wife say? "Why don't you invent a machine that could do it—i.e. transcribe from the spoken word to the blackboard? No need to be there in person". Now that was a dumb thing to encourage in him! I instinctively frowned reprovingly when I heard her say this—some advice! Fill the pockets of anger left untouched by his analyst, and by time and experience, fill it all with servo-mechanics—that was the gist of her advice. He must learn to unwind. Let him learn how to laugh at losing at this stage of his life—he has become a prisoner of success, just as much as he was once a prisoner of fear of failure.

T.D.: There is a lot to be said for the anonymity of the loser, the fundamental mediocrity that is our common lot as humans.

U.D.: I found it so funny to let his little son win at chess when I played with him. Claude was like a person stunned; he shook his head in amazement when he told his wife, "Look, he won the game with her... he won... " My amused grandiosity changed to irritation as the incident reminded me of irreconcilable difficulties between us.

I didn't have a thing about chess like he did; besides, I never let him win at checkers with me when we first played and he preferred not to play the game with me again.

I loved the evening at his house when we drank whisky and

listened to Teddy Grace singing the blues again—He lent me the records which he wrapped lovingly to have them copied. What peace in that house. God! What peace!

T.D.: There is no hate worse than that of jilted love.

U.D.: Who left whom? When alone with his wife for a moment—what with all the demands of the children for her attention . . .

T.D.: Though overwrought and obviously overworked, she remained smooth in her movements, her voice kind, sensitive.

U.D.: There was a struggle going on beneath the surface between compliance, dependency, and control in the practical spheres of life. I realized then that I liked her. When I opened up to her, I felt her retract, frozen into being sociable on a superficial level, a prisoner of conventionality. We would never be friends…

How am I to know if I ever did any good for people? I've seen and treated THOUSANDS of people and tried to help each in therapy. Not just 300 in a lifetime, as my daughter's textbook in psychology gives as an average for psychoanalysts. I've already treated thousands. I've even saved a few dramatically, thanks to my medical training.

I am thinking of the case of M.M. at the Long Island Home in Amytiville, where I did my first residency after a year of rotating internships at French and Roosevelt Hospitals. By then I was married to Henry, with my baby daughter in tow, my son just on his way inside of me. This woman of about forty, who had been a cashier at the check-out counter in a supermarket, was admitted for depression. I was assigned to treat her. She complained mainly about being so easily fatigued, to the point where even telling her gripes over and over again made her feel tired. Something in her voice, in her sad little face, in her eyes, caught my attention. Her husband had just left her and their 9 year old daughter for another woman. She was worried about the future, and I felt she had plenty to worry about, and did not find her neurotic. In reality she was the first patient I had met at the Long Island Home whom I felt was not mentally nor emotionally abnormal at all. Her "Saga" was what really undid her and almost cost her her life. The specific reason for which her family had insisted she come to the hospital was that she had suddenly become paralyzed in her upper limbs while working at the checkout counter. On another, but simultaneous level, her girlfriend at the adjoining register was ticking off ciphers, but while doing so, she had slipped a $5.00 bill sideways into her uniform. M.M., who was also a friend of the manager, knew that he had got wind of the whereabouts of disappearing money from daily totals. She was aware too that he was watching her girlfriend from holes drilled in the ceiling. It was at this point, knowing her girlfriend would be caught in the very act of misappropriating the money, that she felt incapable of raising her arms. She had warned the girl without coming into the open about the manager's plan...

At the L.I. Home, a most capable psychologist, a Dr. Ky (to whom I gave a lot of grief by repeated complaints about having to be on night duty three nights a week and getting only one weekend in three off), tested M.M. He emerged with a "brilliant" diagnosis of "CONVERSION HYSTERIA"! They had not seen one in years. The Director advocated the Kalinovsky Special (my name at the center for ELECTRO-CONVULSIVE Therapy) to help her over her depression. I asked the staff to wait—I said she was my patient, after all, and I had some say over it. I couldn't quite put my finger on it, but one thing was certain, she was neither neurotic, nor psychotic, and there was no reason to hasten with a course of (ECT). I prescribed a mild tranquillizer. She said it made her worse. (It was months before I discovered that what Dr. Z., the other resident psychiatrist, and I prescribed was often changed by the directors without our knowledge. Later they apologized and gave as their excuse that they did not trust the judgment and experience of Dr. Z.—I had made it clear I did not trust theirs.) I asked M.M. to come to see me more often in my office, hoping to get some clue as to what was really ailing her. I noticed that after about 10 or 15 minutes of a session with me, her eyelids drooped. I quizzed her: She mainly felt fatigued, when? Without having been given the suggestion, she implied she became what she called paralyzed, when she undertook tasks which involved repetitive movements, like cutting meat, putting up her hair. I was constantly reminded of someone, but I could not place the person. I got out my textbooks of clinical medicine. I felt there might be a metabolic disease that bothered her, maybe Calcium metabolism. I stayed in my office at night reading chapter after chapter, hoping to put my finger on what I felt was a medical affliction. Dr. Z. came by one evening and asked what I had in mind. I said I was certain there was something wrong in the metabolism of this woman's muscular system. He asked what was I thinking of? I said something like Calcium metabolism, I didn't know quite what. He laughed with his good natured humor, and asked,

"Are you going to tell me that she has a Myasthenia or something like that?" and walked off.

That was just it! That was exactly what she had: Myasthenia Gravis! Only two years earlier I had treated an older woman who had looked like her on the Neurology ward at the University Hospital in Geneva. We had treated her with a new drug and kept her alive against all odds. The drug had to be flown in from America. The case had made history—how could I have forgotten it? I called in the Assistant Medical Director when I made M.M. exercise and gave her a shot of prostigmine which made her feel better. He put his finger to his temple and turned it around significantly to indicate I was, "ZOT—FERUCKT—Crazy" and stalked out with the head nurse, ordering ECT for the next morning. In addition to this he wanted her to receive an injection of Thorazine to quiet her down. I called her family that night and asked them, just to satisfy my qualms, to take her out of the hospital early in the morning to Dr. Bender, a Prof. of Neurology in New York. The next day at noon Dr. Bender called the medical director to say M.M. had a classical case of Myasthenia Gravis and not to give her Thorazine, nor ECT, for it would undoubtedly kill her by choking. The Director's Assistant never apologized; still, he did not change my prescriptions after that. The staff said they were told I was "inciting to riot" and had rendered Dr. Z. a discontented physician. They thought Henry and I would be better off elsewhere. They said in view of his aristocratic background, he was a degenerate for being unemployed and wanting to move in on the grounds at my expense. Though they all stressed Henry's good looks, they openly despised my lack of resoluteness toward him. When I lost the job at that hospital, after one year, sure enough, Henry at once found a job in California and flew off. I excitedly phoned Henry to tell him what had happened at the hospital. He said I was no doubt making too big a thing out of it. He wondered why I took minor setbacks so much to heart:

"After all," he said," your work—that's the only thing you're any good at really—you didn't even know how to cook an egg properly when I married you."

T.D.: What about Ferdinand from Gratz, what happened to him? Why did he die?

U.D.: That was the co-therapist's fault. True—I should have made a stink and been more assertive, as I was with the above-mentioned case. I said he, Ferdinand that is, must go to the hospital again—the first time I sent him, he went to Columbia University's State Psychiatric Unit in New York City. The psychological testing done there said he was potentially suicidal. His intelligence, despite the language barrier, was of the genius level. The son of an Austrian physician, he felt he knew enough about medications to keep administering new ones to himself. He had constant, abstract sounding complaints of headaches for which no organic basis was ever found. He attributed his headaches to a change in barometric pressure. Boy! He always found one somewhere in America to coincide with his pain! Every time he traveled he consulted a physician who prescribed for his headaches, his depressions. He claimed his headaches started when he was placed in an American open air camp for German soldiers after WWII. The inclement weather and exposure had he said made him ill for life. He always added on, never discontinued the previous medications.

When I returned from vacation to rejoin the group therapy which had been run by the co-therapist alone in my absence, I said,

"I want you in a hospital, for I want you to get off all these meds for a while." The co-therapist openly contradicted me on this. His argument was that he would still have to face his problems. "Yes, but I don't want him in this state with all that medication in him… "

I never expected the psychologist to contradict my clinical nose. He was a totalitarian, a bully! He had to override me, and it killed Ferdinand.

T.D.: Ferdinand was mad! He looked exactly like the Mad Prince whose picture hangs in the Mexican Museum in the large park in Mexico City. That one too was mad, genetically schizy, and you know it!

U.D.: No! There's no proof whatsoever to any of this. Ferdinand was a depressive with too many self-applied drugs. I gave him all the samples of Fiorinal he asked me for. He killed himself with the last batch. I had given them to him for years! I stuck to Albert Ellis' line then. Analysis was met with enormous resistance. He wouldn't come off his homosexual repressions, either; he just sat and sat on them.

T.D.: Didn't he call for the Priest? The stupid convert—like all converts—they become more Catholic than the Pope. Didn't his wife and the Priest let him sleep in the middle of a Saturday afternoon to his death the next morning?

U.D.: I felt the co-therapist, his wife, the Priest were all in cahoots…

T.D.: The lesson: no more co-therapists who are strong men in need to prove they are better clinicians than those trained to be such. A clinician is a clinician, and has a nose which must be followed. I must put my foot down more forcibly.

U.D.: The co-therapist would have crucified me in front of the patients, as he did later when I began to contradict him in the group.

T.D.: The patients were getting anxious, it was as though mummy and daddy were fighting…

U.D.: The co-therapist never owned up to his mistake, did he? He has shown a weakness time and again, in avoiding the recognition of suicidals. That's a fact! He lost at least one other that I know of.

T.D.: When I was in trouble with Henry, my husband, (which continued chronically) and wanted the children tested, he always made himself available. He tried to help. He tried to tell me time and again, "Henry doesn't give a shit. He's an extremely narcissistic type of a guy. I like him, he's a likable guy, but when are you ever going to realize he only cares about himself? When did he ever buy his son a coat or a pair of shoes? You say he cares—how does he care? He's just out to undo anything you set up for them, and there's nothing you can do about it."

U.D.: He—the co-therapist—is still a friend—He's always offered such reasonable, level-headed advice, but he has no imagination.

T.D.: Who needs imagination when you're in deep trouble with circumstantial obstacles to imprison you?

U.D.: He's inclined to bite the hand that feeds him, like he did with Albert Ellis, to whom he owes so much.

T.D.: Most men do this with their mentors—it's a vicarious way of killing off the father in order to attain manhood themselves. They feel impelled to overtake him to render him ineffective, and when they can't, they attack verbally, they criticize, they become catty.

The dykes have broken. The sluices are open.

> *Que ma quille éclate*
> *Que j'aille à la mer*
> *Rimbaud.*

I'm going to read "Carlos In The House of YU" The way it was first written, to make myself feel better. If I could only bleed monthly again—an apotheosis, a cycle, the regular lunar waves define your existence concisely. Presently, coffee and cigarettes spin one off without constraint, discipline, or divine universal order... One master in behavior therapy postulated that besides eating, sleeping, and relaxation, SEX is a potent anti-anxiety agent. If by sex, Joseph Wolpe means intercourse *per se*, this might lead to doubtful results in some individual cases. Were he to include in the appellation of sex the fullness of sensuality, or even its imagery by evocation, I would consider his postulates of the four ways by which one counteracts anxiety as entirely validated by experience. Anxiety requires the participation of one's neuro-vegetative system (increased heartbeat, perspiration, clammy hands, dry mouth, tensed up sets of muscles, dizzy spells). Without some of these physical manifestations one does not experience anxiety. Therefore, it is easy to understand why neuro-vegetative activities (for instance eating, or the evocation of sex) usually associated with pleasure would inhibit in the end the discomfort experienced during bouts of anxiety. "CARLOS"? I must have a look. Reread also "Grandfather Incest" which led to "Carlos in the House of Yu."

Rereading helps. Reliving the very experience.

CHAPTER 7

Grandfather Incest

That summer, ten years later, my senses were awkwardly
reawakened. The stimulus was an inordinately
complimentary, semi-retired colleague. He entered upon the
rather empty and desolate stage at a time when I was seeking
companionship within the fraternity of medical men; a lovely
young patient with a drinking problem, the mother of two infant
children, had suddenly died. She was, to all appearances, much
improved for having been able to give up drinking, and yet she
died. Misdiagnosed as being intoxicated when it happened, she
died by choking, in a coma. This was attributed to a thrombus
which traveled from leg to lung. News of her unintercepted death
was sad, sobering, disturbing. The thought that she had been in
my office the week prior to her death would not leave me.

On that occasion she had looked truly awful. She had said
there was nothing further to talk about. She agreed to undergo

psycho-diagnostic testing—a parting gesture—with the future in mind. This was initiated, but never terminated. She did say she had hurt her leg, and was kept awake by the pain. I questioned her sudden gauntness and sunken cheeks, which she attributed to weight loss resulting from an ascetic "water diet", together with a regimen of megavitamin therapy. I remarked on her technique of "massive assault on all fronts"; she protested that she was enchanted to have shed the weight. Her complexion had been most attractive in the past, strongly feminine, rotundly Anglo-Saxon, but now the bloom, the radiance of the healthy young woman with rosy cheeks, was gone. "I wish you would not plunge into this so forcibly."

"What do you mean? I love it… I haven't been that thin for I don't know how many years… "

"It's nice to be thin, I agree. I always found you so beautiful as you were… Promise to call, and at least consult a non-shrink… Promise?" She had promised. We counted on the many people in the field of medicine who surrounded her to intervene, if anything seemed out of the ordinary. Attention was paid to abstinence, dieting, but what with the busy life she led, none was paid to her personally.

At moments like this, the carefully built edifice of independence from one's colleagues collapses like the proverbial house of cards. One wants to be physically near others who know death intimately, people who live closer to its inevitability than I in my solo practice.

I met this older semi-retired physician in the dining room of a teaching hospital. He was willing to listen, discuss, and compare. He said he knew of a case that resembled the one under examination; he was reassuring. During times of doubt in one's professional life, the opinion of peers matters greatly. It can help to alleviate the burden of guilt. He, and an older and retired psychiatrist named Dr. Smith with whom he had come and I, were still seated in the hospital's cafeteria when most of the staff had already gone. I was gradually reassured by the two men, although occasionally I would still whine, "She promised; she was so beautiful... so young still..." I was becoming a nuisance even to myself. Dr. Smith finally said, "The most beautiful woman in the world... even she must die." The other physician said something to the effect of "Even she who has the mostest... ," to which Dr. Smith reflected jokingly, "Every woman wants to think she's the most." The other interrupted, "What if she really is the mostest? Look at our hostess, what if she really is... ?"

"Is what?" Both Dr. Smith and I were taken by surprise. "What?" Dr. Smith left at once. I stayed, feeling increasingly uncomfortable, undefinedly so. Before leaving, the semi-retired internist surveyed the empty room carefully, when he asked me furtively for my telephone number. "I might have someone I'd like to refer..."

"I'm listed in the phone book, under M"

"Why of course, I forgot you're more than a mere Maria..."

Was he crazy? Did I misconstrue? I never thought he'd follow up on the accidental meeting. I thought I'd made a bad impression, and had come across as too weepy, too unperceptive. I had misunderstood his intentions, that was certain. But then, no, I had not.

Predictably then, this otherwise learned, and certainly well seasoned man followed the sad occasion of our meeting by contacting me. To my surprise he then phoned me again. What for? He obviously believed this was the way to start his day. Typically he would begin our conversations by asking: "Is this the Dr. M-B?" It was.

"In person?" It was she, in person.

"How many people have you killed this week?"

Now how likely did he suppose that would have been? But to a psychiatrist in my circumstances, it was a close call. How so? I would reply meekly, but taken aback by his sick humor. "Why, by suicide, of course,"—long silence—"Over you." I was more vexed than amused. His type of obliqueness should have been predictable. Still, mention suicide to an analyst, any psychiatrist, and you strike at an area somewhere between past and present, between the diaphragm and throat—not to speak of hands which finally hold the phone too tightly. Occasionally I would meet him for tea or lunch. When the quality of food was not worth the cost, he would become upset. I gladly paid my own way, for, as I insisted, we were friends and colleagues, after all. He said he had been married. "For how long?," I asked. "Thirty-five years… "

"Thirty-five years! That's a long time indeed. You must have married when you finished your medical studies, did you? That's a long time indeed… "

"A long time of ups and downs, mostly downs!"

"How sad—you're quite vigorous, though, aren't you?"

"Vigorously enamored… " I thought his wife had recently left him, and felt sorry for him—at this stage in life! No wonder he looked grubby at times. His communications to me were full of sentiments of a highly flattering nature, which he expressed incessantly, with machine-gun rapidity. They were inelegant overstatements, peculiar to uneducated people who have lived too long in the metropolis. For a professional who had traveled extensively in Europe when studying medicine in Germany, this struck me as an eccentricity. I did not interpret these recitations at first for what they might have meant. Was he not, after all, denying me the status due our mutual profession? I ignored these long incantations of attributes supposedly mine, of a long-forgotten beauty I barely recognized. But treated as a young enchantress, I moved into the slot with ease and gratefully accepted help, advise in the many areas of knowledge in which he seemed to excel. He loved gardening. The empty stands in the front and back of our house became filled with pink and white variegated bloom. I asked advice about finances, too. He gave it willingly, and I began to think it possible to retire one day with an income, rather than die in harness as I thought most of us did. He often asked me to sail with him on a nearby lake. I remembered my English mother-in-law "having to accompany the Dear Colonel" in Torquay, Devon, for fear he might have a heart attack sailing alone in rough weather. So that she would desist in her recriminations, the poor retired flight-lieutenant sold his beloved skiff.

I finally accepted, and learned to sail with my older colleague. On his boat, instructing that first time, he screamed like a bloody Wehrmacht Commander. He had said earlier, "My wife won't sail with me. She says I remind her of Hitler... " That was easy to see. Still, what a pleasure: the sun, this large shimmering body of water, a companion. Suddenly, by contrast, I felt the heavy loneliness of all the preceding years. He said he had a mother in a nursing home on Long Island, New York.. "Still?" I exclaimed, admiringly—it seemed unheard of to have a mother at this stage in life. Our drive to and from the lake took an hour or more each way; and since he drove considerably more slowly than I did, or just about anyone else on the road, we had ample time to converse. Unfortunately a pun was frequently the main source of his conversational fun. He also revealed stores of esoteric knowledge about branches of ornithology and zoology, which fascinated him. The habits of avian species especially made me take note. When I hinted at some of my menopausal difficulties, he responded by quoting from this unusual background: "Did you know that a pigeon doesn't need anyone else? Just looking into a mirror, the mere sight of herself, and she ovulates. A case of fowl self-love… "

"A case of narcissicm in ornithology, so to speak?"

"No. Well, yes. It's just that she doesn't need a mate for bait… "

"Do you?" I wondered disconcerted.

"All she has to do is look into a mirror and she ovulates. Why don't you? That would settle your imaginary complaints."

"I wish I could."

"You would… "

"Have they studied other birds of that class?"

"There wasn't enough glass for the garce."

Some scientists will, of course, mention a bird as a unique specimen when in reality they haven't had time to study the others. Professor Van Tienhoven at Cornell at least taught me that much.

"What else did he teach you. Anything I dare know?" When consulted in the past about general medicine, my kindly colleague had volunteered good advise, for he exuded confidence in his field. With regard to problems relating to intimacy it was wretchedly difficult to elicit his opinion. I insisted on obtaining his acutely weathered evaluation. I patiently persisted with: "Van Tienhoven believes estrogens might be unadvisable. He considers the hormone—even certain topical creams—the lesser of two evils when in dire need. You see I have difficulties, so I wondered, what if it often hurts when you make love?"

"That often? Hope I'm the better of the two evils —You know many cases of dyspaneuria are psychological, you ought to know that."

"I've always suspected my problems were due to long periods of abstinence."

"I'm, I've the ideal remedy… "

"*A voir*—that remains to be seen… "

So I would, but not as I had expected. During our trips to and from the lake, my companion certainly expressed a genuine interest in dogs and their mating habits. He repeatedly mentioned, such and such "whelped" (with an explosive belch in sound). He even mentioned his own daughter analogously. There was no legal father around for that one. Were we back to narcissistic pigeons?

"God helps those who whelp themselves… "

"What about estrogen to treat women for a menopausal or senile vaginitis?" I persevered with a moronic inability to unglue myself from this central preoccupation in his presence. A senile vaginitis. What a misnomer in our medical texts! It was not an infection. Wherefore the ending 'itis'? It was not exactly due to senility either, for women less than forty years old have been known to experience this. We were dealing with a precociously smoothed out inner lining—like autumn leaves waxed by the sheen of time. Gone were the rivulets, the ripples, the steep banks, the circumvoluting climbing turns, the delight of hills traversed by furrows and ridges. The tides of estrogen waves were slowly receding, and leaving softly shining, arid beaches, with glazed surfaces as delicate as crystal. He responded to this reassuringly by saying he did not in the least mind 'a frictionless vault'. "There is of course the danger of the fall before the steep unencumbered climb."

"What about estrogen?" I asked again, most irritatingly, for he seemed impatient to proceed briskly without further ado. "All that menopause talk—a time for pause—most of it is in a woman's head—a pain in the wrong place." Back to that, with him as with so many men? "That's what the men say—who don't know."

"And the women who won't… " Perhaps it was too late now anyhow? It's never too late to do well. Punning might avert itself like any form of mental illness; a communicable disease. I always considered mental illness the most contagious disease ever to children. Two of my companion's three children were successful professionals. His youngest, a daughter, was a child of the times, and had dropped out for a while. His oldest, who received training in my specialty as a physician, had said to him, "Punning can be a way of remaining uninvolved… ". He was undoubtedly compulsive about this. I had suspected other peculiarities, and these could simply not be sloughed off much longer. For instance, on four or five different occasions he took photographs. He would ask me to pose for him hurriedly by some curiously delightful spot, a waterfall! We must stop at once and take a picture. Alas; To his chagrin, no film! He had other eccentricities, too. He kept applying for positions at far flung places like the American Hospital at Pago-Pago, in the Pacific. We would fantasize going there together. Of course, we went through the informative bother of investigating every aspect of these (to me) amusing day-dreams. The fact was he really applied for these positions. He took refusals in his dainty, punning stride. How did he feel about his family? All I managed to detect was a true feeling of resentment against his mother. Was it Carl Jung who said that people who have parents alive for an inordinately long time are often held back on a psychic level in their maturational processes? He might have been one of those cases. His mother was described in terms which led one to see her as a strong, castrating female, one who always managed to place his father in a light that made him feel amiss whatever he did. He felt genuine sorrow when he evoked his father's memory. In this I could well sympathize with him. What I failed to accept was that there was an area where his feelings toward his mother might indeed spill over in other relations that involved women—even young, very young women… Where had I heard the rumor that he had a weakness for very young girls? Gossip no doubt, without foundation. Well, his love making approaches were out of the ordinary, to say the least. Most reminiscent really of his punning (as opposed to a mutual dialogue). Even after getting to know him better, his true feelings remained mysteriously hidden. Nevertheless, I found it pleasant to be asked out by this colleague whom I found increasingly and poignantly likable. Once, after we had eaten out, he would not accept my offer of an after-dinner coffee at my house. My daughter was still home and was having friends in. I wondered, in passing, if he had lost his head over her. It was extremely difficult to imagine her—my ebullient daughter—taller than he was and so capable—as a Lolita. I went so far as to ask her, and we had a good laugh together. But she really enjoyed him, the New York Times he brought her often, the talks. She considered him a smart fellow. He found her a delightful girl. When did all these silly suspicions begin? I remembered snatches of a patient's recitations, some of my own discomfort with this woman the previous day. Some older physician who had recently been appointed, she had said… mothers were going to sign a petition of complaint addressed to their town board, for they would not allow him to see their young daughters. She sounded possessed, and leered as she looked past me. I had been concerned with what it had meant to her at the time. But what if she meant him, my friendly, talkative, congenial colleague? She didn't know the physician's name. He was to leave the next day for an extended holiday. He asked me to stay with him in his car to allow him the opportunity of saying good-bye "properly." I looked at him more closely. The furtiveness at times, the peculiarities... No, not ever. It was his age really that disconcerted me. I had never been intimate with anyone that ripe. It meant overcoming a certain reluctance, that was certain.

The patient I just mentioned was herself incestuously enamored, and lived her life out through her daughter. She had gotten herself vicariously caught up in the girl's love affairs, and I was unable to extricate her from this child. To me, the mother was obviously crushing the girl in her own development. I had repeatedly attempted to bring her back to her own void, the one in her own life. She would agree, "Yeah, yeah, but my daughter... " I found her unreachable. I was reminded of some fishes in a deadly, unworkable, incestuous symbiosis. One containing the other, or the inside one having to crush the outside one to explode into its own existence?

Why all these ruminations about incest? I had at least warned my companion about the intentions of these women. I had spoken about complaints in the area where he practiced part-time. He barely responded, slightly amused, his eyes refusing to meet mine. Incest. What was it now? The old Flemish grandfather figure, there he was! Immense in my eyes when a child. He had a physique opposite to that of this man, but the same odd, high coloring, and the same furtiveness. In the sixth or seventh grades he waited daily for me near my school at the Rue Quellin, in Antwerp. He seemed enormous. As if accidentally, he would rub his elbow and then a full arm against my emerging breasts. Once he reappeared in Ostend as I stood in a crowd.. He pushed, and pushed against me in a crowd… Complaints at home (only after months of this) led at once to an investigation from which I was spared. My sister Paula said he was a respectable elder, a grandfather to a large progeny, a wealthy Flemish landowner, and willing to pay in exchange for silence. It was a sickness, she explained. He was given a warning. Months later he reappeared again in Antwerp when armed with a stick as though it were a flag, at street corners I warned other girls and pointed him out to them. Why would I associate all of the above with my kindly colleague? He was strange. How? Well, you just could not really touch him. This time in his car, when he asked me to wish him on his way "properly," I kissed him in a filial style demanded by the occasion. He kissed me back with surprisingly quickened breathing as he seized my limp hand. That was odd. I felt curiously his reaction of sexual arousal—to what, I wondered? I looked at him in the dark of the car, rather concerned about the four neighboring houses and their numerous windows. He seemed to hold in his breath briefly, made a few writhing motions on his side of the front seat, sighed deeply, then screamed out in a most unbecoming, rough, boyish voice. What was he doing now, I wondered? He said goodnight and adieu curtly, opening the door to let me out. He had spent his passion.

When he returned from vacation, the daily punning on the telephone resumed. The weather was balmy, warm, and sunny, day after day. I was not busy. My children had left for a vacation to far flung places over the globe: Denmark—Alaska—There was also talk of going to Zambia. I gladly accepted his invitation to join him sailing for a long weekend, and to spend the night on his boat. He said his wife had left for Florida to divorce him. I felt sorry for this older man, alone, dainty looking, dignified by age. I eagerly looked forward to sleeping on board and finally to enjoying an uninterrupted time with him.

This day on his sail boat, below deck, the water was lapping joyously against the hull, a dance beneath us. We lay close to each other after swimming in the very cold water. He seemed to love the smell of my wet hair, and breathed lustfully in my ears. I felt affectionately close to him beneath his well-aroused body. I heard him take ever deeper breaths of the fragrance that surrounded our hair and wet bodies. I felt slowly carried away by the intensity of his reactions, the delight of the floating boat, the murmurs of the lake beneath us. The sun felt golden and enticingly near. His fingers explored cursorily, and I thought for a moment, "Why! He is examining me professionally!" I looked at him appreciatively with awakened physical interest. I observed a few sudden bursts of noticeable sighs. Then, abruptly, he got up and left, apparently much preoccupied. The hatch, as I had urged him, was left open. He said he wanted to see how close to shore we had drifted. I felt held down by the movement of the waves which took me along on their rocking stampede each time a motor boat sped by. Closing eyes wearily, I realized that earlier, in the arms of this frustrating and frustrated companion, hidden fantasies of incestuously flavored experiences had re-emerged. Here was the old Flemish grandfather figure out of my school days... These now changed excitingly into memories of other perverse older men encountered in childhood... thoughts of darkened corners imbued by the scent of seaweed and male urine in movie houses on stormy days in Ostend, of the North Sea, erupting over the dykes, streaming down in the center of town, inundating the market place... Awakening, breathless with surprise, to secret longings, associated for years afterward with the pealing of bells on holidays and Sunday mornings at the sea-shore. He had told me earlier about some of the girls he had truly liked. They were very young women really, unsuitable I believed to such a grand-fatherly suitor. I thought of telling him later that night about the strangely awakened memories. When I joined him on deck, he looked nervously at his watch. "What time is it?" He asked.

"Does the hour matter?"

"My wife expects me home for supper," he muttered nervously with contained laughter, "Make haste! Hoist sail!"

"Your wife? Have you two remarried lately? You're always in a hurry, why don't you sail us back?"

He was obviously not going to spend time on the subject of what had transpired between us, nor discuss the re-emergence of a wife. A misunderstanding? Actually, what difference did it make? With more time to spend between us he might have been up to even more nonsense. I watched him sail without grace in his movements. He sang like a howling, rough voiced, street mendicant. Without thinking, I asked, "If you were to be a dog, what kind would you choose to be?" I had been told that his wife had a knack for dog-breeding, and presided over national dog shows. After reflecting a moment, he said, "I believe I'd choose—well the kind my wife prefers to breed." It occurred to me she might have developed an enthusiasm for dog-breeding because of this son-of-a-bitch: An attempt at rematching, perhaps? I noted for the first time that his head belonged on a different and more forward plane than his body. He appeared at once metamorphized into a most unattractive dog-like creature... what with the perpetually hungdog, ingratiating smile. The whole thing was silly. I had no reason to take my frustrations out on this obliging fellow who just couldn't level with anyone about anything. What if he were a manic-depressive in a manic phase? Perhaps additionally simply neurotic in the sexual-social maze. On the return trip he slept peacefully while I drove rapidly. He awoke in time to ask if he might visit for a short while. Silently we walked up to my front door. I turned, and said without a smile, "I have to hurry; I have just enough time to meet an important date for a dance… " He stood there with mouth agape, for once dumbstruck, un-punning… I closed the door firmly behind me, repeating without conviction, "Just enough time to dress and make myself beautiful." I had caught the look of surprise in his eyes and I thought for an instant I had awakened recognition in him. Separate and alone again, I debated whether to resign myself to prolonged isolation. The semblance of closeness to another had been a sadly deceptive experience. In retrospect it had ended rather farcically, really; A voice reminded me of Freud's saying that one doesn't love or marry older women, one honors them. Love is for the young…

Was the promise to go out to a dance a form of rebellion against one's circumstances? Are minor deceits our comic, semi-tragic lot? Why resignation indeed, rather than a true, uproariously hilarious breaking out? I had promised to go to a dance and would keep to my resolve after this day of sun-drenched sailing, especially as it had trailed off heartbreakingly with this doggedly evocative grand-fatherly figure.

Carol, my secretary, was willing to participate in what we considered our breaking-out debut that night. I remember dressing with a vengeance in fury and haste. My afternoon companion's essential rejection helped me in my determination. I chose a long gown with a high slit on one side; it had been bought in Hawaii, and was of native tinted cloth. The colors were luminously enchanting, like the afterglow of sunsets on Diamond Head. They evoked dark orchids at night.

CHAPTER 8

Carlos In the House of Yu

From our table I looked up at the bar of the "House of Yu," I noticed a man who stood alone, away from the others. He was markedly broad shouldered. I caught a boyishly rakish, furtive expression while he drank his dark beer slowly and looked at me. He wore a short sleeved shirt, open at the neck, and simple black trousers. He seemed strong and physical. An Italian worker passing through, or perhaps a European recently arrived in the area, I thought. Our eyes met inquiringly. I sat for quite awhile, listening to the music, watching his reluctant unsmiling interest in me. Someone came to invite "either of you ladies who cared to dance" I said at once that Carol, my companion, did. When she left, he finally invited me to the dance floor.

He moved timidly to lead into the music. He exuded an aroma, as though his shirt had recently been starched and ironed. We barely spoke at first. The little that was said was hardly heard above the spirited sounds of the jazz tunes. We stayed on the dance floor during the orchestra's short intermissions He soon realized our conversational difficulties were due to my foreign accented and low voice. He said he had traveled in Europe and mentioned by name some of the cities he knew. Had he been to Antwerp? Instead he knew Ghent; he pronounced it "Jent" as in "June". While we compared views on the European capitals we both knew he seemed unable to get used to the way I mumbled. In a vengeful fit of testiness I might gladly have asked him to repeat after me 'Scheveningsche Vischersvloot', an historic password used by the Dutch to detect German spies. But I responded intuitively to the fiber of touchiness, even defensive mistrust in his attitude, and refrained from clowning. He appeared hypersensitive and unusually serious minded. He seemed uneasy with the unfamiliarity of the surroundings, uncomfortable with the present boisterous crowd. I felt alert, carefree, and stimulated by the scotch I had drunk.

There was adventure to be had, I could see this now. The music was played by a group of engineers and high school music instructors who performed almost nightly both for the fun of it and for the money. My dance partner looked curiously at the intimate hall and the polished wooden dance floor. Paper covered lanterns shone white around the red Chinese lettering, and Hawaiian skirts surrounded the orchestra's podium. Heavily painted wooden reproductions from Pacific Islands, with Easter Island heads peering down their long noses, ran the length of the walls. Totem poles appeared unexpectedly in dark nooks. Surrounding the dance area was a low wall of lacquered black. Tall bamboo shoots grew from this wall up to the ceiling, and through these we could see red candles flickering yellow flames on the red cloth which covered the tables in the large dining area.

Where we danced wooden masks stared dark and unsmiling through hollowed eyes. Red carpeting ran from one end of the rooms down the hallways, leading to large niches designed for private dinner parties. The establishment was unpretentiously lavish, and while he held me I noted for the first time an air of exotic allure. The paper lanterns throbbed with the music and the bouncing couples. Having surveyed the area with him in mind as he led glidingly, I finally asked enunciating each word with care, "Do you dance much?"

"My steps don't much indicate it, do they? It's such a busy place, hard to get around somehow."

"You're doing fine by me. I don't dance that often myself, these days."

"Do you live here?"

"Yes, I do. How about you?"

"No, I don't. It's the first time I've come here."

That was quite obvious, I thought, wondering why he took it all so seriously.

The orchestra intoned a very fast and highly bouncing number. Widely swinging couples began to jostle us. He said "this is not for me," and took my arm to accompany me quietly to my table.

This was a busy night! In the dimly lit barroom what a crowd! Where had they all come from? Near the entrance some forty men stood four deep by the bar and huddled by a concert piano, where well voiced persons played and sang WW II tunes during the orchestra's quiet interludes. There were fewer women, ranging in age from young school girls to the grandmotherly independent American working woman type. What a scene! Much action, I thought, almost unbelieving, as I watched men enter as complete strangers and leave not too long after with a smiling young woman they had just met at the bar.

I had come to the dance hall that night on the crest of a highly assertive mood, a mood of recklessness. I had thought, "I'll show Carol how to go about this... " She might have sat in hundreds of similar clubs during her youth while I was traipsing around halls of learning. This night, she had sat passively at first, though I knew she was tensely expectant—a tall, blue-eyed, serious looking blonde. She appeared quite stately in her matronliness, which had begun to show in the last few years. She had barely looked around the barroom at first and refrained successfully from seeming expectant. My approach to her had been a commandeering tone of "I'll show you Carol, we're going to do this and this... " That meant of course to get ourselves invited to dance by the right partners for our evening out. To help us over the reefs of the evening, we had ordered drinks at once.

I drank easily that night and sipping a second scotch I viewed some three men who looked like interesting partners. One of them was now dancing with Carol, and she did not return to the table it seemed, for a long time. While I sat alone, sipping my drink carefully, this mood changed considerably as I began to realize I was being coldly observed. My previous dance partner had been following my smiling, not unseductive inquisitiveness as I surveyed the men. In the mirror which I faced from a distance and which overhung the length of the solid wooden bar stand, as wide as the room itself, I caught his cool, but curiously wondering glance. I looked away self-consciously. I was approached by a few men, the "older connoisseur" type, but I refused dances and drinks. I looked again at him, directly this time, and saw him standing apart from the crowd, at the right end of the bar. I noted his strong shoulders again. They leaned gracefully on folded elbows over the rounded edge of the bar. One of his legs rested easily on the elevated step at the base of the solid oak bar, while he, swung it around playfully. His other leg was bent at the knee which he leaned against the heavy wood. He turned his head and looked at me seriously, but his gaze was still tense. I saw his eyes were immense and strikingly blue against his dark wavy hair. He laughed suddenly with roguish mischief while I smiled in recognition, and I nodded a "yes" as he motioned with his hands to ask about a turn on the dance floor.

Dancing with him this time, I was attentive to what he said and avoided anything which might lead to misinterpretation. For the remainder of the evening I remained at a distance, but I was still aware of being close to him and did not take notice of anyone else. I abstained from humoring and clowning. It was late and almost closing time when we finally joined my secretary, who had found "the" choicest dance companion (a rather unattractive Arabian, I thought). She and the ideal dancer were now seated together at our table. During the course of the evening, we exchanged partners. I was not comfortable, and was content when returned to my own stranger. Carol's favored one had noticed my impatience with him. He had told her derisively: "Geez, she couldn't wait to get back to that guy!"

Neither of the men drank much. My companion mentioned he had "just gone over the hill". This was said lightly, but then he added wearily that he felt it at times. Did he mean he was fifty years old? He appeared strangely young. "Marriage means a lot of troubles, lots" he exclaimed with a heavy sigh, as though what he mentioned was the most difficult aspect of getting on in years. He loosened up somewhat and expressed the age-old desire that when he reached this stage in life, he would leave and just go—walk from the most Northern part of Africa, across the Sahara desert, and then go on down till he reached the Southern most tip of South Africa'... I asked him at once if he would be willing to take me along. Inclined to be on the go as a youth, I told him, "My mother said I was born with a bicycle between my legs and a cigarette between my lips." It seemed he laughed only when intentionally startled.

The summer's exceptionally warm weather led to a comparison with our seemingly endless bleak winters. He too came from somewhere near Lake Erie, where winters are snowbound and lasting. This lead to a discussion of activities available for the heavy snow months which predominated much of the year. "Do you ski? I've come to love it." He mentioned his preference for cross-country explorations. Championship cross-country exploring on skis involved the ability to shoot on target while under stressful conditions, he remembered his only small accomplishment (mentioned in a way that made one wonder if he were perhaps an expert) in sports consisted of target shooting, in which he said he had won some minor trophies. "Have you now?" I replied, for he had said this with a marked offhandedness.

He spoke eloquently and knowingly of guns made in Belgium. There was a small-town quality about his unassuming mannerisms, which almost seemed affected. His speech was often punctuated with short, deep sighs, and once or twice I wondered whether he was troubled. What mainly caught my interest was his ponderous reticence, his essential quietness. When I mentioned him later in glowing terms to Carol, who could only vaguely remember having danced with him among some others, she exclaimed, "You don't mean that one, do you!

Why! He's a farm boy from the sticks! A country bumpkin!" She was brought up on a farm in the desolate hills of upstate New York—she ought to know!

While we danced he seemed distant, too carefully absorbed in leading, but when we left the dance floor he sighed and said, "Why, I never thought the night would wind up like this. I didn't think I'd stay this late." We were evidently both reluctant to see the evening come to an end. While we danced, he studied my fingers time and again. Did he wonder about an absent ring? Suntanned as I was, did he wonder about his partner's degree of whiteness? How is one to know what these quiet, passing strangers think?

When did he decide not to leave and stay till closing time? At what point did I find him so exciting? At the table, the four of us were casually conversing. He showed open interest as the evening wore on, but still as if reluctant to get involved. He described his work as difficult: appraising the cost of installing high-powered industrial air purifiers. He had been employed by the same firm since early youth, and following World War II he returned to the same manufacturing company and was steadily promoted. It was hard to explain, but "Can you understand," he asked, "the terror I feel sometimes faced by as many as twenty highly-titled engineers seated across from me at the conference table?"

"I guess it can be troublesome."

"I, the Company foreman, needing to qualify, explain, and justify to the specialists what we plan to do and why it has to be done in a certain way. Many of the men are younger and they're sharp. They're just out of engineering school. Why; It happened just like that in San Diego a week ago... " I thought he's been far from home, often. Still, to his tormented-sounding questions and statements that needed reassurance, I said, "But you most certainly have the upper hand over everyone of them in view of your experience. This is a pretty new field to most, while with your background, you're way ahead, aren't you?" He looked up like someone amused by a child. I could positively hear the male complacency in his voice when he asked me, "What do you do? Do you work?" and to this he added, laughing mischievously, "You seem to have what it takes up there." His interest still appeared too distant to me, so I answered casually, "Both Carol and I work in the medical field," and let it go at that. I decided then to avoid mentioning that I had a good profession myself, for I feared he might leave. He had spoken as one intimidated by titles. I knew few men who looked forward to knowing a psychiatrist by choice—let alone a woman shrink. In view of his own reticence, I enjoyed the idea of my own mystery. Besides, I was getting pretty tipsy.

The four of us spoke of having some early breakfast at an all-night "Dunken Donuts" counter within a short driving distance. (My daughter and her University friends had renamed it the "Drunken Donuts" spot for the night-owls.) I said, "I prefer some sobering tea. I'm awfully thirsty for something real to drink." Carlos said he too preferred some tea. I realized to my own surprise he would come home with me for tea.

A few years ago, following a prolonged bad time with unsympathetic neighbors and startled courts (surprised by their and my opposing persistence) I finally established a practice at my home. The residence is a simplified version of a laboratory; a nest of practicality without adornments except for paintings and many books. It is situated on a heavily shaded, quiet, tree-lined street, where old homes are meticulously looked after by their mostly middle income, conservatively persevering families.

We quietly entered the dark hallway, which is used by patients as a waiting room and by Carol for her work, and crossed to the near empty and spacious library-living room. He stretched out on the sofa while I busied myself happily with the ritual of preparing a tray for tea. I could watch him from the kitchen, as he sat up again and moved to the corner of the sofa, as though taken aback at being confronted by a large, exceptionally well endowed nude young woman, a recent painting done by my 18 year old daughter. He stared in disbelief at the paraphernalia accumulated helter-skelter from a multitude-of countries. The built-in, wall-to-wall shelves (my only great improvement to the old house) bulged heavily and without much order with books. He seemed enthusiastic about a drawing made by my son of his sister asleep. He remarked openly and with interest that he liked the sketch, and added, "The boy has definitely caught something of the spirit of the girl at rest." He appeared to enjoy the tea, and showed open amusement when I fetched clean cups directly from the dishwasher. Still, I could not help noting that he felt uncomfortable in this work-shop living room. Our dog, a predominantly beagle pup, seemed a familiar object to him—at last something. He recommended himself to my good graces by indicating he was "the best kind of pet to have," nodding his head to emphasize the point. While we drank tea, I played a light dance tune on the record player. Slowly we huddled against one another, and I stretched out alongside him on the rather narrow sofa. Sleepy, relaxed, comfortable, I wished to convey this feeling to him. I had politely accepted the drinks offered during the course of the evening and had reached a heightened level of tolerance. I felt his reserve and nervous preoccupation strangely reassuring. It was nearly two o'clock in the morning. We held each other more closely.

The given name of Carlos now sounded incongruous to one with such deep blue eyes and such ponderous demeanor. I was unable to identify his speech pattern; it was unfamiliar to me. At times I thought I heard strange British overtones. In view of his marked sobriety, what if he were a real ascete? He came from Pennsylvania, and who knew how many sects and branches originating from Calvin and Luther had sprung up in his part of the country? Considering the severe, simple manner of dress, not to mention the aroma of ironed starch that emanated from him, was he perhaps simply Amish or Moravian? Asked about his parents and siblings, he said he was the oldest of eight (Ahah! I thought. I knew he was authoritarian and strong willed). While his mother was indeed English, his father was Italian. What a pair the two must be. He described them as the most noisy, quarrelsome couple on earth. Of his father he said, "Despite his age, and he's well over seventy now, he's the meanest, worst tempered man I've ever known!" He said this with a convincing wince, nodding his head strongly to emphasize the point of his father's bad temper. When he spoke of having grandchildren (not to mention grown children), I found it damnably difficult to believe he had indeed reached that stage in life. Though he had spoken easily about himself and I had listened closely, he was tense again. I wondered for a moment if he feared the sudden apparition of a jealous husband, but no, in all likelihood the tension was more from a divisiveness within himself.

I thought he behaved as though he were afraid. His somber blue eyes were immense, deep as sapphires. They kept looking around as though in search of a clue, and I felt like shouting at him, "Hey there! What the hell are you afraid of?… HELL?… " Evidently he was truly fearful and he took large steps from room to room after he had peered approvingly at the pool, shining and shimmering in the back yard under the moonlight.

I told him at that point that I was divorced, that my daughter was visiting a friend in Denmark, while my son was salmon fishing in the wilds of Alaska with his father. I hoped that sounded pretty far away and cool, even reassuring. When the lights were mostly turned off, I touched his strong face with the barest tips of my fingers, saying, "Do let go a bit, Carlos," and I closed his eyes. I felt I wanted to remain forever in this position against him, my head tucked away between his chest and arm. Sleep! What peace in this man's hold. Utterly relaxed. I felt I might very well go to sleep then and there on his broad chest. He kissed me then. He held me strongly and kissed me gently. I felt his breathing become much deeper as he drew me even nearer to him. I found this exciting. The touch of his cheeks and lips instilled desire in my fingers, which clung to his warm fine face. I looked up and saw him quietly pensive as he let go of me, distant again. I watched the appearance of slyness, the questioning smile that first drew my attention to him, inscribe itself in his features, and to my utter surprise he asked,

"Do you mind the fact that I'm frigid?"

The voice was shaky, insincere, and the facial expression with its sideways, roguish smile seemed meant for an audience.

"Do you mean impotent?" I asked in disbelief.

"Yes, I guess so… " He winced, why? "That's what I mean… " He looked at me, and his blue eyes held a kiddish, evasive gleam. An impotent one again, an announced one at that, who didn't know the difference between frigidity and impotence. Though what difference was there in reality? He never quite seemed to speak his mind. Was this another canine prankster? Was this to be my fate from now on? Why was this man so attractive physically? Were the spontaneous responses going to give out on me too now? Had I taken them too much for granted?

I recovered quickly, really too sleepy and probably too tipsy to care anymore. With a shrug of shoulders, disgruntled, I sat up, muttering crossly, "Goodness, and what do you expect me to say? But this being the case, we might as well be comfortable in my private quarters and in my own bed!" Was this perhaps his irritating way of being humorous even coy? I could not blame him for the aftermaths of the sailing experience with Grandfather Incest. On the other hand, his evasiveness reminded me intuitively of the way he said he had won minor trophies in target shooting which I had perceived earlier in the evening as a gross understatement of his achievements in that field. It seemed to me he liked mystery and incited curiosity.

I lit a strawberry colored candle, took it up the stairs, and showed him to my bedroom. I do not recall getting glamorously and intimately prepared—for what? When I joined him, I was wearing an enticing bikini—as I had nothing else—since the night was very warm. The costume hid the four spherical untanned white markings of body, and he whispered reproachfully: "I've undressed, now, why haven't you?" (Who did he think would overhear us? The Good Lord from above?) Despite his unexpected reprobation, abbreviated silk panties were kept on.

A quiet, pale bedroom. The large bed. Window, with curtains wide open to the quiet street. A lit, tall street lantern, shining white beneath our second story room. A tall and broad tree extending its large branches, with foliage rustling against the front porch roof, also against the window's screen. Foliage swaying just barely at times to cover the lantern's light. Clean, light yellow sheets. How lengthy this manly body appeared in the moving shadows of the candle flame. I crawled into bed and moved quietly up to him. He held me tightly without a word and sighed. We obviously felt well and contented near each other. I thought I could peacefully go to sleep against this man. But under the candle light flickering pale sheet, how strong his body!

Absolute delight emanated from his striking physical strength! I marveled at the mere touch of him. It seemed as if he were wrapped in tender metal, the inner and outer layers of skin inseparable from the sinews beneath them. In the leaping colored light his essential masculine attribute stood surprisingly erect beneath the thin cover. What then had he meant with the sly statement about being frigid-impotent? (I had been right, then, about his mastery with firearms?) The organ of his desire attracted my gaze. I remembered pathology lessons in Geneva once—a young man, strong and well built, had been killed accidentally. (Was it in surgery?) He lay on the pathology table, on the cold slab seemingly still so warm and alive, and we all filed by. Professor Rutishauser, a German Swiss, usually formidable with immense and protruding eyes, was seated, shriveled and despondent looking, near the pathology table—a guardian to the dead man. As I approached, I knew he was staring at us, the few girl students. Always the object of his "humorous" remarks, he said to me as I fixed my gaze sadly on the dead man's youthful face and chest, and then back again at his face, "Come now, Mlle., Madame, whichever, have a good look at you know what, and then perhaps you'll be able to concentrate on what you should be looking at." The man was most gifted down there and yes, when I'd had a good look, I could go on and see what it was we were supposed to see and remember—possibly a mass forgotten in the abdominal cavity…

Carlos here was very much alive and at least as gifted. I feared being hurt as a result of the wretched difficulties experienced in the past were he intent on pursuing the matter optimally.

Deep sighs. The melting aromatic candle sputtered over. We kissed, touched. His warm hands caressed strongly, lengthily. My lips wandered in response with delight over his shoulders and strong arms, covered by curled gold. My cheeks rubbed against the extent of the taut, clean outdoors smelling abdomen and thighs; I marveled at his golden haired loins where an ascending comet was caught between two distant stars. On the heaving bed I realized he was a seriously loving man. He repeated often, "God! What are you doing to me?" I intoned "It's wonderful... " I was strongly excited by him, lively, loose, and tipsy.

He made me laugh self-consciously and soberly when he responded to our emblazoned thrills by emitting a low keyed whistle, his lips slightly parted over clenched teeth... "Here now," he said all of a sudden, while he pulled me up firmly, and turned me around as though I were a doll. "Come closer, come to me," he ordered, placing his long legs over mine, while his taut belly pressed hard against soft, concaving, giving flesh. He placed both his hands high between my legs and gently pulled the panties off, while he sprung them apart. Without warning (I thought) he penetrated at once or rather, he attempted to firmly, then more gently he pressed again and again. I held my breath again and again to suppress anticipated pain... what with my particular difficulty... Despite delight of play and generous secretions which ran moist at the appropriate areas at the entrance, deeper penetration was dry and ungiving. He obviously objected to what the French so aptly call *Les bagatelles à la porte*—frills at the door...

Unaided, he stayed midway, then retracted. He whispered again, "God, woman, what are you doing to me?" Drunk as

I was, what did he think I was doing to him? He separated with both hands again, but silken this time, and reapplied pointedly sideways. Then he stayed. "Dear!" I called out, "It feels wonderful, do stay… " I began to follow his desire. Led by his firm hands which warmly surrounded my hips, they followed blindly in divination of his want. Though inspired by the frenzied stroking, they would not respond as he wanted to the quivering, shimmering manly hips. I clearly felt his need to feel me as possessed and airy as he was himself, like a perpetually flickering wind-swept flame reflected in the rising sea. His manly passion had wings which allowed him to soar. I felt drawn as by slowly heaving waves, a woman swaying heavily from within…
I could not transmute into the tremulous song of abandonment demanded by his vibrating passion. My body continued his, submitted to his, as he resumed and reunfolded. I spun dizzily around his ascending, trembling containment. I begged softly at first, then I pleaded openly for mercy. His proud passion, his Man of Man control insisted, persisted. He devised and reinvented. This was a manly demand for harmony I realized I could not follow. I pleaded again, "Do come… " A vibrant ascent, a virile crescendo into infinity, when he culminated, scintillating. I held him so closely with my arms around his hips, my body pulsed with his heart's throbbing and hammering. I felt an ageless roar of ecstasy in agonized possession within me. How copious the warmth of love's inundations. I shouted with joyful relief, impressed and content, I had not known a man more powerfully self-possessed." Do stay… " I still asked… And he did!

Outside, the night was quiet and very warm. It was raining lightly when I looked up and saw he had dressed. Day had not yet come. In the sky, mauve streaks heralded the sun's rebirth.

Crimson arcs, with soft orange and purple. Tropical skies here in Northern New York. I felt I had come near the flight of dark orchids in the night.

I found him in the living room, sitting quietly on the edge of the sofa. His head seemed humbly bowed as he looked down, and his hands were clutched in an attitude of prayer. My ebullience fell. I offered to fix some tea and food, but he merely shook his head in refusal. Concerned, I remained silent too. While I drove him back to the "House of Yu" where his yellow pick-up truck had been left the previous evening, I finally asked him, "Do you feel you have sinned?" He answered strongly, "Yes, I do!" My hand had reached instinctively for his bared forearm. He pulled away strongly. I asked again, in earnest, and without the slightest amusement this time, "Do you really mean this?"

"Well, yes, I do," he said, ponderous and disturbed. I wanted to drop everything and put my arms around him.

Sitting down, getting up, my pelvic bones felt bruised for days. It was as though I had bicycled from Antwerp to Ostend (55 miles) non-stop, after years without exercise. The pain was an enthralling reminder of him. Joyous, hopeful day-dreams erupted I would see him daily, or at least be with him often. Realization came slowly. He might not call again. Anais Nin's experiences were vivid in my memory. She stresses the fear of sensuality in American men. She said once in her diaries that she had sensed something in her life here in America which she had not experienced in France, that "sensuality is a vice for Americans, and they are ashamed… And they visit their resentment on the one who lured, charmed or seduced them. Cruelties of love take place when the love does not answer a need."

Britannica's Atlas helped me locate a town near Lake Erie where he resided. That much had slipped out before we knew each other better. Collaborating with telephone operators, I located two men with a surname similar to his. I had seen a name engraved in tarnished gold on a withered empty wallet and he had said slyly, "See, that's my name."

I thought of sending him the book Aku-Aku by Thor Heyerdahl about the secret of Easter Island. In my house, he had recognized an original small statue of volcanic stone from those parts. The book would be sent without a note. But then, to which of the two addresses?

Two weeks later, Carol (an outspoken 'Secretary General,' her voice on the edge of hysteria) banged excitedly on the office door during a session, shouting loudly, "It's for you! Personal!" It was Carlos. His voice was quiet, and he sounded inarticulate, but imperturbable. I cried excitedly: "Where are you, for goodness sake? Where are you calling from? I've really wanted to hear from you!" He had been summoned to our area again. Would I meet him at ten o'clock the next evening? He expected to take five hours to drive from his home.

I wore the same dress, a flowing Hawaiian sheet of radiant but muted, shaded colors. It was a lovely cover on one evenly masked by a dark tan. The moment he appeared will I am certain remain with me. He stood sideways in the doorway. He seemed stunned by the lights and hesitant about leaving the threshold between the Motor Inn and the barroom. He looked well groomed, but recalcitrant, erect, severe, and somber. He approached, his blue eyes immense and flashing, a tall, quiet, domineering leader, without words. I caught his eyes, but he looked away. His gaze followed the few people in the room. I noticed one other woman, a youthful brunette seated at the bar, conversing casually with the few men standing nearby.

I thought he walked in her direction, until I gestured toward him and he joined me without a smile, without transition in his gaze. He said he had not recognized me because my hair was all done up and piled high on my head. It was true, I had been to a beautician that day. When a waitress came he ordered," Give me something to drink!" She was surprised to say the least, and when she pressed him to be more specific, he said in a most unmannerly way, "Give me the same she's got in hers," pointing a finger into my glass of scotch. I asked him why I had not heard from him. He mentioned that he had tried to reach me on six different occasions. Six times! And to think I thought... He said he always got some answering service. If only I had known this! I asked him if he had told them it was a friend, but he had not. He said rather irritably that he had driven five hours that night without rest. He said, "I just had to find out what this is all about... if all this is for real." and then turning to me finally, he added with eyes flashing smiles, amiably, "if you'd been for real... "

He admitted having had a hard time remembering what I looked like. I confessed to similar feelings about him, but said how struck I'd been by his good looks. He was also much taller (by at least one foot) than I had remembered. He gulped two drinks while informing me he never drank hard liquor—not even stimulants like coffee or tea—except on very special occasions like the marriage of one of his children, or when he became a grandfather. What was it then about this man that made it so difficult to perceive him as fully grown, let alone over fifty years old? Had I misunderstood him, or was it due to a hard, invincible armor he carried around with him? Schizophrenics usually look at least ten years younger than their stated age, depressives on the other hand... He seemed a lone, regal, but young leader of man We had returned to the "House of Yu" where we first met. What did Carlos really look like? Burt Lancaster with a distinctly mystical quality immediately comes to mind. On the way to my house this second time he became expansive. Drinking what I drank definitely made him speak more flowingly. I felt I might know him finally as he was with his wife, his family. I was fearful but curious, and seated next to him, I quivered.

At the dance hall he had bared inner sadness. He had said, "I keep wondering where this world of ours is going? What is it coming to?" To him its waywardness was best compared to Germany and its people. I was off guard at first when he spoke of this, and I sensed an increasing tenseness in me, my heart beat throbbing in my neck. Against all intuition I prayed rapidly that he would say something to the effect that the German people were an emotionally deprived people, thwarted, twisted from early childhood onward in response to bullying fathers and victimized mothers, outsiders to their own feelings. Was this what Carlos meant? Wasn't this what E. Erikson had said all along: "All mankind starts in the nursery?" How did he, this primal seeming man in his tight contemporary harness feel about this? I had time to compose myself, he was so ponderous. "Do you remember what I said to you during our first evening together?" Did I remember his statement about his innermost conviction, namely that "Life is a mystery to be lived not to be solved? "Yes, I did, for he had lashed out at me twice with it. This was one of Carl Jung's most fundamental tenets:

"We limit ourselves to the attainable, and this means renouncing all our other psychic potentialities. One man loses a valuable piece of his past, another a valuable piece of his future… The serious problems in life, however, are never fully solved… The meaning and purpose of a problem seem to lie not in its solution but in our working at it incessantly… This alone preserves us from stultification and petrifaction."

I had scribbled these quotations out of "The Portable Jung" and showed them to Carlos. He related them to what happened to the German people during WWII. "How could you?" I asked perplexed and worried. His answer: "When I think that one hundred eighty thousand young men were killed, maimed, or taken as prisoners by the Russians! When I think that the cream of humanity was butchered like that, I have little faith left." I stayed very quiet. Did I as much as mention the Jews, all those butchered by this elite? I said no more than, "It is estimated that one hundred fifty million people have been killed legally so far in this century." These figures surely mean little to the ordinary mind like amounts expressed in light years. Forty-four million people were killed during our war WWII. A gigantically looming figure beyond the reach of personal meaning. I had lost the loquacity, and expansiveness in his presence, and told myself, "For goodness sake, show some reserve." He danced a polka with enthusiasm, his Burt Lancaster smile was sweet, and his tall body poignantly graceful as he bent over, to bring his body closer to mine for the first time that evening. He tried to lift me into joyous springing leaps. My feet rebelled, and suddenly I felt miserable hopping up and down with him in public. He showed concern: "Is this too much for you? Do you want to sit this one out?" Without waiting for an answer, he took me back to the table he had chosen, farthest from the crowd. Where we sat across from one another he said with concern I had looked peaked and pale. I showed him the three and one-half inch heels on my new shoes. He said, "I don't feel fatigued in the least. That yellow pick-up truck is difficult to drive. That's good. It keeps you awake on a long drive, and I didn't have to stop once."

What control!

He knew the way to my house. He had taken note, as he pointed out, of a very large tree. In excitement and turmoil the previous evening, among other things, I had tried to give an air of intimacy to the living room. He noticed a difference. I thought he surveyed it with cold objectivity. How unadorned this place suddenly seemed compared to the wealthy and well decorated homes of some married friends, supported for a lifetime by a man. When I drove him to my house that first time, he had seemed uneasy. Now relaxed during the drive, we continued to converse. I mentioned in passing the difficulty I had had in locating him, suddenly aware that Carlos was not his true name either. "I tried to find you... "

"Don't ever call me; Don't ever write to me!" I muttered something about Aku-Aku, frowning reprovingly at his outburst. "I wasn't going to say who it was from. After all, I realize... of course... " Had he been haunted repeatedly in the past? "Have you been constantly pursued by females, perhaps?" I asked coldly, with simple curiosity showing. "Well, no, I've never gone out on my wife except once; that was two years ago. She wrote letters, and it's been hell at home ever since. Just once... and she just won't give up!" He sighed deeply. If he put up a performance like he did with me, then "poor woman!" I thought. He continued, "There are girls, young ones and pretty ones in the office, and there's one in particular. I know all I have to do is give a sign...

I'm EXTRA careful! I don't want ANY trouble!" He was certainly warning me!

"I've been told it's bad business to get involved with employees. Now my brother-in-law in France has a shoe business and some twenty girls working under him. It's bad to mix business with pleasure… There is poetic justice, you know… " I stopped there, remembering I must not clown or tease. Soberly I continued, "I understand. But then, why contact me again? Why have you come back? Do I remind you of someone you've known once?"

"No. Do I?"

"Yes. A film star, really… "

"Who?" He asked in eager surprise.

"Burt Lancaster without the dumb screen smile."

He nodded approvingly, and said with laughter and pride, "Why! Just yesterday, a little girl asked me for my autograph in a supermarket. It's been happening for years."

"Did you give her his autograph? You know, you're quite aloof, you're somewhat severe, austere… You're… "

He nodded, knowing what I meant. I hinted at having some difficulty with his touchiness. He seemed not to hear this, and just let it slip by.

"You know, Marie," (he hadn't given me his right name no wonder he must deform mine) "the men who work for me in the ditches, when I go to see how they're doing, how far they've come along, have told me they shudder… they're somehow afraid when I come around. I don't say anything to them. They know by the way I look if they're doing all right."

He was obviously pretty smug about himself when it came to work, but I understood the men.

This ponderously quiet fellow with a commanding bearing had managed to subjugate me with some unconscionable appeal. I became certain of this. He appealed with an irresistibility from the past. That was it: with the fascination of the fishermen I had known during the long years of childhood and adolescence. That most certainly was what it was—all those summers spent in Ostend by the North Sea: I lived by the clean beaches that stretched out as far as Holland, beyond Scheveningen, swept by heavy tides. The ebb and flow rocked one on the lifesavers' boat which I, as a special privilege, was allowed to climb into during departure time from the shore. As a child I watched and laughed and babbled with the Flemish fishermen in charge for the summer. They knew me at first as "that one from the Congo". Unlike the swarms of tourists, I came daily, weather permitting, to wait for them. I carried the sun on my brown skin. Usually I stayed quiet, which they liked. The Flemish fishermen wore a golden earring in one ear lobe to keep the evil spirits away from the sea. At times it got very rough, with heavy green swells. The men taught me to dive and to recognize strong currents by the dark emerald streaks which lanced the sighing, white-crested, jade green North Sea. On special days the sky was blindingly blue, with thick, fast-moving, white islands of clouds. At sundown I detested having to take leave and go home to our jewelry store-fronted house. It was situated across the once famed Ostend Casino, near the edge of the delicately stoned boardwalk. Climbing down the steps of the lifesavers' sturdy tall boat, I gazed after the fishermen… in the strongest light of day when the sea receded and the luminous grey haze lifted—in the crepuscular hour… They were young and vigorous with their one golden earring, their cold dark eyes flashing against hard Nordic and Spanish features. I could only glance hungrily at them from long distances. From their "Patates Frites" emanated exciting smells of foods forbidden to us. At home there were the four girls and my mother; my father rarely joined us during the summer time… With my mother's insistence on adhering to ancient rituals and taboos, how was I ever to reach out enough to overcome the multitude of overpowering reservations of our small, highly inbred, almost all-exclusive world?

Carlos—another unreachable world. Class, religion (whatever his was), upbringing, for certain, cultural worlds apart. Though from a family of eight children, he stayed within himself and alone. Was this part of what brought us together, this strange alienation? Parents divided by different backgrounds, a desire to reach out despite (perhaps because of) barriers at this stage in life when old obstacles might not matter any longer?

In the house, I saw Carlos walk decisively toward the waiting room. He read my regulation hung certificates and diplomas. Insolently he trespassed into my mystery, then returned to the bare living room and said in a neutral tone of voice, "So that's what you are. Well, I didn't... " He suggested we not drink tea and asked to go upstairs. I lit a candle and followed him without a word.

Close to him in bed I felt strongly excited. "I truly like you... "

"So do I... " He was extremely affectionate. How warm the night! Our bodies were slippery as though dipped in ancient ablutions. His astounding masculinity, his most private part, pointed proudly and perpendicularly to the ceiling, illumined by the tree rustled street lantern. The flame of the red candle licked upwards. There was moonlight, candle flame, street lantern glitter splattered against the ceiling. Spawning shadows glided in a dance from wall to wall.

He exuded his peculiar aroma of ironed starch, a fragrance of wood-burning, of sun-baked, scorched sweetness. I envisioned him in the noon of day. A strong, serious, feeling man, rustling waist deep in tall, windswept fields of feathered fronds of oats swaying in the gold of sun, the sea distant below the horizon... I wanted to contain him, hold him, absorb him through all my senses, prolong for at least this night the pleasure of him. I felt as though I had waited years for him, in this very room... Reawakened to the meaning of desire, my mouth, lips, tongue, sucking his nipples sharply as an infant, traversed the sculptured curves of his chest, the taut smoothness of his abdomen, and playfully teased his masculine organ. Effusivenes' delight! I heard his bewildered cries of deeply sensed pleasure. This time there was no fine whistle of excitement... His touch teasing as silk, I tried to imprison it very close to me. Hesitant, he moved away slowly. If only he would not—just a fleeting feeling. Without warning he swung me around to face under him... In a commanding gesture he penetrated slowly, deliberately. There was an unspeakable moment I clung to, feeling completed by him.

An attraction with its particular tides moved us beyond immediacy... An ancient voice incanted, a rising, receding liturgy... He carried me unto a gliding stage: a life boat rocked by the heavily sighing North Sea.. Coasting dizzily on the wind of turbulence, I felt an unending joyous longing for him. I heard him say "Woman... I can't take it... woman what you are doing to me ... ?" I heard myself moaning pitifully... I pulsed with his unfailing, soaring containment. He insisted on bedazzling while I pleaded for him to give in... When he deliberately allowed himself to culminate, I felt his trembling slow climb, in a deep tidal heave quickening in greater frenzy toward the distant horizon—a sharp crest arose to meet the sky when he crashed with foam iridescent splashing rainbows against the sandy warm shore.

He was uncomfortable with the heat of the deep summer night and admonished me for not using some air coolant. How unusual to have had that many warm nights! As we lay very still, he said with puzzlement, "You know, I've never had this happen to me... a woman has never gone down on me... " (Down—up—depending on your perspective.) "Down?" Now what did he mean by that? "Don't you like being kissed all over?"

"Yes, I do, I do!" He sighed unusually for a man that self-controlled. He was commenting again, perturbed about the heat. "Should I fetch a fan?" I thought the heat was radiating from his strong and powerful body and that I reflected his. I fetched hand towels, dipped into a cool soapy solution. The candle's flame sputtered its last drops while I washed both of us down. The ritual was delight in the quietness between us. We slept in each other's slippery warmth, eventually pulling a cool sheet between our bodies. The moon, silver, joining through the thick foliage the yellow glow of the street lantern, splashed light at the foot of the bed. One of us awoke. We made love again.

It was early morning. I stood by the window elated, though menaced by sadness. A single star hung suspended in the sky. It winked a few times in the quietness of the dwindling night, alone in a sky luminous with emerald, streaked with tropical indigo, purple. The scenery of voluptuous dawn colors was unexpected as always in these grey winter spheres. I held on to the vision of sky being overtaken by daybreak outside the window. I felt I must prepare for sudden parting, loneliness. I felt sucked in by its familiar well where I might touch my own strength again. I thought of my son—how long would I have to wait to see him again? A few months earlier in the Alps in Switzerland I remembered being alone waiting for him to join me. I was in the high mountains. One afternoon among the tallest peaks I could smell the seas from the other side of the mountain brining lips with salty white foam. The weather turned. I thought I might never be able to come down again. I heard the wind being hurled across these glacier deserts, echoing from one mountain peak to the next; like a sandstorm the icy cold cut the skin with the sting of sharp tearing needles. The glacier caught the last of the light in a rainbow. The mountain head stood as impassible and severe as ever, but seemed suddenly dwarfed against the immensity of sky. To be alone means to be alone…

Carlos called me to him. He reached out for me and pulled me back to the bed alongside him. His blue eyes were serious as ever but radiated deep blue, smiling hunger. He slid me alongside him, his beautiful large hands placed me obediently against him as he simply penetrated. No pain, no reticence, for though I had already left him I received him, determined to let happen between us whatever he fancied. Deep whirling thrusts; delight of pull at the center of me; he was leading me dizzily around, while I dissolved in his brown golden haired hands. I had no say in what was happening. I felt myself gently brought down to earth while he determined not to bring these heavenly sweeps to fruition. As he teasingly coiled up to me, he kissed my breasts, a short, boyish, affectionate kiss to each—there was just enough to fill the palm of each of his honest manly hands, and he said, "One doesn't always have to come. They say it's good for the prostate to keep it in… " I sighed with warm contentment and agreement, though I had never heard of this before. He lay very still and appeared reflective, then he swallowed hard a few times, his blue eyes pensive, somberly serious, so serious… What was he going to say now? Would he reproach me for being so difficult? Eventually he said, looking ponderously down at me, "You're an experienced woman… " Surprised, I replied hesitantly with a frown, "Well… yes, I've been married twice… "

"Well then," he asked firmly, "HOW DO I MEASURE UP?" From deep within me there was a laughingly strong feeling of recognition. I had somehow guessed all along he would ask. I had finally found the boy. He reminded me at once of my adolescent son. When still very young boys will wonder aloud, "Is mother going to marry me when I'll be big and strong as Daddy? And will there be enough left for me?"

When adolescents, they're afraid and feeling the onset of desire, find a proper substitute. Still, they crave the admiration, the recognition. "Say Mom, don't you understand," my boy had said once when I questioned his capabilities, "that's what makes the wheels go round… the way your parents feel about you… ". How was I to tell Carlos that he suddenly reminded me of my son, who reminded me in my love for him, of Claude? Goodness, all the spinning around had gone to my head!

When I visited Claude after he had been married for many years, he symbolically asked the same question as Carlos. We were both parents by then. Our children had met. My children were already in the car, waiting to be driven off, and as we were leaving, he emerged from his large old house, atop the shores of the Mystic River, and ran back towards us. He jumped on a unicycle, and cried out in his deepest voice, "Look, Maria, no hands… look!" He spun into widening circles. I stood waiting, admiring. When we made ready to leave for good, he called out again, "Look! Look!", while he mounted an even larger unicycle, his hands free. I nodded admiringly, shouting, "Bravo!" in a last loving gesture.

When Carlos went through his unheard-of love acrobatics, deep within me I knew he would eventually say, "Look, look, no hands!" He was also asking, "HOW DO I MEASURE UP? You, the mature, the experienced woman, the mother, look, I'm the best man—will you choose me? Am I the greatest?" Had the adolescent within him come awake under the impact of our certain separation? He wanted to know: Had he ultimately outdone his father, and so all other men? They had given their best, these good, honest men had, but would they ever outdo THE one other? I exclaimed to Carlos, "Never before have I encountered anyone so utterly self-controlled! You are certainly the most. Bravo! Besides all this, I like you immensely... " Did he want to hear the latter? Could he understand it? For some reason beyond the rational I felt a sensual hunger for him that would take the remainder of my days to satisfy. Did he want to hear this? I was certain he would not return. His mind had not caught up with his magnificent body, with his warm loving feelings and refused stubbornly to unite with them, to consummate the man. It was therefore difficult to accept he had returned when he expressly made a point of letting me understand that somehow I was "at fault" for what was happening between us. Though he was good and kind with his hands and strong body, he treated me simultaneously by word as though I were a malevolent seductress. As though I were the one who had entered him to possess him as a demon. "That's just it... that's what you are...", he had said. I was also the other woman then, the not all-loving mother, the witch who haunted him.

It was five o'clock that early summer morning when I drove him to his room at the Inn. I wore my best daytime clothes. He said he had to attend to work at eight that morning. Before he left me in the parking area, he turned to me humorously, but with the boyishly sly smile not meant for me, asked if I wanted to join him in his room for a while. Laughingly I declined his boastful invitation. As he was about to close the door of the Inn behind him, he turned back and retraced his last steps. From a distance he stood in the brilliant morning light, humanized, joyous, a tall, imposingly vigorous, youthful figure of a man, so unbelievably handsome. I hated to see him go… ' I wanted to say to him "I must tell you, Carlos… I feel you've been good to me… You're a good, strongly powerful man… " There was sadness in the glorious morning light. He raised and turned his head sideways at a rakish angle and prolonged his serious gaze.

CHAPTER 9

Free Association Two: The Winged Angel of Death—St. Exupéry, the Pilot, the Author

What did the publishers say to my first book "Dialogues Between Krishnamurti and Zarathustra?" They said I ought to write a novel like? Who was it? Surely it wasn't the French very young and popular novelist Françoise Sagan? It was. Little did I know then of the wisdom to be found in novels. Creative artists can be mysteriously aeons ahead of their contemporaries. They have clinical noses for societal diseases.

St. Exupéry was a round-faced man, the tallest of giants. Why did I think, from where I stood, far beneath him, that he appeared dissolute as he looked down and passed me over. I was dressed like a real fool; that boy-girl thing had bothered me all of that day. I wore flat, rubber soled shoes. I never was comfortable in them at that young time of life when I was too large breasted—I wore a silk chemise over a severe skirt. At this gathering of sophisticates for the cocktail hour at the hotel Pierre, near Central Park and 5th Ave in New York City, I must have looked like a forlorn school girl. Some of the men wore the uniform of French Resistance officers. I stayed glued against the wall, my bulging leather briefcase under my arm with typed loose leaf book preciously ready for presentation. I wore no lipstick, and my curly hair looked fit for the jungles of Africa. Certainly not fashionable then. I probably stood there like a true mental case wondering about the same old idiotic fears: Would he guess about what happened between Claude and I? Or was it rather the pilot bit? Ah, yes—that is important. That was actually why I went to the party in honor of the French Government in exile. The book was an accessory concern for an introduction to Antoine de St. Exupéry.

First Flying: How old am I? 1 became ill in school and co-pupils took me to the headmistress, and two of them brought me home. I'm perhaps in the 5th grade, 10 years old. They skipped me up in the first grade, because I knew how to read. Who taught me? I don't know for the life of me but consequently I never learned the alphabet (only taught in first grade) till I held my first student job as an assistant librarian at the New School. You must have said this already… how childish! What of it if it is childish? This is just what I am trying to recapture here. When they brought me home, they took me to the store on Pelikaan Street. My father was alone. He took one look at me and blanched. I must have thrown up, for I remember being in the little courtyard with him, at the back of the kitchen, and he pumped water over my burning head. The next thing

I remember: I am very ill with a "brain fever" (I guess). I am delirious and hallucinating while lying in a very large bed and the room is crowded. I am on the first floor of our large old house—it must be in my parents' bedroom—or is it in the living room? There are many concerned-looking old men, some with long beards, and they are pushing each other to get closer to where I'm lying and have a look at me. I am dying I think, and they are praying—there is sad chanting. It does look similar to the scene you would expect to see when someone has died in a very religious household, and the men have come to pray. That's it! I've got chickenpox with a meningitis. First appendicitis, then meningitis, then something else. In between all of this I am screaming. It is evening—it is night. I see all of them around the bed. They stare, sad and worried. All my sisters are there and my mother. I don't see my father. I'm burning with the heat—a plane is on fire—it is falling and falling—I'm in 5th Grade—it must be around *1933*. I kept screaming about planes they said. Later on, according to my mother, they had to tie my hands to the bed, then they were placed with my forearms in plaster, in order to prevent me from scratching at the vesicles of chickenpox. This spell of illness must have lasted a good three months. From then on for years, into adulthood, when very tired, I could feel my tongue expand oddly to gargantuan proportions, the corners of the room assume different dimensions and proportions to one another from what is normal. One knows this for there is a nauseating feeling that goes with it. I understood patients who told me what they similarly felt:

A woman patient who was too ill to come to see me when I visited her at home told me that she had dreamed very painfully the previous night. She remembered vividly she was trying to get something as large and cumbersome as a camel through an opening as small as a needle's head. I shuddered for I suspected a highly organically determined dream. Mis-perceptions, organically founded distortions, sound and feel like this.[1]

The burning plane—I believe I can still see it now—I was screaming and talking away at a rapid pace in "Chinese" said my sisters who did not know Chinese. When I came to America, Europe was burning, and I knew people who had gone to 'work camps.' My most absorbing wish, a constant day-dream, was to learn to fly, to get to be part of one of the European resistance air-forces, and without telling anyone, return to fly over there, and bomb to smithereens the buildings that housed the jailers of the imprisoned chosen people. BOMB THE BUILDINGS... see them run to freedom! I still thought at the time they could escape from their camps in that manner. Mine was a sort of Kamikaze mission before I learned of the Japanese sorties. This day-dream of popular heroism must belong to the myths of all people, especially to the wish-dreams of young people who righteously arise to the defense of endangered loved ones. To die for love's sake while destroying the enemy—what deep reverberations in a youthful heart! After the fiasco with St Exupéry who deigned to communicate with me only to say they did not use women pilots. Did I want to "Voulez-vous coucher... ?" Did he mean with him? He needed help for certain at that point and I didn't see how I could assist him into bed. He was highly inebriated.

I went to the Polish Consulate (after all my mother was Polish, and my father's Dutch nationality did not help. The Dutch Queen had no air-force at her disposal). I do not remember what I told the clerks, but a concerned Polish Consul received me in person. In retrospect the scene must have been

[1] The biblical imagery was of course also determined by psychological factors: out of loving concern her family thought it best to have her meet her usual obligations to them. To have done so was no longer feasible. Hence her feeling of having to do the impossible. Within a few months she died of an inoperable brain tumor.

hilarious. He seemed most worried and upset and went step by step with me over all the possibilities and the expense. How would they get me to London once they had expended the money on training me? Who said they would be willing to let a young woman fly? Why was I so keen on flying anyhow? He seemed to realize, on an intuitive level, that there was something uncanny about my determination.

The Belgian Government instead offered me a job at the Consulate as a secretary, which I accepted. My idea, of course, was to at least get my foot in the door... my spelling was deplorable! Eventually I left them, but they saved me three, even four years of undesired undergraduate schooling, as they were willing to give me a paper which stated that were it not for the outbreak of war, I would have been able to enter the Free University of Brussels in Belgium (that was of course were I able to pass the difficult entrance exam of the "Jury Central" for students who skipped grades.) This, as well as the help received from Sidney Hook, the Chairman of the Philosophy Department at NYU, gave me an entry into third year college. Instead of going through the misery of years of humiliation in a local N.Y.C. high school as a recent immigrant, I was able to take off on wings... but not on flying wings...

Of all this I never spoke to Claude... but I married two pilots, each on active flying duty when I married them. That Claude saw clearly—not I—for by then I had forgotten all about the heroism of my savior complex. A Dr Martin Wangh, a psychiatrist, wrote an article once about Europeans who survived the holocaust they had in some manner witnessed and now walked about with a world of repressed and much unresolved hostility in the fiber of their being. That, I felt, was a "right on" article. I was struck by it and then looked for the name of the author. I found him to be the same Dr. Martin Wangh I had met years before on a cargo ship on my first return journey to Europe in 1947. I asked him then if perchance he knew a certain Edgar Wangh who had directed his father's bank in Ostend, right next to our jewelry store. He said Edgar was his brother. He asked questions—I was still struggling in the thick of denying anything related to my past—he was offended—then forgave—then when I wanted to open up, he wouldn't anymore. I saw his good article and found a picture of our store front in Ostend and his brother Edgar is on it. There is another man, (maybe the same Dr. Wangh?) and my sisters Sara, and Fanny near Edgar—I believed Fanny and Edgar liked each other.. Dr.Wangh said he had met the most lovely, hot blooded young woman of all times in my family, that she was dark as a real gypsy. That must have been Paula. Ha! They always mixed us up, despite the differences in coloring and age so obvious to us. When they mistook me for Paula, or Fanny, or Sara, I swooned with happiness. Didn't my own father get us badly mixed up? Well, certainly our names...

Watched the tube in my room here at the Statler on the Cornell University Campus. Snow high on the Matterhorn, near Zermatt, in Switzerland. (Ate some Swiss cheese and made myself a large cup of hot Chocolate). The chronic difficulties with eating habits: Once started I have found it difficult to stop eating. It's been this way for many years now. Abstaining is no problem, except for the instilled fear of becoming ill when not eating... To think that my parents fought throughout my childhood because I would not eat! My father would shout at my mother at the sound of my screams, "Leave her alone! If she wants to eat, she will—if she won't, she won't... leave her alone!" This drove my mother absolutely berserk, and she blamed him for undermining her authority in the eyes of her child. She said

I would die of inanition, galloping tuberculosis, the lot. Then they said I truly got a touch of the latter, or scoliosis of the spine. A woman doctor found this to be sort of the case when she examined me with all the other pupils in our classroom in 7th grade. She drew on my back with a piece of red chalk and made me parade, wordless, over and over. I suppose she found the curvature way out of line. Off they had packed me, years earlier, to a convent, a sort of sanatorium/ health camp run by the State, with 800 other schoolchildren from different sections of the country. *99.9%* of the children stemmed from coal mining families from the Walloon country (thank heavens, for they mainly spoke French). At the health colony, which was directed by charitable Sisters of Mercy I was affectionately designated—for a change!—as L'enfant Jésus—The Jesus Child, a literal translation of my father's angry "Josell Punim" as he found I cried too often. The sisters thought the name becoming because of the long curly hair, the dark coloring of my tan,, and my sad "soulful" look. I still lived in fear of wetting the bed, and under threat of being taken off by some Boeman (Badman) who leaned—massive, round, and high—actually it was the water tower for the town of Wenduine—between us and the sea.

The hot chocolate—how good! I love it, for it is getting cold out. I've lost some six pounds in the eight days spent here, although I've eaten well, when I felt like it. The Statler Hall where I am staying is part of the University Hotel School in full operation. There are many colors of students from all over the world, and I hear French, German, Jamaican accented English and Haitian music in the voices. In the culinary arts, they eat their own attainments the first semester! I still prefer snacking to major meals at a session. I really prefer eating at one of the students' major cafés: Willard Straight Hall. There one can listen to music; it is spacious, and very high-ceilinged. The music stems from a large juke box, and is carried by many fine speakers across the enormous hall. The old neo-gothic structure has multi-paneled windows that remind me of cloisters. In the daytime the light pours in and one can see some of the campus grounds, the law buildings, and other beautifully erected stone structures in the distance. An arm of Cayuga Lake shimmers through the foliage. Yesterday while here for brunch, I watched a group of French-speaking young men, then I returned to writing these associations. Two hours later when I went back to my room, the boys were still there working on their studies.

My daughter came with a friend and I took them for dinner at the formal dining hall here at the Statler Inn. I like her friend; I do not believe she cares for him as she finds him too intellectual, too aloof. He is a sculptor now but was a pre-med student here at Cornell for some years. He shows great sensitivity, also lots of unexpressed feeling. She is still very young… They both enjoyed dinner a lot, it seemed. She is openly very critical of my eating habits lately—no doubt I've become eccentric with being alone so often and for prolonged periods of time. She might learn one day that her own Oedipus complex is responsible for some of the times I've spent alone. This evening, I am MUCH, much calmer, thank heavens. For now I feel I've had enough of this. Things have fallen into place pretty well, haven't they? I still will have to check on that passage in N. Wiener, which I thought was an allusion to Claude, or people like him.

T.D.: FOR CHRIST'S SAKE LET HIM GO! He doesn't care for you now. God only knows if he ever did! What difference does it make at this stage in your life? You fool! You bloodiest of all fools! FORGIVE HIM—LET HIM GO!

U.D.: NO! FIRST I MUST UNDERSTAND HIM! WHAT REALLY HAPPENED THERE WHEN THE TWO OF US WERE TOGETHER?

T.D.: How much better can I do that? LET IT REST NOW—LET IT SETTLE!

U.D.: I am calm. I am definitely feeling better. It would be nice if someone else could type the written notes. I don't care to look at them again, so soon. Will others care to go through all of this?

T.D.: Yes, they will.

U.D.: Why?

T.D.: Free associating in honesty with past material hasn't been in print that much. There might be a most valid reason for this… it might be a bore at that. To see. It is worthwhile to find out how well this could work.

U.D.: <u>EXORCIZE HIM through writing</u>. Anais Nin said that was what she was doing re. Gonzalez. The inspired woman who recently published her book "The Zipless Fuck," or rather "The Fear of Flying," did the same, by acting out behavior with the aid of Adrian, who taught her the experience of living as though there were no tomorrow. An entire 2-3 week period of guided permissiveness! The experience with him was the highlight of the book. At the end of the thrilling time spent reading her, after all the giggling at her humorous descriptions, I sadly realized I liked none of the men, except for the first German analyst who treated her. Still, one certainly got to know them well. The language of love-making has, I believe, received definite setbacks during these times of over compensatory daring on our part as women. I wonder if clinical language could not be made more poetic, appealing, than what one reads lately.

T.D.: Theory. This is not the idea!

U.D.: Through Anais Nin's diaries, Henry Miller emerges as an intense genius, human, strongly lovable in the end. Was he her first love? Unfortunately, she conceals. I, for one, enormously want to see this tacit understanding on what is considered good taste in good art revolutionized absolutely to its opposite.

T.D.: Less concealment. The less the concealment, the better. It's needed In all areas, especially psychoanalysis. Yes, I see no reason to hide in this respect. In her book "Fear of Flying" the author mentions a talk given by a Dr. Feuchtenberger on the loves of creative people. I thought it was very good, but the message applied to too many other people, not just artists. Artists are no doubt more deeply affected than others by their emotional experiences. The libido theory, on the other hand, does not apply any more essentially to them than to everyone else. Strange that Erica Jong too is one of four sisters. I was unable to put her book down, and got very little sleep, but considered it worthwhile. More hot chocolate. Felt very sick suddenly and upchucked the lot. Can't go on. Just enough of this for now. Might peek for a minute at "Carlos in The House of Yu". Sick again. Don't inhale! *Mère—Amère—*America— *Suffit!* Enough.

Claude as Mother Substitute. While eating:

About the Scoliosis—The convent had not done the job then?

Well, Mama came to see me there once. We sat beneath a large tree. It was warm. I cried and begged her to take me home with her.

> *"Elle pleurait comme une Madeleine,*
> *Elle pleurait, pleurait, pleurait,*
> *Elle pleurait comme une fontaine,*

Toutes les larmes de son corp y passaient
Oh la la, la la quel cafard!
Oh la la, la la quel cafard!

This funny song reminded me always of the above scene with my mother. She cried too. She exclaimed I looked so well, but she could not take me home with her till I was all well. I wanted to show her how well I was and to illustrate I showed her how good I was at acrobatics on swings, on anything on which I could twirl with body and legs. I would improvise a *grenouille* (a frog's contortion) on a single rope of a swing; she admired, but she left me. I became enamored of a young nun (a novice?) who wore civilian clothes. I found her beautiful, and she liked to laugh. Another close friend there; I remember her looks better than my own at the time. She must have been a year or two older, for she was also taller and her uniform bulged where her small breasts began to point through. She was very blond, almost platinum and silver frosted by sea air and sun, and completely blind—sort of two holes instead of eyes. Her skin was blotched, eaten by sea and wind, the huskiest little voice I ever heard from a girl... her fingers in her nose and eating the products thereof. That was fascinating. We led each other wherever we went. I always waited for her, and we stood queuing hand in hand. In the sand dunes we stayed together and she taught me how to braid grass. I would spit into the arched top part of it, and it became a mirror and I would tell her what one could see. The dunes—later like the wooded parts of Cape Cod really—<u>arches</u>—<u>mirrors</u>—<u>leading the blind</u>—<u>knowledge</u>—<u>dream of Claude</u>—<u>the arched chair</u>—but nowhere else is the air so imbued with iodine and the aroma of seaweed, carried by the ever-present winds from the North Sea. Did I finally become continent for urine there? How old was I then? They sent me three times. Well then, this was when I was about seven or eight. There with 100 girls in the dormitory. I was continent. There was the threat of the Bouman (the mysterious shape of the water tower outside) while *99* Catholic girls suddenly fell on their knees when darkness came. It took a long while to learn this was how they said their prayers. They fell by the side and all around me and I did not. They never made a fuss about prayers. I just did not and no one told me to. Really losing self in details—get going. At the convent I hated butter, I hated milk. At home I hated "pap", i.e. the runny warm chocolate pudding my mother had me eat at each meal to fatten me up—I just hated to eat for her. I loved it when through the coughing and choking and the wanting to throw up my father would lift me on his knees and console me, and tell my mother to leave me alone. Loved his prickly skin. The lovely curly black hair… the smell of tobacco on his tweedy jackets—God forgive me! What if I had <u>wanted</u> all that commotion over me and the wretched meals? I doubt it.

Later I began to love mayonnaise, ice-cream, and boys, and chewy gum drops, while I trained for extracurricular gymnastics with the boys in the speed-running competitions. I won the last leg of the 100 meter relays for girls two years in a row. My family said I had become decent at last; a completely changed personality emerged they said "like overnight!" I had finished the first year of the Modern Section of the 9th Grade. I had done well—restored the honor of the family at the Royal Atheneum of Antwerp that year. I came out second in a good class of 30. Aunt Antoinette my mother's youngest sister, whose children usually did remarkably well in school, said I must have copied the answers to the examinations from her children. Her children were not even in my year's class. I was proud and wanted badly to tell my father the good news. I believe he died just before

I found out the official results of my exams at the Atheneum. I know for certain he would have said, "Didn't I always say you were good with figures already when you were the tiniest tot?" Our entire family constellation had begun to change. Charles, my sister Paula's boyfriend (she was a mere 4 years older than I) who to begin with was also her Latin teacher, was not a diamond dealer; he was the first different one to join the immediate family. He studied at the Free University of Brussels, bringing logical thinking with him, crystal clear thoughts I could understand. He brought the outside world to me.. This is leading nowhere! Stay with it. On the predominance of Mama's obsessions re food.

T.D.: You lost your thin-strength—you've never resolved this.

U.D.: I would not sit with Claude at first; I thought it too intimate an act to eat with him alone. He said he could see my point. It made me unbearably tense. My hands would shake, and sometimes I could not swallow.

T.D.: Well, I also thought they might be starving in Europe.

U.D.: Some, perhaps, but that was not all there was to it. Sometimes I was unable to talk, even when there was someone else with us.

TD.: Remember on 8th Street at our usual restaurant in the Village? That other girl, when Evie left, she was my new flat-mate, was much older and much cleverer by far than I. After teaching for many years she wanted an advanced degree in Sociology I believe it was.

U.D.: I just blocked. I probably felt left out of their conversation, I couldn't join in. Claude looked at me. She pressed and wanted me to speak up. He held my hand reassuringly under the table, laughed in his coughing way and said, firmly, "Say, leave her alone for a bit… " I couldn't open my mouth—later at night when alone in his flat, that was quite a different story…

How I loved holding him, every part of him between my lips! It felt so silky, a dark velvet delight! His delight—mine—I would hold him for half the night. He pushed the occipital part of my head lightly against him, with the tip of his fingers as though I were his musical instrument, toward him, more and more and I felt I was entering him, becoming part of him. I re-entered the womb with him. I could finally lose my head in my mother's breasts, between his smooth, large, low hanging testicles. I could reach the nipple at last and feel smothered between those beautiful large silky breasts—she never allowed me to touch when it mattered. I tried early in adolescence once. I just wanted to playfully hold, in the fullness of a palm, to pinch lightly, to squeeze gently. She was absolutely shocked and dramatically took the pose of one offended—a hand to her heart, rejecting. Claude finally let me. Get hold of the feeling of waiting—to wait to have a child—upset at putting down date on this page.

Taking histories 8—10 hours a day, for I went back to work Wednesday in my office. There is always a date to record—for whom? How often does this material get reread?

Thought just before—Waiting—dates—correct ones this time! 1953-54: Graduation University of Geneva. Full fledged Doctorate in Medicine with published thesis. Internship *N.Y. 1954*. First child (kept) conceived in *1954*, delivered '55… I was not as young as I thought when I had my daughter! Waited so long to have her, my very first child. Sssso much waiting ! Switzerland? All that waiting. How many, how very many times raped there? And before that? And to finally have a child!

Here is the waiting relived through my daughter now, the thought of having to do the fitful expecting and waiting all over again through her periods. A bad turn for her preciously soft, unfinished, perfectly proportioned curvaceous body—pregnant? Yes, that's it—reliving the whole bloody <u>waiting game</u> with her now. Waiting to see if she is, watching for signs, wondering. What if she did carry his baby? Strapping big boy it would be, I'm certain. She came home all bruised that day, with a friction burn on her side. She said he had dragged her onto a sofa; she was sleepy and inebriated. He—pitifully beyond action. Why the hell did I let her go out with him? There were two men with her, and I thought the other would not let her out of his sight and that they would bring her home, there being one too many. The big brute of a man! I can understand her though: teachers, professors, an absent father figure—does one ever get over that?

How many years of waiting, worrying? I attended surgery regularly. Because of this fear of pregnancy in Switzerland I became a serious disciplinarian of watching operations at the University amphitheater. in Geneva. A <u>periodical breather of the blood-imbued air. Despite our gauze mask I was certain the miracle particles were bound to sink in c/o the alveoli—into the blood stream—into the uterine mucosa and make it shed. Make it shed. Make mine shed!</u> That was the waiting song in Geneva to the tune of "Three Coins in the Fountain"—MAKE MINE SHED—MAKE IT MINE... MAKE IT MINE... MAKE IT MINE... Breathe the thick bloody air coming from the operations—women in surgery on the table—<u>And it worked!</u> And it did shed! And I would menstruate! (Especially when not pregnant and when just late??) There is finally a science based on the same principles as the intuitive ones I "smelled" out during the monthly bleeding waiting game as a student. <u>Waiting to be a mother</u>—How many years? Some 10 years! The waiting became unbearable in Geneva. By then I was longing to be like my sisters, instead of unlike them as before. I wanted especially to be like the prized ruby, my sister Pauleke, who seemed so well looked after by her husband in Antwerp, Belgium, while she cared for their children. I came to school with her elegant discarded clothes. I had to examine someone the day I wore her good wool Swiss Hanro dress, but I wore no stockings. My long hair stood away from my face and neck like that of an ancient native of Central Africa. I had been waiting fearfully to hear my name since the beginning of the semester in OB-GYN. I thought they skipped me. Prof. Von Wattenville (who later delivered Sophia Loren) called my name just as I ran in that day in a straight line from bed ! Barely 8:02 am. Hundreds of boys in the large amphitheater. I walked down the hundred steps to hell (to the low central platform) and realized I forgot to put on a slip and that people might see through the woven, clinging Hanro wool cloth. Melle Berryman! Von Wattenville's delightfully expectant blue eyes always seemed a bit reproachful to women, certainly that day. I usually sat next to Van Eeckhouten for GYN. classes. He was an older, middle-aged Belgian student who had spent some twenty years in what was then called the Belgian Congo and was said to know strange things. We liked each other. A few days later I walked out on the Professor when he dictated letters to his secretary unrelated to the case on hand, gloves on fingers, while the woman lay there shivering with legs spread apart, and the bare cloth covering her openness trembled. I did not slam the door, just said I must not be a witness to this, and said I was sorry to the woman. They told me he said I was right, and on the exam he gave me the maximum grade. Well, I did all right as a student intern in that department, but not that day in front of everyone. I was to palpate and examine the patient. A big 200-fold 'OUCH!' went up from the boys—because of the inadequate size of my hands I seemed to have really plunged into her. She told me she didn't feel a thing and not to worry.

I never found out anything regarding Van Eeckhouten's wife and children. I knew he had them somewhere. It was a big mystery. See—See—I'm not the only one who withheld from friends one loves the most important things, as Claude and I did.. At that age when one is young, the thing that counts most is the PRESENT—THE PRESENT UNDOES THE WAITING—IT NEUTRALIZES EFFECTIVELY THE AGONY OF WAITING. *Voilà!* There it is! That's what the Gestaltists (the therapists) said all along. I thought it had meaning mainly later in life. The present totally encompasses the future for the young. They are still somatically close to the growing process and the perceived memory of changing soma. Later on you cannot successfully pull them inward again as Gestalt Therapy does—except when there is a crushing conflict that stops the *ensor—élan*—soaring flight to the outside, the future

Interferences with Learning: The great men, teachers at the New School for Social Research. Many interferences with learning from them. Most important to me at the time: their German accents! Their bloody stinking accents! Unbeknownst to me, these precipitated one back into the arms of the Gestapo who, mere months earlier had prevented me from not being affected by them. An ancient jungle law sprang to the fore—kill to survive; hate or be swallowed. Like ants, they were suddenly everywhere in Paris, their mud-green uniformed presence wherever one went. They were beginning to assume the airs of those who take liberties. In the streets, in the parks in bloom, in all the beautiful structures open to the public, one couldn't take a dreamy walk ever without encountering their threatening appearance. They walked, nail-studded soles loud against the warm pavements, always in groups of three or four, never as a person, alone. I'd venture out in search of the heroes found in books over the last two years. Often rested in passing on the benches I wanted to touch; I wanted to breathe the air traced by their lives — Jean Christophe, Verlaine, Rimbaud, Bergson, so many others, the heroes of an aspiring studious literary adolescence. They were as alive as the greatest hero of all: Jessie Owens, the speed runner from America. He was a Black King, handsome beyond compare... a magician from "A Thousand and One Nights", who repeatedly undid Hitler publicly for all to view on the Newsreel movie-screens in Antwerp. The *1936* Olympics were held in Germany. The King, Jessie Owens unexpectedly wins the most spectacular competitions.

Hitler stomps and raves in public, his racist lunacy in evidence. In the movie houses in Antwerp the Flemish public laughs at his ridiculous demeanor... He's been upstaged! I feel identification with the world's fastest runner. He's different. He's a King escaped from his pursuers through his superior endowments... He's thumbed his nose at the lot... I love him.

I had just learned about Krishnamurti and his masters Tagore and Ghandi. These Indian philosophers appealed more strongly than all others at the time. A year later, in America, I was told by one of my philosophy professors, Marcel Barzin, (the very same man who had earlier taught my brother-in-law Charles at the Free University of Brussels) that my enthusiasm for these Hindus implied a pitiful gesture of abnegation. He said to me: "In times of greatest political conflict and national strife when war is threatening, (America was not at war yet) there has always been a group of men who have promulgated the attitudes and beliefs which tacitly imply pacifism." I understood he viewed their convictions as a conspiratorial attempt against what he well knew to be the inherent bellicose nature of man. Prof. Barzin took pride in his fighting spirit. He said he detested sitting in a boat, waiting passively for a fish to bite on the wormy bait. Was he perchance implying that I had turned cowardly? Abandoned my people? How was one to tell him? In truth my interest in pacifism (since it was this which he denounced in Krishnamurti and his disciples) was the only lifeline I was able to get hold of. They were the only thinkers who helped me cope with THE anger, the engulfing hatred lying barely beneath the paper-thin surface skin. My young fantasies during German occupation days in Paris, Bordeaux, the exodus back to Paris, were of the most murderous nature toward the Nazis. Sickening waves of endlessly heaving hatred… How to tell that to Prof. Barzin? When 17 years old, not long before I met him in New York, I had nightly fantasies without which I could not sleep. In Paris, in Bordeaux… to lull myself asleep, repetitively each night I would go through the same ventures, seducing soldiers, counting, numbering, guessing—estimating the number of "bully boys of the Third Reich" whom I killed one after the other, in my fantasy. How many before they round me up? How many will pay for this life of mine? If we all did this.., till sleep would come.

As we get older it is easy to forget how difficult it may be for youngsters to confront anger, defeat, helplessness, hate. How insurmountable at times are these sickening waves, these heaving anti-social, (or social) surges in the process of growing up. The young need us then… How are they to overcome the panic? Though adult strength already has pulsed in their bodies, in their feelings they remain murderously angry with the helplessness that still holds them back. Their unstable emotionality stirs us, and their anxiety contaminates us. We turn against them in anger for what we feel within ourselves. To protect forgetfulness we reproachfully turn away from them. Stinking, crying shame... Pacifists... Pacifiers: Drugs, liquor, explosive acting-out behavior... "Hang on!" The storm is bound to settle... In turn they will forget. They must, as all women do—suffering so much pain in labor, they too forget, always. In my case, as an adolescent, crime prevailed where I lived. The self-protective fantasies of criminality were transmuted into acts of being an heroic savior. Were it not for this attempt at capturing some understanding of what brought on the mood of misery during these first years alone in America, I, too, would have forgotten.

What other interferences of learning? The language barrier, of course. "THEY" had taken my song away from me. "They" had taken that sharp, smooth, fast-running—no longer lisping as in childhood—tongue acquired as mine in French.

T.D.: Who?

U.D.: They! The contingencies of war, the invaders...

T.D.: I emigrated without preparation, and found myself with a lisping, hesitant, whispered tongue again, fumbling in its expression...

U.D.: Claude loved to hear me search for a word: "An instrument to protect one against the rain... " He'd smile and say that was a pretty clear definition for what I wanted to communicate, and wouldn't offer the word "umbrella." Bob, my first husband, in response to my loud exclamations of enthrallment at the glistening "foques" (pronounced by me like "fuck") at the zoo in Central Park, New York, grabbed me forcibly by the arm away from the surprised crowd. He made certain I knew words like "seal" for "foque". He set himself the task of speedily enriching my English vocabulary.

II. A SMOOTH LANDING IN AMERICA

When I arrived in America for the first time, I came off the boat, the 'Nea-Hellas", following a rather long trans-Atlantic voyage which started in Portugal. It occurs to me that I was the only passenger who had an unshared cabin, first class at that. In Lisbon, I offered Greek-Line officials all the money I had on me (that is all of $500), whereupon they said they had a space for me. That was in October of 1940. They must have been surprised. So was I at what I thought was my ultimate good luck. The waiting queues extended the length of four or five streets outside the shipping line's offices. It was good luck. The woman who was to share my cabin was a Mrs. Livingstone—I remember her name as she kindly never turned up for the trans-Atlantic voyage. In the middle of the ocean passengers believed we were going to be torpedoed. I could not have cared less by that time, as long as we did not have to return to occupied Europe. Franz Werfel, the writer and his new wife, the widowed Mrs. Gustav Mahler, were neighboring cabin mates. They made pests of themselves—speaking German. Also, they were edgy, irritable, and objected personally to me for playing the piano in the large deserted lounge—while the ship tiptoed around mines. They wanted me to refrain from breathing loudly as they did, or at least refrain from playing Beethoven's Moonlight Sonata… Did they fear to disturb the mines in their slumber? They had indeed much to loose — but then, having known them, I found them the ugliest older people I'd ever met! I always wondered who the fellow was who saw me translate, dictionary in hand, word by word, Cronin's "Good-bye Mr. Chips" during the voyage (my own system of learning English). He was neither young, nor really old., tall, extremely lank, he wore an odd little cap. I never heard him speak. He looked after a very young boy. He was usually accompanied by another English speaking man, who was younger and by far less distinguished appearing than himself. The latter was very gregarious and outspoken with me. Through him I received a message from the incognito passenger that I was doing it all wrong, and should instead read such and such and do it so and so. He was known from what the ship's young Greek physician told me, as The Important incognito first-class passenger. This cold, distant preoccupied seeming man might have been Thomas Mann's brother Heinrich.

Don't believe I've ever been able to afford again as luxurious, nor as expensive a voyage across the Atlantic. I would consider it quite a waste really under normal circumstances. My mother had given me five sparkling new bills of $100 each and some small change. I smuggled this $500 right from under the noses of the thugs. One of them said to me at the French-Spanish border, on the successful exit: "If we find any money on you, anything, don't cry, just tell us if you have anything… " I was mute: I could hear the sound of my heart pounding. It said "Hate you—*cochon*—pig—hate you ." "How do you expect to leave from Lisbon? You say you're going to America. Where's your ticket?"

"Friends… They are waiting."

"Who?"

"People assigned by the Wagons-Lits-Cook people… "

"You said friends… ?"

"They are friends." An elderly man employed by the Wagons-Lits-Cook in Paris had warned me of this. They were unable to provide tickets which indicated available boat transportation, but gave many helpful hints and a few of the available and necessary papers to get out of Paris. I thought of the clever idea of hiding money between the glued two halves of a fluffy powder puff inside my powder compact. I always had a childhood compulsion to open dolls and look at the hidden inside—the genie in the bottle—and later would sew the incisions together again to hide my inquisitiveness. My early curiosity finally paid off. While they searched our luggage, I went to sleep under the strain of all the concealment. There was too much unexpressed feeling. Often in times of crisis the soma takes over with its own older wisdom. It pulls one inward, as back to the womb, a state of lesser consciousness. Here, on my way out of hell. The other passengers woke me to board the train which was to take us to Portugal.

At the next stop, in the Spanish town of Irun, they dragged a young Dutch Jew out of our compartment. He belonged to a family of diamond dealers from Amsterdam, Holland. He quickly asked me as he took his luggage down to take a large diamond ring which he wore and give it to his father who was in the States. I said I would. Then as he left, accompanied on each side by secret police of some sort, I suddenly ran after him and returned the ring unobserved to him. It had suddenly occurred to me that he ought to keep it, for he might need everything he could lay his hands on to buy off the swine. I told him in a few words of the experience with the jailers at the internment camps in Bordeaux and of the times I had seen when they could not resist our precious little stones. To think I met that same Dutchman some 5-6 years later! It was in New

York, across the street from The Russian Tea Room on West 57th Street. I was with my first husband. The Dutchman was with a group of people, his wife and parents... They looked at me without sympathy, with suspicion when I exclaimed and loudly called and ran over to him. In response to my explosive cry when we recognized each other, he temporarily became most excited, babbling without rhyme nor reason (in their eyes). One must have lived these minutes as we did to understand how preciously dear life can feel. Simply to be alive and well how wondrously miraculous in and for itself! Our meeting Monsieur Norbert Wiener would agree, I'm certain—was an anti-entropy phenomenon, *par excellence*. I felt like taking giant leaps down 57th Street chanting for all to hear: Anne Frank is alive and well in New York!

At Willard Straight Hall, at Cornell University in Ithaca. The large purple juke-box is playing. And many young people sit studiously at solid wooden benches and tables—eating, reading, writing. I spoke to Evie on the phone; she might come for Thanksgiving. Hurray! I have not seen her for nearly two years. After I spoke to her, I remained excited but unfocussed. It snowed heavily on the way over here from the hotel room on campus. Belgian appearing slate roofs on stone, neo-gothic buildings and snow. Trees and whiteness shimmering in the quiet darkness. Small sprinkles of round, pebbles and ashes everywhere. Will Evie really come and will she like the atmosphere here? She has reached an impasse in her life. There is still time to turn around and change course, make a clean break from a life dedicated to the care of others. The temptation is to continue to lead a self-sacrificial existence dedicated to an elderly mother and others in Europe. The alternative: Become independent—earn her living. Get into a profession and take her acquired skills back to Europe. But how can I convince her of her great capabilities? The strong push must be now! Else she'll be swallowed up by enduring family ties. I see that last alternative as the penultimate end. She might feel reassured about regained vigor once the last stage of menopausal changes have been capped.

Back to spewing up from the past. Lately I have been unable to retain food during these writing exercises. It's as though one's insides had to get into the act. Were it not for Evie, how would I ever have held up under the strain of the New York State Medical Board Examinations? Five whole days of exams in a row. I stayed at her flat, and she mothered, fed, and showed constant concern. I can't remember ever having been so lovingly cared for. An hour past the last day of those long ordeals I turned maniacal, and couldn't stop talking! I have done a lot of priming on the occasion of her announced visit. Unless I expect to be with a man I don't usually do this. What the hell am I really up to? Just trying to gain some objectivity as to where I stand with regard to my appearance. Changes can be so lightning quick at this stage. It's not as if she'd stood still during this time either. At menopause we don't all decline at the same rate, nor at the same time. There is a period of some four or five years when we age rapidly, more so than men do. Then we settle in and the majority of women do well for longer than our male counterparts. Were Evie to follow in her mother's footsteps, she might remain most seductive for a long while yet. Could I love her, were I to find her physically repulsive? Certainly not! Then I must see to it that I am not an object of pity either. A long time ago, when employed by one of the hospitals and completely snowed under by work and worried about the children... no money, nor time for buying nice clothes, hairdressers, what not... She and Henry and I had met in New York. We were walking on Broadway. Henry, strikingly tall, wore his clothes superbly, and looked his distinguished, impressive self. Evie wore a beautiful new spring coat. She appeared so soignée—elegantly pretty, that day, as always. I was marked by dark circles under tired eyes, feeling overweight, a fatigued mess... Evie and Henry walked side by side, slightly ahead of me. People stared at them. What an attractive pair! I felt left out, trailing behind in frumpy clothes. That was rough! I felt jealous and simultaneously ashamed, sorry. All the old sibling rivalry revived momentarily. I didn't rejoice for her, but I should have in view of her not that good looking much older husband whom she usually had to walk around with. What was it my mother said? "Evie is always impeccably attired. What refined elegance! True, she has no children, but she's one hundred percent better off than you. Look at the life this man is offering her. They travel, they enjoy. They have everything. What do you have? Nothing! No diamonds! No decent living quarters. No religion, no Sabbath, no rejoicing. You have a handsome fellow; other women can enjoy him. For you there is nothing—you labor like an ordinary work-horse to keep him in clover. All you've got is a fellow with looks and where does that leave you?"

I said that was totally false; I was looking to the future. The children brought joy. Even the work at the hospital brought joy—sometimes. Gads! It is true though... I wished I could at least have lived those years of motherhood to the fullest—I waited so long for them! It is of the essence of women to be waiting, always. No use denying it: the show was badly planned.

* * *

While Henry stayed in Luxembourg for months and months, unemployed there a good deal of the time, I wrote him a most feeling letter which at last expressed what I felt was the truth about our marriage and what had gone wrong between us. He brought the letter back with him and handed it to me saying: "I don't want to receive letters like that from you ever again. I want this to be well understood once and for all… "

* * *

I believe this entire exercise won't suffer from skipping at this point. I mean I feel adverse to copying notes that still seem full of contention inasmuch as I have clearly been unable to accept without sadness, anger, and a measure of self-contempt the situation I have repeatedly found myself in with respect to my last marriage and divorce. I don't mind copying where it says "he wasn't nice right from the beginning. Meeting him on the way back from an excursion in Canada by bus. He had been flying in the bush in Northern Canada just before I'd met him. True, he wasn't nice from the beginning and the interns at the hospital where I worked went out of their way to help him, even find him a job in New York, even though every one of them advised against getting seriously involved with him He took their many kindnesses in his stride as though it was his due and we all owed it to him…

N.B. So very many pages on the interactions with husband Henry!… We were forcibly still much involved in view of the children's visits to him and his manipulations with me as usual about money. My inability to let it rest and to accept the inevitable. Strange that our textbooks do not mention miserliness, pathological retentiveness, as part of other than obsessive-compulsive personality disorders. And why is the latter predominant in men rather than women? I know how the

Freudians look at this but it does not take women and their own earliest attachment into consideration in this respect. This, I must be reminded is not an exercise in theory of psychoanalysis.

* * *

It's nearly five in the morning. I wish I could go on a while longer and have breakfast downstairs, a real breakfast, then go to sleep. One of the buildings across the street has a beautiful vault-shaped window with orange colored lights aglow. It is reminiscent of an enormous tablet on which you might find large writ inscriptions as of the ten commandments. These treasured vaults! A dream came back to me today from my analysis: A box in a box, in a box, leading to the holy Sepulcher.

U.D.: Did I really manipulate these two children of ours? What the hell is a manipulative personality anyhow? Ambivalence experienced in their case to an outstanding degree.

T.D.: TRUE. Exploitative of others?

U.D.: When have I ever… ?

T.D.: When didn't you? You give all the love one could ever wish for and then what happens?

U.D.: What does, sot?

T.D.: You begin to expect, demand as much in exchange, if not more. And if they can't give it, you pull out, like a blaspheming witch. You won't stay on the giving end, will you? You know as well as I do, that's the only way to go.

U.D.: You mean no endorsement to make the relationship valid? Even a simple check needs an endorsement to be valid.

T.D.: Don't play games! You know as well as anyone that children can't begin to endorse till they're about 12 or 14—or even later. How many times did you regret them? God knows the children showed love more than you are willing to deal with here… They are such wonderfully open children!

Didn't the boy tell you clearly he couldn't stand to see you alone, sad the way you were, most of the time? Didn't he feel sick with guilt about the sadness, the emptiness he certainly never brought to you?

U.D.: Dr. Albert Ellis woke me up—he finally said, "Get rid of them!" Gripes should be carried to their ultimate conclusion. It opens the way to a healthy compromise.

T.D.: What the hell did you tell them during your outbursts, while going to pieces for (let's say) being late? Were they told that in truth their very existence was the most joyful event in your life? Didn't you imply by your deeds in non-verbal terms: you half-breeds! Your bastard of a father won't help in the least, and there you go and can't even be home in time for me to drive you to <u>your</u> stinking lessons (which neither of them asked for)…

U.D.: Ambivalence, repressed hostility, displaced hostility, that's it! Displaced hostility from parents to the men in my life and from the men to the children. The MEN! What have I done to their lives??? <u>Claude</u>—He now has a woman who hasn't grown with the marriage. A marriage of mutuality, and he hasn't got it.

T.D:: Rubbish! Besides these matters are less important to him than to you. It's time you learned that to some men, especially exceptional thinking men, marriage doesn't mean as much as their work.

U.D.: I urged marriage. Once his mind was made up, of course, then the partner doesn't seem to matter as much. It's the decision that matters. His wife-to-be stepped into an opened slot. No, I do not believe a replica of himself was what he needed, nor a physical replica of me. He could have done better. Why did he have to marry a (compared to him) minor mathematician? He was enough of an innovative scientific genius to lead (let alone amuse) an army of them. He didn't need being immediately seconded by one. So she built him a *téléférique* to go from the house up and down to the banks of the Mystic River. Well, she's a sweet, outstandingly sensitive girl and the right partner for certain who not only had worked in the same outfit as he during WWII, but also gave him, was able to give him the understanding he deserved. Especially now you must LEAVE THEM ALONE ! How much longer are you going to keep at this? Who knows if they even know you exist by now?

U.D.: They know! They know! Barney O. told me so. Another cold-hearted scientist that one. The worst thing for him was to have spent that year before the war in Germany with their sick racism to contaminate him here and there...

T.D.: Cold? Far from it—in the contrary... And so what? He does exceptionally good work that benefits a world of others—He also thought he'd found the answer to a better way of teaching reading to children through a newer statistical approach to phonics. Didn't he have some twenty guide books on the subject sent to you from Harvard University? He might have felt guilty for some of the things he said to me when Claude and I were not that close any longer and I said I wanted to study medicine... and become a psychoanalyst (as my teacher and ideal Karen Horney). He said I looked too exotic... Really! Not American enough ...

U.D.: My friend Winnie Love in California, when she met him at her house where I stayed with her, said he had been a quiz kid. One of the first. As Norbert Wiener described himself:

"The infant prodigy or Wunderkind is a child who has achieved an appreciable measure of adult intellectual standing before he is out of the years usually devoted in a secondary school education. The word prodigy cannot be interpreted as either a boast of success or a jeer. It calls to mind either people like John Stuart Mill and Blaise Pascal, who had proceeded from a precocious youth to an effective adult career, or their antitheses, who have found the transition between early precocity and later effectiveness one which they have become too specialized to make... Thus the child prodigy who is not in fact a prodigy of moral strength as well must make a career success on a large scale, for want of which he is likely to consider himself a failure, and actually to become one... to the grown up, it is lovable and right for the child to be confused, to be at a loss in the world of adults around him; but it is far from a pleasant experience for the child ... "

T.D.: Well? Didn't Barney O. go exceptionally far in life?

U.D. He never really liked the likes of you. He never really liked the likes of Claude.

T.D.: Oh? That's not certain at all. Well, he seemed very shocked when Claude told him

"I won't do another thing for them... " and whatever else ... that Barney said Claude was doing then ...

U.D.: Barney's wife? She might be the only very human being he's really loved.

T.D.: So—WHAT—ABOUT YOUR MANIPULATIVE-NESS? What have you done to Bob, your first husband's life? Where did he go when you left him? He grabbed at straws, a wispy sort of a woman 20 years his senior.

U.D.: She loved him, yes...

T.D.: They say she was bitchy and had never enough; she never acted as though he gave enough. He was seemingly her son-husband.

U.D.: He feared having children. So! Maybe he needed to remain the beloved son. True. Wouldn't have been hard to do. He gave so much of himself.

TD.: He didn't ask that much in return, did he? Well at least he loved the philosophy lessons you knew and he went into philosophy himself for a while, then evolved into psychology.

U.D.: Didn't I ask him to stay on and study medicine with me when he came to see me in Geneva?

T.D.: Wouldn't that have been convenient for you? He smartly knew he didn't want that!

U.D.: He was the one who told me in Geneva that Claude had remarried, and he said that his new wife looked remarkably like you.. That really just about did me in.

T.D.: Didn't you deserve that—but good—from Bob? ... He is married for the third time now—it is not good.

U.D.: Not bad at all, really. He's done well in scientific research, has been described as great, as a human being who's been able to help many.

T.D.: What the hell did you do to Henry on his way to Argentina? What good did it do him to get you forcibly pregnant? And were you sure he got you pregnant that first time?

It was Henry's—Henry staying at the Y.M.C.A. to be near the hospital and using the intern's quarters to shave, wash up.

U.D.: All the interns said, "Don't, Maria. Henry is not for you." I was certain I got pregnant that first time around. I wished deeply it was his child. The dates said so. He was certainly the handsomest built man I thought I had ever known. From the back as strong and straight as a regal black athlete. He seemed calm, self-possessed. Little did I know... He told me about his family background and a duty to live up to his name. When I mentioned my own religious background and previous marriage in passing, he was upset but then decided that it was all right as long as I did not mention this. I chose to think he was being very funny, but he meant it very seriously. No one said I was possibly ruining his life and future too. Henry was jobless. He introduced himself as penniless, just back from flying in the Canadian Bush. He was truly not "nice" from the beginning. You've said this over and over again. Delete the rest. The main thing to remember: I did want this child of his and mine—with him. Imagine being an intern in OB-GYN. for some three months. Every delivery became harder; every new-born a world of sweetness. A miracle clung to with envy and desire. I HAD WAITED SO LONG! THERE—THERE—WAS THE LONGEST WAIT—

T.D.: He gave you a beautiful child!

U.D.: I gave him two beautiful children.

T.D.: Who used whom—you fool—in this?

U.D.: You did!

T.D.: You used him as a stud, a magnificent sperm dispensing stud!

U.D.: That's a lie! I hadn't any intention of letting him do anything. He forced me while we were on the roof and he asked me to sit on his lap. The nuns smelled evil and were roaming in and out of doors. Who ever heard of a decent man who did not use precautions with a girl he barely knew?

About my first born the doctors were emphatic about her being at least two months premature. So for goodness sake, it could not have been "that forced first time! Not possibly. The other probability? I lost the first and was able to keep the miracle that came after. That's it, of course! How in the name of heaven did I not realize this before? The stinking, pervasive, all invasive guilt—the destructive consequences of it messed up the relationship from the start. It was not as if he had had any experience with marriage previously. It's ten past six a.m. Don't pull out now. *Assez—Fini*—I've had enough of this.

T.D.: You want everything your way. That's manipulating! Just as your mother used people, so do you, and from her you wouldn't take it.

U.D.: You don't even know what you're talking about. Every time the children went to see him, he tore them apart with pleas for them to stay in whatever God forsaken place he had landed though he was not able to remain in one place nine tenth of the time. He wanted them to stay for their good and future well-being no doubt? I've had enough of this—I don't want to be some namby-pamby..

<u>SUPPER</u>: Filet of sole, a bun, half a glass of nice French Rosé Wine. I feel too full again. Had a light lunch of cheese and a small roll here at the Hotel School.

Walked down College Avenue for some cosmetics. Evie is definitely coming in a day or two. Yesterday morning I did gymnastics in the room, facing a large mirror. Today the muscles of my thighs hurt as I walked. I'm in dire need of more than swimming. Undeniably the masquerade continues daily in the ineluctable footsteps of the aging process—mornings in the mirror... each day new marks of disfigurement. If it were not sad it might be funny... A surprise each day! A stranger is emerging who demands familiarity at once. Women's resilient skins? Not anymore. It is 18 degrees F. out tonight, it is finally snowing in oblique thick flakes. The air is crispy, barely wet, invigorating. I bought a pair of overalls for my son and will send them to him in Anchorage as a holiday present. I trust he will want to ski in these—I will sent his ski boots also. By air? No. By post—it is better through Henry's post office box—what if Henry is not there again? He spoke of a strike He did slip in having put

214

funds away for Rex's school for this year. What about next year's schooling? You compulsive... No, I didn't say that much to him on the phone. (I was home to see patients for two days, 9 hours each day—on the third day, four, five more...)

Now I'm completely down from my high. Henry called from New York City. My daughter handed me the telephone and said to him, then to me, "Come now, you two, no getting upset!"

Yes—as Fritz's under-dog = U.D, top-dog = T.D. has it. UD—TD alternatively—I = UD, that is better. This manner of speaking to oneself as an outsider has a pretty self-righteous ring to it, and also sounds phony and too far from what is felt specifically, for the convenience of what is said generally. True feelings have been hiding deep down lately.

U.D.: If only I could lose myself. Deep down I feel it is good, this finding out. Some patterns are really emerging. I still can't really believe I'm a manipulator.

T.D.: Look again. What do you think all this whining and blaming has been about these last years? He gives you this name he's so righteously proud of...

U.D.: That's just it, the righteousness of him all the time. And he isn't that smart either.

T.D.: I dare say. He might have hit the jackpot, if he had not met you on that Canadian bus, on his way to Argentina. If not for you he would not have remained in New York, where he found the people ugly, their manner of speech ugly, everything ugly. He called it a jungle. You were after him the moment you set eyes on him. You were captivated by his proud ways. He stood alone and proud and held his own with the custom officials. He even found you ugly at firs for you were not his type. You sure weren't that good to look at anymore... You've gone through all this before...

U.D.: Well, for a long time I felt guilty about how it all began and treated him royally to make up for a possible deception... how many times are you going to go over this? You've just found out the deception was a self-deception!

T.D.: You never did look as you used to, don't fool yourself. You just went uglier and uglier and lost that nice afro-oriental family touch. Look at your son—he has your features. Isn't he something?

U.D.: No, he looks like a very refined Hindu, but it doesn't suit his straight-backed Scottish-English body. His eyes are too large and prominent—a touch of exophthalmia like me

T.D.: Looks, looks, looks! You'll never cure yourself of that obsession! I wish I could write myself out of that one. You're not a good woman. If you ask me, you're still getting back at Henry. Each day you get up late, you show him.

U.D.: Well, what of it? When I'm lazy, it's my business now.

T.D.: You're one hundred per cent better off than *99%* of women.

U.D.: Am I? Doesn't the loneliness matter at all?

T.D.: That must be your doing. You have a respected profession. You've even saved some lives. That's all right. You sewed that girl up in OB-GYN, with dumbstruck Dr. Milton Rosenberg not believing his eyes, standing by speechless, except to say "Go on, go on... " You sewed her up there, at French Hospital, and he said "Go on, go on... " with part of your glove sewn into the episiotomy repair, and you couldn't get your finger out after the delivery, what with the episiotomy done and over with...

U.D.: I told Rosenberg I was unable to find those three muscular layers they all talked about. I saw her later, by the way. Neither she nor her husband complained, and I asked her specifically whether I had made her too tight. Laughter all around… they were happy, she said.

T.D.: For certain, you saw them later?

U.D.: I certainly believe I did. And following this experience I did very good jobs, especially on girls with out of wedlock children. The perineum did not show a thing. Not even the lace makers of Bruges could have done better. She was so happy. That poor baby of hers to be given up; suffering already in that hard metallic incubator. Just born, and he cried with real tears…

T.D.: What a waste for everyone to have let you do surgery. You were just a dead weight there, just as much as Henry became a dead weight around your neck.

U.D.: You see—you see—you say so yourself!

T.D.: If you ask me, (and you do seem to want to know) you did him a favor letting him go. We all know that much. But what is all this blaming about? So you both made a mistake. LEAVE HIM ALONE! Don't try to manipulate him again and again.

U.D.: But he tries to manipulate me all the time—through the children.

T.D.: How can he when he's so far away? He doesn't ask you for anything.

U.D.: What about all the money I spent… all those responsibilities he never shared?

T.D.: If he were dead you would have had to spend it— wouldn't you?

I just returned from the Olin Library. The heavy snow and strong winds are slightly different from our town. I saw Oriental Princes (as Rutishauser, our Prof. of Pathology, called the Arab medical students in Geneva) march on parade, seemingly inspecting their subalterns as they mounted the steps to the library. I understood soon after: The ground, a mixture of ice and wet snow, was treacherously slippery, and ahead of us a lone student fell, his glasses catching the light from a lantern.

Not feeling that great about my self, what emerged wasn't that pretty. Still, I have a feeling of relief. Could I have gone that thoroughly into weaknesses at a Marathon lasting weeks at a Gestalt Institute in California, for instance? The impact of others might be much stronger. I never felt it as deeply at the Marathon held by Dr. Albert Ellis for two and a half days in Toronto, just three years ago. I did learn a lot, but not necessarily about myself. Except for being told by one and all that if I did not lack confidence as I seemed to I might really be something...

Went to the Rathskeller around 1 p.m. Light lunch. Had half a grapefruit, a roll and cheese. "That's how it was—the Monday before Thanksgiving—" said the T.V. announcer late tonight. Lately I have felt unable to retain food and less and less inclined to eat. I'll become ill if this continues. Is all of this due to the force feeding from early on? I was able to resist it as a child. What did it lead to? A scoliotic back. I lost some 2" in height there, and never became as tall as my mother.

Scoliosis and **Instruments of Torture**

I remember the torture chambers when I was about thirteen years old. The corrective devices! My mother and the school both insisted on the exercises with the medieval appearing machinery—the self flagellating instruments of torture, a redress by atonement through mechanisms inspired by executioners (that is as prescribed by the Jurist Schreber's father).

In Antwerp the hard wood and metal machinery of Dr. Ginsberg's Institute—there were hangings there three times a week. MINE! Twice after school, during the bleak and rainy late winter afternoons in Antwerp, then once on the day of the Sabbath. That, instead of going to school for half a non-writing day. There was one machine in particular that hammered one's back—I remember the sudden chill as the lancinating hammering struck at first. The stabbing pain shot out the front! For years afterward anyone who would greet me with a jovial slap on the back (a habitual comradely approach in Antwerp) barely escaped being murdered. It threw me into tears from acute pain followed by a burst of fury.

Tante Antoinette—touching, lovely, sweet old Auntie A., my mother's youngest sister. Gads she just died this week. She was so good to my daughter when she visited her there in old Tel Aviv. How touching I found her French accented pleadings when I too went to see her, "Eat, eat of my honey cake… " She sat with us, barely surviving, this last winter. Armand Nr. 1 didn't make it to her bedside in time either.. Neither she, nor my mother had physician children, who could save them at the last minute! Poor Tante A., poor Mama, some physicians you've made! Didn't I once save my mother's life? After I almost made her lose it, that is. When she came to stay for a few days, she wouldn't stop sewing and fussing about the house, though I had the only housekeeper—Mrs. Thomas—of all those ever in the family, that she got along with. Dear Mrs. Thomas said she loved her and respected her! She said she was a wonderful woman and she deserved respect! When my mother disciplined the children she was convinced that without the fear of God I was never going to be able to train the children?

My answer: "You don't need fear—they've known enough fear. They've already suffered enough for a lifetime." I meant the early separations, of course, and also my unhappiness during my pregnancy with my daughter. The months of late night work during pregnancy interning at French Hospital's accident room; the stabbings, the bloody muggings in the whorehouses nearby, the interrogating police all night!

What about Mama in all this? Well, during her last visit she wouldn't stop being helpful and doing... At night she cried with pain due to chronic arthritis, her heart, her osteoporotic bones... I bought her good French cognac and that helped some at first but then it didn't anymore. I couldn't stand to see her in such pain, but she just would not stay put and rest. To hear her agonize at night—I finally put her on Cortisone and she said she felt better than she had in years. I had just had a D. and C. and she insisted on waiting on me, hand and foot, and just about paralyzed me into inaction. She kept going stronger than ever. I asked her to stay. I loved her and told her I would make it nice for her. "What!" She cried out, "There's way too much work to do here for someone my age, away from life and activities... " She said I wanted to bury her alive in my place, "this *dorpje* (small burgh) in the hills" she called it with smiling sarcasm.

She returned to her own flat at the Hotel Greystone on Broadway and 91st Street in Manhattan and there had what I suspect was a massive infarct. The E.K.G. showed it was probably recent and her third or fourth. When I examined her before she left she cried softly and said I had the gentlest touch... That silken flesh... Those delicate brittle ribs... Those still velvet smooth breasts... She finally let me touch her then. The cascading folds of satin skin, still so touchingly attractive to me... I knew finally her day had come. She knew it too, for else why did she ask to go back to Belgium and for me to take her... Well, this time I knew it was for real. She wanted to be buried near her father and mine. I alerted the family and said we must all chip in and support her and let her keep her treasures for her grandchildren, since this was what she wished. I felt it was my decision and it was none of Henry's affair. The three other sons-in-law objected strenuously. When I took time off from the hospital to accompany her, she changed her mind at the last minute... the stock market... what not... I stayed on, Henry left. A few months later Paula came for her. By then I owed my mother a small fortune, and I paid for her fare on the boat that took her to her death six months later. At the last minute again she said she wouldn't go, but Paula wouldn't hear of any delays. She helped her pack some ten trunks, most of which were not even opened before she died. We were to give everyone of them away to various charities. On the boat she wrote each of us a letter stating exactly to the minutest detail what she wanted each of us to have after her death. Most of her wealth (and it was a miracle she had anything left, the way she gambled on the stock market) was left to her grandchildren.

Fanny, my father's darling, spoke her mind years later. She called Mama. a castrating, punitive woman to my father. Fanny said she had suffered through her bad character, that she had been an envious and unkind woman, especially to those she considered her inferiors. She said she was pathologically jealous and unloving... To me she represented a tower of strength. I barely knew my father. I wish they hadn't fought so much. I wished she had remarried again, after the time in France during the occupation and was left widowed again. I wished she could have found happiness. I always wished I could have done this for her... If only she would have let me...

Where does this leave us with Auntie A. and Sabrina my beloved cousin and friend who was sent to try out the anti-scoliotic torture machines with me? Aunt Antoinette no doubt urged her imploringly: "What do you risk by trying—perhaps it'll do you some good too!"

There was nothing wrong with Sabrina's back. She was in awe entering these enormous rooms, empty, except for the gigantic, eerily cold machines. Sabrina looked horrified as she saw me hanging by the neck and grasped my hand in pity... I hung and hung by the neck and showed off. Did it help? Who knows? I still did not know any better who I was, as distinct from my three sisters, nor did I have a more intimate feeling of my own body. Though my back did get straighter and stronger.

I believe my identity remained a mystery to me until I was psychoanalyzed. Even then, only toward the end perhaps...

Found out I've really not been "hot stuff" as the saying goes... How will all of this benefit others? If I remain healthy, I have about 1,500 people left to see and treat in my lifetime. Actually a self-exploring marathon is bound to benefit. So many others have been through similar experiences! How many planned children are there around anyway? How many women have felt ashamed? Unable to share? I must trust the outcome, for once. Haven't I lately? I must have as I kept writing, despite strong feelings of being overcome by shame, of feeling accusing, mocking eyes on me, translating inevitable accusations of exhibitionism, mainly on the part of older and wiser men: "Following self indulgence, exhibitionism is bound to follow..."

Freud.

Trust it for once! I have sometimes, but not enough, not often enough. The TV. in termination said, through the voice of a nice looking Rabbi, "Especially the benefits bestowed upon you by almighty God." So be it. Peace. It has stopped snowing. In the distance on the other side of the lake the separate lights shine clear as reflecting crystals. In the hills of Ithaca cottages are still lit. It is a lovely scene despite the cold of night. Lately colored clusters have appeared in the luminous windows. The holidays are to come. Gentle hills, brightly lit, gentle hills.

Maria: *"Thumbing Nose at the Lot of Them."*

CHAPTER 10

Free Association Three: At the Rathskeller

The waitress who cleans off tables is a delightful girl, reminiscent of a very young Margaret Mead. She gives an impression of strength, wholesomeness, though there is a great softness of youth which still envelops her features as she bends over the heavy wooden tables. She says she has graduated from Cornell but does not attend school right now, adding (regretfully) that she was possibly not dedicated enough to her field, which was anthropology. Openings for women were not what they were supposed to be. She reminds me that it was "Only last year that they appointed a woman full professor for the first time and gave her tenure here." I told her it was hard to believe, we were in 1978 after all. Surely all this would be turned around by now. She emphatically denied that this was the case. I told her that I practiced as a physician in a town Southeast of Ithaca. "Oh!" she exclaimed excitedly, and with humor this time, "That's the big city! We laughed. She came from Pennsylvania where her people still lived. I wondered if it were Carlos territory, but no it wasn't. She wanted to know if I had specialized, and I told her that I had, in Psychiatry." Hey! This suddenly sounded very good. The girls at the University seemed happy to see me around. I've rarely felt so appreciatively received as a professional as I have here. When I go away from home I seem to forget, and a part of my persona often gets shed. Afterwards it feels good to meet with it again, until the continual demands pull one down once more. Psychiatry is definitely one of the most draining branches of medicine.

One o'clock in the afternoon. Up till five o'clock in the morning, for I was unable to stop reading the Freud-Jung letters. I realized that Jung in his youth was quite mythomaniacal. What astonishing productivity though—in both men, at that. What a beauty Mrs. Jung was, how warm and loving. Locked within her femininity, within motherhood. At times, however, rebellious about her image as the weak other side of Carl, unable to get herself across as an individual, "the beautiful woman" she still aspired to be. I surmised this from her touching letters to Freud. She tried to exorcise the demon between the two men, before it grew gigantic and destroyed the relationship. She tried... I am convinced that had the two men been of the same religious background,—had Jung belonged to an older religious order, as Freud did—they would have been able to continue to help each other with inspired innovations, each surging on the wings of the other's creations. Jung's puritanical Protestant background was bound to hold him to earlier loyalties. He tried to make the break. To him it meant plunging ever deeper than Freud into mythology, ultimately into mysticism. He struggled to liberate himself from his father, who became strongly displaced unto Freud. He had to prove himself worthy of being a man on his own; he needed to overtake Freud and leave him behind. He might have attained such in friendship, had Freud not felt impelled to play the role of unerring father. If Freud had found another disciple as gifted as Jung to further his cause in Bleuler-land, the two men might have stayed together. The emergence of Freud's sister-in-law, Freud's love of her, which he never acknowledged to Jung... What a tragedy were this true. An outrageous dissimilation for the history of psycho-analysis. To become enamored of Freud in a filial manner entailed being partially swallowed by his demands to work alongside him (for he badly needed the help of inspired disciples, and there were obviously too few for his insatiable needs). Jung felt swallowed, and in fear of being smothered—though he seems to have done an enormous amount of work defending Freud's cause in Switzerland. Still, the demands continued. It appears the more he did, the more was asked of him. Some letters on both sides seem missing.—Is there still concealment involved here? Is it bad to want to shed one's professional Persona frequently? Well—think of the way you felt about Baudouin, (not the King—the psychoanalyst who treated and trained you.) Didn't you think he thought about your problems when you weren't with him? No, not really. I thought about my own problems. Why then go into such a dither of an uproar when you saw "Mouton", the curly one, sitting one day in the quiet antechamber?

What about the repercussions when you found out Dr Worms—Wagner whatever his name, who was—in therapy with him too? This Dr. Wormser (or whatever) was a refugee from Germany, who had married into Swiss upper-upper crust, and was said by some colleagues to have denied his Judaism. I confronted Baudouin angrily with this. Baudouin, for once, seemed to come alive and was *énervé*,—nervous. (The only other occasion on which he got "nervous" was when I told him in passing it was perhaps not too good an idea to remain sexually abstinent for long periods of time as I had done.—He said, upset himself, "Well, there is no reason to get yourself upset about that… " I was not upset—I just wanted his opinion and he gave it to me in a manner unworthy of the master.) As to Worms—Wagner, whatever—he was a strikingly handsome, highly articulate young man. Baudouin said "nervously,"

"Well, he might be a Jew—*en partie peut-être*—partially… ?" Whatever that meant, Dear Monsieur Baudouin. In part? He almost said he knew—when in reality he had not tackled that problem at all with Worms, let alone with me. One of Baudouin's earlier books contained some pretty uncomplimentary remarks about Jews. I mentioned this to him. He said calmly that when he wrote the text (a diary which consisted of social comments while he traveled in Germany during the thirties), he just didn't know better then; he had come off the fence since and changed his mind. It seemed the explosion brought forth cleared the air between us. I should have known that I was not angry as much about this colleague, this Dr Worms as with myself and my own tenaciously repeated denials about "origins".

I applied for admission to Columbia University's Medical School with a little old cross (found in the street) clearly worn across my bosom on the picture which decorated my application blank. What compromises… Cowardice takes many forms in the land of the brave and free… What was all that about? To think that on the day the photographs were taken for my application to medical school, I had found the dumb, nickel-plated thing in the street. After the picture-taking session, I attached it to my beautiful diamond and sapphire bracelet and walked to Uncle Harold's hotel nearby on Broadway and 110th Street. Uncle Harold had just arrived from Mexico. I was convinced I had saved him and his wife and children from the Nazi thugs. Auntie Sofia, his English wife, was a sister to the brothers who made family history by being named physicians to the Royal leaders of England. They were the famed brothers with whom Uncle Harold had traveled early in his life, they came from their small towns in Russia, to work as dockers in Mexico and study medicine there. Uncle Harold was the SAINT'S youngest son—there were five brothers and as many girls.

After I left Uncle Harold and his four boys and wife in occupied France, I wrote from Portugal to the third brother of the famed ones, who resided in Mexico. Uncle Harold had said without mincing a single word:

"Write to my brother-in-law in Mexico and tell him to save our lives, else we're finished."

I wrote a long imploring letter, explaining that if their help were not immediately forthcoming, all would die. Well, being 17 years old, what with my mania for writing "touching" (my sisters called them "exalted") compositions, when I arrived in the States, as I walked down the gangplank—surprise! These Mexican millionaires were there, as well as one of the physicians. They could at least have told me they would be there and waiting for me! The physician was a kindly, soft spoken Ear, nose and throat man who had married a girl from Antwerp. She came with him to meet me. What a joy to have them there just then as translators! Uncle Harold's youngest boy, meanwhile, had disappeared during the exodus, and my uncle had consequently become most religious by the time the child reappeared. The small boy, totally English speaking, about 2 years old at the time, had gone off to play and never turned up till many years later.

The Mexicans had come to meet me at the boat in order to talk to me directly, discuss strategy, and get the very latest bad news. That was on October 13, 1940. Thank heavens they were there! Why? Well… at least they showed me to a hotel. Did they do that much? I don't believe they did, at that! One of the Mexican's daughters eventually gave me a booklet put out by the New School, and that was the most helpful thing they did. Before I got off the boat I clearly remember there was a Government Official, a custom's man. He had said: "You can't get off the boat unless there is someone to pick you up." Unaware of the Mexicans down on shore, I said, "Well, I have an uncle who came over from Holland. He lives in Brooklyn, and is a policeman." For some reason the myth had circulated in the family, in Antwerp, that my Uncle Adolph, (my father's oldest brother) was a policeman in America. In fact, like all the others, he was a *diamantaire* (a diamond merchant). The agent looked around smiling and writing all this down said, "You're being met by your uncle." There were other diamond dealer's children on the boat, including a wealthy young couple I met during the voyage. It was their waiting uncle who took me with him in his chauffeured limousine to his hotel—The "Park Crescent" on Riverside Drive, where I was to spend my first night. I was frightened only for the few jewels, my inheritance, which I wore on my blouse, my wrists, and my fingers. The official looked all of these over. Still there is mystery here… He asked, "How are things over there?" I must have told him an inimitable mouthful… He filled out the forms for me and said: "You don't have any jewels." He looked at my small camera and said: "You don't have a camera." He then added something which I will always gratefully remember, "You know what? You've got guts, kiddo." Then with a big smile, "Don't forget to go and see the World's Fair... "

I have kept that first spark of gratitude toward this new country—it has never left me. It reinforced the impression I had gained in occupied Bordeaux from a Mr. Henry S. Waterman, the American Consul to France. When he questioned me about my plans for the future, he dealt with my dead seriousness without a hint of amusement. I said I wanted to be a philosopher, a scientist, and to continue with my studies in philosophy. He gave me a paper in lieu of a passport. This no doubt, saved my mother's life as well as my own, for I was up to much nonsense by then—namely, the daily secret outings to the camps, at which game I was bound to be caught eventually. What with my compulsive counting of dead Nazis to lull myself to sleep... each and every night the fantasy continued along the same lines: I would seduce a German soldier. With the gun I would then steal from him, I would kill the next soldier. Then I would destroy the evidence of the next one, who came to look for the first two—then the next, then the next... In view of the initial excitement, the string of destroyed and buried bodies became longer each night before I could fall asleep. I believe I got as high as eight, or even nine, for every detail was attended to, visualized, and carried out—but I reached fifty in theory.

During the occupation days in France, we behaved in our daily, ordinary life like ordinary human beings with ordinary moments of heroism and compassion. That summer, Uncle Harold's oldest son, John, who was considered the handsomest male child of the family, and I took long walks together near the seashore. On one such occasion we saw a group of German soldiers running in the distance crying out and signaling toward the water. We saw one fellow thrashing against high waves far out at sea, while another group of soldiers nearer the shore was shouting out to him. I jumped in, while John, a poor swimmer and more practical, ran for help. A few French farmers came to assist, and we dragged the soldier out of the water. He sounded tipsy. He was sunburned to a crisp, smelled of beer and seaweed, and blabbered on endlessly about love of people, all people being the same, and gratitude. He begged us tearfully not to tell anyone what had happened. All his buddies had disappeared, no doubt in fear of trouble. John and I never questioned our gesture, though that same night I continued the chain-reaction fantasy, but began the vengeful delight by giving myself first in love to John, before seducing and killing the others.

Thank heavens, John was watched day and night by Uncle Harold, who commented on his son's admiring follower: "Marieke is a good-looking girl, but why is she so broad? Paula—now there is a girl—a real Gypsy, a real beauty." For one thing, Paula was already married to Charles. My backside had indeed grown out of all proportion with all the anti-scoliotic machinery and the athletic activities of the last years... And my chest and shoulders had become worthy of a true Dutch swimming champion.

In 1945, with beating heart, (uncle Harold was the first member of our immediate Antwerp family to be seen on American soil)—I went to visit him. I had not seen him since the sad imploring scene in occupied Paris. I had just a flicker of misgiving. Following his telephone call to say he was in America and wished to see me, I began to wonder if he might in any manner resent me or my mother who was in Cuba by then. The tone of his voice in response to my cry of joy left a lot to be desired. He received me in his small, dingy hotel room. He appeared unshaven, unkempt, and rather sad. He had grown enormous around the waist. He! Always manicured in the past, the chosen youngest son who had married so well! In Belgium, like a true snob, he spoke mainly English—never French, and a mere hint of Flemish. I had always felt intimidated in his presence.

Among other things his odd English accent made me realize I had not known him well. Today I would recognize his manner of speech for what it was: an entirely local London accent. (Henry would no doubt describe it, with feigned shocked amusement, as "The East End".) He asked again about my mother, without expressing the slightest enthusiasm. He told me he had been interned in a refugee camp in North Africa, until the Mexican family had extricated him, and he had immigrated to Mexico. I asked politely, as was required by old custom, "How is business, Uncle?" He said, "Very bad, very bad indeed." I remembered my mother had written to say Uncle Harold owed her money. Did I expect a windfall? Instead, he looked at my bracelet of precious stones, which I thought he might remember from my father's store. As he bent over to have a closer look, being a jeweler of sorts himself, he asked accusingly, "What is that?" He was pointing to the hanging symbol made of plated nickel. What was I doing with a cross? The next thing I remember is that he showed me the door. "Get out—I don't want to know you!"

"But Uncle, I found it in the street!"

"Why are you wearing it then? Have you converted? Get out at once!" He literally threw me out. I went sobbing all over Broadway, drained as a wrung-out rag, and walked all the way down to the Village, only to remember that I did not live there anymore.

I had been told that to be admitted to Columbia University's

Medical School, one must be a "pure Christian", (whatever that still meant to me at the time—probably a member of the Gestapo), male, at least 6 ft. 3 in. tall, blond and smooth haired. I got my hair straightened and wore it in bangs, which lasted long enough for the photograph to be taken, plus I wore the desired symbol of Christianity. I was admonished not to admit under any condition that I was interested in psychoanalysis, or in becoming a psychiatrist. Such declarations might classify one as heretical. I voluntarily submitted to psychological tests to exclude the latter possibility. At Columbia's University Medical Center, the test took many hours, and then I spent many more with the head man, Dr. Sigmund Pietrowski himself. He thought my interpretations of the Rorschach inkblots showed some after-images from the Nazi occupation days—the clomping boots. —There were also healthy images, like the girl who walked in the rain with shiny rain boots on, and the girl sitting under a tree to dream and to read. He asked me what happened on the "Draw-A-Person Test". I had set out to draw Claude whom I knew intimately by then. His arms and hands, too difficult to draw (possibly?), were placed behind his back. When it came to drawing his sex, I suddenly did not know if there were three, or two, or one, and really got into a fix… To my shame Pietrowski got the drawing out again and proceeded to spend an enormous amount of time dissuading me from my love for the mathematician. He went into a long harangue against mathematicians like Claude. He compared them to "true scientists" like himself. The message I came away with was that he, Professor Pietrowski, was the better of the two men and nothing on earth could convince me of that! He thought my choice of medicine was not a bad one. The difficulty he felt was that I had *l'embarras de choix* (a nice way of saying I had too many interests), but he would recommend me to the Psychiatrist in Chief, Dr Nolan Lewis. He reminded me not to tell the admission's officer, a small disagreeable man named Dean S., that I was interested in psychiatry. Needless to say, I never got in. Even if they had admitted me, I do not have a clue as to where I thought the funds would come from to attend that school. The two other applicants whom I befriended and with whom I studied pre-med at Columbia University were admitted—one of them was a very large girl, daughter of a well known New York surgeon. She had a bad reputation, which was well founded in every respect. She dropped out before the end of the first year.

The second successful candidate was a very serious, nice type of a fellow, a German Refugee. He did very well, but decided at the end of his second year that there must be many easier ways of making a living, and went into business. Dean S. was probably a good small town business administrator, but he certainly had a poor clinical nose for choosing candidates for medical school. Franz Alexander, the analyst, tried to get me into a medical school in Chicago, but women were out. The GIs came first.

The day the Germans were catapulted into official surrender, I returned to the photographer's studio where the pictures had been taken for my application to medical school. This time there were no religious adornments. I wore the wedding ring, Bob, my first husband, bought for me. A Carmen, with a flower in my hair; I had a picture taken as I thumbed my nose at the lot of them! I then scrambled to the University of Geneva, where I had been accepted as a medical student.

The episode with Uncle Harold as it emerged here now appears pretty unreasonable, even under our past circumstances. It is most probable that I was ready to be married to Bob, who as a Quaker was a member of an outside tribe. In all likelihood my Uncle had got wind of this, which would explain his coolness toward me. The silly bracelet episode was undoubtedly the last match needed to start the explosive interaction. After what he went through, it was understandable.

What does all this material lead to? The continued mythomania, the false appearances to gain acceptance, these are a form of self denial which lead eventually to the cowardice of self-manipulation. Were these the trailing aftermaths of a few months with the Nazis in occupied France? Less than six months of extreme turmoil could not have wreaked that much havoc. Painful experiences which one knows are anomalous and which are clearly assigned to circumstantially determined bad luck (which stems from outside sources) do not necessarily change the fiber or texture of human character. Not even when the ill-fated happenings which occur during a period of increased inner turmoil, as adolescence is bound to be. Beyond childhood one is affected toward regression or growth mainly by the experiences that reverberate from within. In my case the groundwork was laid during a childhood of esoterism among distant, at times hostile, strangers. During the war one lesson was learned, however:

"To be yourself can kill you". Now I am living through the experience of having to be myself—or it will kill me. The situation, the circumstances and this stage in life, at a time when all values are healthily turned inside out and over—has made this feasible at last!

Why then did I leave Claude, when I found out I loved him above all others? He didn't push, he didn't insist... That was no doubt the meaning of perceiving him, when I drew him under the pressure of being tested, without arms, or with arms tied behind his back. It might also mean, "Look, I'm a good boy, I keep my hands behind my back!" Good boy "in his Sunday best"… Also perhaps: ineffectual as a man in our relationship—"as unarmed", without arms. In the Mephistopheles dream: the old fashioned chair was arched, but without arms! His psychoanalyst charged a good sum and that did not leave him swimming in gold. By then I did not have that much either, and he was not overly generous at any time. Why do I say that? He was quite careful except when it came to books. Very unlike diamond dealers, who treat a fiancée regally when they take her out on a date. Yeah… but these are the same precious stone dealers who do not marry girls unless they come along with a small fortune, as every one of my sisters did. My inheritance was spent on being schooled except for diamonds, which I hope will go to the children one day. All except for one piece, which was absconded by a "friend" who had been recommended to me by my mother. Swine! Gurfein and Sons, 5th Avenue, N.Y. The number of crooks with great reputations, who came her way during her years of lone widowhood was astonishingly high. It was my fate to meet so many of them in New York. Of Mr. Gurfein, Sr. she had said: "You must go to see my dear friend Gurfein, who married my widowed cousin!" I did, and no sooner did we meet, than he suggested I sell him all my jewels. I had told the customs official on the boat that these were not meant for trade, and I saw no reason to sell them on arrival, but I was willing to give French lessons to Mr. Gurfein, Sr. for a while. His newly acquired wife kept out of sight. Five years later he finally got hold of the most beautiful piece. It was the same fated bracelet of diamonds and sapphires, an original design of my father's which I have seen reproduced with minor variations to this very day. A few days before I married Bob I went to Gurfein and Sons office to get an estimate of its value. I was always able to enter the Sr. Gurfein's office without question. He said to leave the bracelet for an hour or so and he would tell me what it was worth. I returned a few hours later to take it back with me to another dealer (a Max Geldzahler, who was a friend to both my parents, and had dealt mainly with my father in Antwerp). He said he thought he might be able to get me a bit more than the $2,000 which he estimated the bracelet might be worth to a merchant. That was in 1945. Suddenly Gurfein Sr.'s unsmiling, bleached blond, elegant daughter would not allow me beyond the desk. She said her father had gone out and she handed me a check for $800. Refusing the check, I asked her where my bracelet was. She said it was sold, and I asked her politely but firmly, "Get it back immediately, please." She told me that the man who bought it was an out-of-town dealer, and she didn't believe she could reach him… I walked away from 54th Street and 5th Avenue, and out of sheer force of habit, headed straight for the Village to cry on Claude's shoulder. Always that beautiful, long, strong-necked consoling shoulder… "This town is replete with sharks and crooks," he had said. A few days later I was married, but to Bob.

Claude still came—he still came! We remained friends, the three of us, in New York City, Bob, Claude, I and many others.

T.D.: Who helped me break away from Bob?

U.D.: First of all, Bob; then there was that intelligent fellow from Antwerp (the one who eventually married a known politician's daughter). I gave him the fish tank and all the exotic fish Bob and I had tended with such care. His parents would not hear of a poor divorcee student. They were no doubt right.

T.D.: Why marry Bob in the first place?

U.D.: I didn't want to get married, but through Mama's good matchmaking intentions for me, the pressure was on. She said I must marry Julio, whom I met in Havana. Julio was an older man, a Russian Émigré, who had made a fortune for himself, became a millionaire and was named "The Cuban Tie King". He had the same double sized head as the actor G. E. Robinson (to whom he bore a close resemblance) which brought a cravat to advantageous prominence. When on Mama's initiative, he came to fetch me in New York, I begged for time; I thought I would get the "Havana Pages" published and become self-supporting. Mama pressured me to get married; she said she would not help out any more, now that I had "squandered all her money" (My inheritance from my father!) in America. It looked as though I was finally out of funds. All my hopes were with the "Havana Pages"—one might call it a first novel. The book dealt rather obsessively with my mother, but also described the diamond dealers, refugees from Nazi-occupied Antwerp who had settled in Cuba. They had created a thriving new industry of diamond cutting in Havana. The book spoke of a young Philosophy Professor, Leonardo Santa Marina, a refugee from Franco's Spain, whom I had befriended in Cuba. It was no doubt my first attempt to extricate myself from my dependency on my mother, from Claude and my shame, by writing it all down.

A well-married Englishman called Ron, who owned an elegant small town-house on McDougal Street, was a neighbor of sorts to Claude and me. He offered to edit the book and make the thing presentable to publishers. He said he knew that business inside-out. We met for a week-end of work at the Henry-Hudson Hotel near the West River. He had entirely rewritten two chapters. The tone, the style... I was unable to recognize them as mine... my stammering, foreign-sounding

English. Sophisticated, world traveled Ron had smelled out the divisiveness in my nature in no time, and he made a point of this in the rewriting. The chapters read like a detective story; there was an air of mystery about everyone, a whodunit quest from page to page. It was glib, well written. In panic, then fury, as I read his well typed, extremely well presented material, I cried out at last "That's Mickey Mouse writing, it's not mine!" I thought I would lose my mind. Not in a million years could I have written English as smoothly as he did. The self identification with my own barely readable book was absolute. He was a practical man, and a generous one. He offered a reasonable compromise; why didn't we co-author the "Havana Pages"? I told him then and there I was soon to marry Bob, a cadet officer air pilot in training in the Navy, and that he would do the needed editing. I must have decided to marry Bob at that point. Ron advised me, "It is the most foolish thing you can do, marry someone like Bob! I'll tell you, he sounds just as unsuitable for a girl like you as this fellow Claude is. At least that one manages to be remarkable. You'll never make it with an American chap, not in a million years, my dear. You're old world to the core, and you'll never change." It was Ron who called Claude "a man's man". That was when I came down with German measles and Claude nursed me for an entire week, bringing food to his flat where I stayed every night during my illness. Ron visited the two of us every night. Claude used to sit across from him and stare at him, not unlike one of Ron's Siamese cats, ready to hiss, spit, and scratch. "You can't ever get more than an absolute YES or NO out of him" Ron had said laughingly of Claude, with his inimitable worldly charm. Claude insisted on nightly closeness as soon as I felt less ill, in hopes of catching the measles. He dreamed of taking time off from work at the labs without having to suffer guilt. Despite everything, he remained healthy. After a week of playing lover-nurse, he came home from work and announced abruptly, "I think you are well now. You had better come out for supper." Was he sick of Ron's daily visits? I felt easily comfortable with the sudden dependence on him. Did this frighten him? I, for one was sorry it was over. When we went out to eat, he looked dissatisfied and worked a lot on paper napkins, covering them with rows of neatly printed, strange looking symbols.

Ron would say to Claude, "I swear!, This girl here, Maria, really!" (Contained laughter while he hid his mouth charmingly with one hand.) "She'll walk a hundred blocks to save a nickel, and then surprise! She'll casually drop in on your party with diamonds in her hair!" It was hard to know if he approved or disapproved, and useless to tell him I didn't like subways... Claude would merely respond with a hiss between his teeth or play with his pencil, probably miles off in thought. I didn't like the comment for it reminded me of my mother, who was known by the foreign community in Batista's Cuba as "an eccentric millionaires". She'd really gone odd during the exodus, and there were days where she seemed to drag herself sadly around, covered by pitiful rags. On special occasions, and sometimes seemingly without rhyme or reason, she would appear to be her old self again. She would be rather eccentrically clad for Havana, but stunning in her French clothes, her diamonds in evidence, but not too obtrusively. Prime ministers (she called them all "*Monsieur le Ministre*") and Ambassadors representing strange sounding countries came to visit her nightly in the lounge of the Plaza Hotel, in Havana, where she resided. She seemed to hold forth with a strange excitement about "The Communist threat," "Communist plots against world peace", "Communist murderers and spies... " things like that. These men might have consulted her about diamonds. They seemed to think well of her. I really didn't quite understand what she was up to. She had become more obsessive than ever with the exquisite pain of compulsive thrift at all cost, and I learned to avoid her. She advised me strongly to marry Julio. She described the life I would lead with him in glowing terms. He would "allow" me to finish my studies, even "allow" me to write. When none of this seemed to carry the needed weight, she implored me to marry him. Then she said the one sentence that stunned me, "If not for yourself—do it for me. I implore of you—DO IT FOR ME!"

Whenever he came to visit in New York, it wasn't as if I hadn't tried to like this Julio. I really tried to like him, but just couldn't stomach him in the end. Bob was definitely the better of the two choices, for he appealed to me. I don't want to talk about it. He is, and has always been, brilliant, most articulate, well-spoken, above all, he was markedly uninhibited compared to Claude and me at the time.

I believe the biggest mistake Bob made with me was to spring a sudden demand on the morning of our wedding. That very morning (my bracelet was already sold) he suddenly insisted that we be married by a Protestant Navy Chaplain, or "we might as well call the whole thing off". We went through the ordeal, neither of us with any relatives or friends as witnesses. He was to leave the next day for Ottumwa, Iowa. Really, he didn't like flying that much. Our wedding night brought him despair, he sobbed in the belief that he got me pregnant, for he did not want to have children, ever. (He never did.) He was highly supportive of a first abortion one year later.

Finally a pattern emerges: Always using one man to give

strength to let go of another.

T.D.: I used Bob to let go of Julio, the Cuban Tie King.

U.D.: Julio... An accident induced by Mama's cravats—*cravache*—spankings—in the shape of threats to withhold further funds. She actually cut off funds.

T.D.: Bob was to neutralize Claude, really. Before I married Bob, didn't Claude then say definitely he wanted to marry me, but wanted me to wait till the end of his analysis? After all, I prodded, pushed him into it. He said he loved me... to wait, "Baby—please... " What did I do? Did I wait as he asked me to?

U.D.: I married Bob. Just then there was the fiasco with the Havana Pages. Bob and I realized we had made a mistake after I stayed a few months with him near the Air-Force training school in Corpus Christi, Texas. He insisted I return to school; I ran to Claude, who took me back and I stayed with him a few days, not knowing where to go... He had this girl Anne then, who lived in the house next to ours in the Village. She was blond and almost attractive. Her picture stood like a symbol of possession on the piano in his flat. The piano had been partially consumed in my absence and fed into the fireplace by Claude, since the owners were not heating the place enough. We were able to keep each other warm for a few nights. Without warning I showed him some of the new love-making techniques I had acquired through Bob's sophistication in that area. It stopped him in his tracks, in his graceful mid-air flight, and he asked startled, "Baby, what do you think you are doing?"

"Didn't you like it, Claudeke?" Well, he thought it was unusual, to say the least. "Let's not do anything like that again... " We went to sleep as we always had. I held on to him, my arm around his waist, as for years I had held on to my sister Sara...

two lenses, concave, convex, with the hue of love to hold us together.

Downstairs, at the Rathskeller. An Austrian student of philosophy is eating a few tables away. He is dirty looking and talks annoyingly loudly in German, holding forth disdainfully on the great Bertrand Russell. He mentioned the physicist Schrödinger's writings (on topics other than physics) as the most advanced theories he had read. He also said that Einstein and another man had worked under his father-in-law. It occurred to me that the student who looked and sounded as though he still needed to have his ass wiped was probably a visiting instructor in philosophy of science... Everyone is talking about Wittgenstein... I found him in Russell's autobiography. This here Austrian sounds pretty bombastic. In addition to calling him oversexed, that word bombastic, was regularly hurled at Henry by Grandma, (his mother). Imagine living for 20 years with a husband who wouldn't touch you... in Long Island, NY., where she visited (till my mother came which, as intended, made her flee in no time), she told all the neighbors and the postman about this imposed chastity which she had suffered for over 20 years. My mother had a similar problem for a few years before my father died, and called a family counsel and the Rabbi to deal with it. She was convinced my father had a regular mistress whose existence no one could prove, though she placed each of us on alert in case she required us to participate in some detective work. Though still young, my father was already quite ill and had only one desire—not to be left alone with her once my sister Fanny was married and gone from home. He made one attempt, a few weeks before he died, to have me come his way, to see if I would eventually take on Fanny's role, and stand up for him. Too young to understand, I insisted on neutrality. He died in time, the night before Fanny's wedding…

M., Henry's father would not touch his wife because on his return journey from China, where he had stayed in monogamous continence for five years, he got himself some "dreadful disease" (as she called it) which he was to nurse for the next 25 years. On his death bed he called for her, she said—she did not respond, being too busy with the cleaning. The preceding year, they had finally bought their own house, situated on the highest point above a lovely hilly wooded area in Torquay, the bay sparkling blue in the distance between the pine trees. Speaking of compulsive cleaning—she certainly punished her men by it. Imagine being condescended to (or thinking you are) all your life because you are not born into the right class, group, school, enunciation. It is almost as powerfully binding, if anything can be, as wealth in America.

What brought this up? Well, by marrying Henry, the cure (I had started in analysis) over this complex about my "origins" finally came about. When definitely? Well, really after the children were baptized. The morning of the event I spoke to the Reverend Casswell, a Jungian trained Methodist Chaplain who worked at the State Hospital. On that day he walked into my office, and in response to casual greetings, I said I was not well, and no doubt looked it for he closed the door hurriedly behind him and made me sit down. To my surprise I cried and told him, "Henry wants to see the children baptized today. I feel disloyal to my people, my father, my mother's father, who was a miracle Rabbi… I feel to have them baptized will alienate them—I fear this will create a… chasm . It will be different between us… " I was caught by a flood of tears. He looked me in the eyes and said quietly, "Everyone wants a father.., needs the love of a father…

" They were baptized that day. Henry baked a baptismal cake that was hard as a rock. Our friends (mainly a woman who had pushed for baptism) came to partake of the frustrated feast. My mother and Mrs. Thomas said there were irregularities in her relationship with Henry.—What with his being home, unemployed, recovering for six months, and a history of "raping easily" when confronted by aggressive elderly females.

T.D.: How did I allow all of this to come about? Now there's a pattern.

U.D.: As far as I'm concerned, it was the hypocritical proselytizing that turned me off for good.

T.D.: Meaning?

U.D.: Well, finally I knew where I stood—definitely, not on the side of the proselytizers. We had to go through all this agony, this monster shit, to make it clear to me.

T.D.: How so, dummy?

U.D.: I felt I had been had. This gave me the upper hand from this point on.

TD.: Sounds pretty idiotic. The upper hand! Really!

U.D.: Well, that is how it felt. It feels right, now too, to this very day.

T.D.: I had been had? As usual it's my own stinking wavering that caused the trouble in the first place. Sitting on the fence—a weakling's habitat,—that did it. Remember? I described it; self-manipulative cowardice? Unable to take the nonsense that went with discrimination, prejudice.

U.D.: I wanted the best of both worlds for the children.

T.D.: The whole minor episode could not have been brought about without my tacit understanding and encouragement. For who was it who said in that comfortable new home in this homogeneous community with more churches than I ever remembered seeing: "These children need some religious education… ?"

U.D.: There wasn't a soul in their right mind around to simply ask: "Why?" Not a single enlightened soul to ask—"Who says they need it?" or "What for?"

T.D.: Who was it really that went shopping around? Not Henry, was it? Suppose I were the real fraud?

U.D.: Now everyone knew Henry to be a bigot and an anti-Semite. No use denying that.

T.D.: Didn't the Director of the hospital at the time?

U.D.: He was a nutty convert, married to the wrong woman.

T.D.: And his physician wife, and the assistant director with the wonderful children, and these people, new friends from above the hill, all belonged to the same Episcopalian Church, in which at least Henry could be comfortable as a son of the Anglican Church. What was wrong with that? At least I didn't have to drive them on Sunday mornings. All these people helpfully picked the children up while we both stayed in. He didn't take them.

U.D.: I stepped into it unwittingly because of convenience, true—it seemed expedient in this sort of reactionary small community.

TD.:Manipulations—expediency—ambition—recognition. Finally one of the Big Crowd! Spare the children the Hitlerian agonies, as Henry wisely advised!

U.D.: It just felt increasingly uncomfortable, that's all. Truly, Baudouin never worked on this with me, no more than he did with Worms, the other physician.

T.D.: It was our problem, not Dr. Baudouin's. Or was he avoiding this too?

U.D.: PERHAPS. More likely I didn't hear. I was not ready.

T.D.: True. He reawakened mystical longings. We nurtured the sublime.

Once before the finals, my analyst, Dr. Baudouin, had not heard from me for two weeks, and I did not call to cancel our usual appointments. He called (the only time he did) for fear I might try to do something to myself under pressure of the examinations. I was all right, but just fed up with him and his silences. Roman—the Romanian—helped a lot. Roman—A long beard—Deep Judaic mysticism—His virginity intact. How did you know? Anyway, he sang so well. I remember standing together on top of Mont Blanc how his voice resounded. He sang beautiful Gregorian Chants. How unbelievably clear the sky was when we hung up there—White cliffs avalanching to unendingly deeper and further snow over buried villages. While with him at those heights, I was unable, for the first time, to look down without feeling sick. (This is usual, I trust, following an unresolved suicidal gesture.) As we rode down on the train, he called to a little boy who was staring at him to come closer and said, "Come and pull on my beard, I know you're dying to do so" The boy, in disbelief, crawled over to him and pulled his beard, while Roman sang, "ding, dong… "

Roman was the only young fellow in Geneva at the time with a long beard—a true Hassidic beard at that. He had large, very dark, malicious looking eyes, pitch black hair, a dark complexion, and his beard was already tinged with silver, although he was barely 30 years old. I was told by Baudouin that while he was teaching students about the Jungian concept of an Archetype, one fellow looked back accidentally and almost dropped off his seat when he saw Roman. He exclaimed, "I've got it! I've seen the living archetype of Christ!" We sat on park benches in Geneva and he read the book of Ruth to me and made me read to him. I almost loved him, but when he spoke of marriage his behavior changed, and I took fright. Then there was Baudouin, who interpreted my dreams more and more in terms of my repressed religious aspirations.

I had a dream of a box located in a holy safe. There was a box inside the box, and one inside that one—I can still feel the touch of the beautifully, delicately grained wood, like jewels. It led inside to the small chamber, where there was a Holy Sepulcher and where the Holy Book of Laws rested. I longed for it. "Only Religion can replace Religion." Religion, as a consequence of infantile dependency needs, is never to be lost. Is it ever resolved? It is part of the instinct of self-preservation, not sexual, not libido, Jung thought. To him, Religion is all-encompassing. To Roman it was, too. Monsieur Baudouin said, "Roman has opened the door for you to dormant mysticism… "

My oldest sister, Sara, knew how to pray in Hebrew—the sacred language some still consider it to be. They won't speak it everyday. That's a sin!

What the hell did you have against Him, the Saint? The bastard had some 10 or 13 children, all of whom worshipped him and most of whom went hungry as children. How saintly is that? Uncle Harold—the same—goes on a pilgrimage each year from Mexico City to Holland to pay his respects to the SAINT, a miracle of a miracle Rabbi. Every year he follows the same route—a sort of transcontinental Via Dolorosa, with first weeping station Antwerp. The last time he went there, my sister Paula opened the door and thought it was one of the religious beggars of the many Judaic Sects who live in Antwerp again and who march up to her flat once a week. She asked the beggar to wait at the door while she fetched her purse. To her surprise

the beggar boldly showed himself into her living room—it was
Uncle Harold! He does not tell his children where he travels to
each year. When on my instigation Paula asked him, "What sort
of Saint was your father, who let his children go hungry... ?"
Uncle Harold jumped up in anger and disbelief at her heretical
words and said, "How do you know what greatness there was in
that man? He was a SAINT!"

So he lies buried in Putte, Holland, among the saintliest of
Saints—there are about four of them. The Grand Rabbi Amiel,
he, and two others, and they say that for all the gold in the world
you could not buy a plot near them. A thick purple velvet cordon
separates the four men from all other mortals and immortals.
My father lies buried among another chosen group named the
Coheenan—the priestly sect.., and so it goes. The Saint probably
took off his white lace gown when he lay down there and gave it
to a poorer man who might still feel the cold...

U.D.: Do you know now where you stem from? On our
father's side Sephardic elixir trickled into our blood streams...
To think I might have fallen for some miserly, second hand,
communally inspired sect in vogue — lies, lies, lies. Bought
for the sake of respectability, invulnerability, like a silver plated
shield against a hostile future. I, not Henry bought the painted
paper idols. In my hands these porcelain faced saints were meant
to crumble.

T.D.: True. I almost bought these, then cried my eyes out
about "having been made" to buy false images, false Gods for
our children. Ha! What farcical manipulations, comical to the
point of tears. When in the name of heaven does one finally
afford integrity, wholeness, the honesty of just plain honest,
non-proselytizing people... ?

Freud at Graphotherapy 1978. Charcoal, 14"x17"

CHAPTER 11

Free Association Four: The Appeal of Subjugation

When working with Monsieur Baudouin, my analyst in Geneva, he would sometimes ask me what the name of one of my dreams should be. Name that dream! This is what I feel I ought to surmise here about some of the free flowing 60 + pp of free associative writing on what I named "The Appeal of Subjugation". It concerns women who dwell on a sub-continent where my sister Sara and I—the not favorite ones, seemed to belong in our family's constellation.

I dealt again and then again with the Flemish vs. the French conflict in our own town, in my particular elementary school and in our own family. What with oldest sister Sara trying to introduce the world of culture and beauty other than what my mother was trying to preserve in her orthodoxy dedicated to

253

a venerated Saint of a father who himself already lived in the past. Now do not wonder again as to why for heaven's sake, I always look for ready made molds to put thoughts into. More safety than in trying to overcome ready set obstacles in a foreign tongue: whether Flemish vs. Dutch, and all the other politically contaminated language hurdles.. The years of compulsive clowning and mimicry of disliked teachers: finally desisted when I believed my mother's inculcated beliefs about getting stuck in imitative gestures as a form of punishment by powerful malevolent spirits.

The pressure of rote learning which led to pressure one could feel right above one's sex, inside one's most natural parts, as though one had to push against them to get the learning into one's head. It could lead to wanting to stimulate oneself endlessly. That was easy to do then: a few exercises as hanging by one's hands between two pianos, just swinging and holding one's breath and that sufficed. It might have happened accidentally at first, when everyone was urging me to join them downstairs and I felt very anxious and probably did not want to go or needed to finish another task first and they were insisting. Unless it was my father who called in wonder—or anger.

He had a habit of calling over the banister "Boys!" We would slide down the spiraling banister, or scramble down the stairs, from different quarters... It sounded like a stampede.

To think a separate but very nearby section of our house was rented out to the most important diamond dealers firm at the time: "Shamisso and Furman". How did they put up with all the activity? Half the diamond bourse came by our place all day... My father called us Boys—he got our names mixed up. But his happy blond child Fanny, called Fanneke most of the time, that one he finally kept to himself for he trusted her and her good judgment and eventually had her work with him in his store. Was the battle of modernity over anciently held sacred beliefs won because of Fanny's strength of character over my mother? She was supposedly the most self-possessed, and had the surest and most common-sense type of judgment. Our oldest Sara said she leaned on her for moral support. Possibly but not certainly for Fanny said she did the leaning and hid behind Sara when our parents fought.

For the longest time in adulthood I loved Sara the most and considered her the gentlest of my sisters. With good music, good literature, she opened the world to the lot of us who followed in her lively footstep. She is certainly the most articulate and the most masochistic woman alive and I easily forgave her the years of cruelty and violence when she went overboard in obedience to my mother by pulling me by my long hair all the way from school to get me the piano lessons she was instructed to trash me with. As a young adolescent she became a somnambulist… walked right down those four flights of steps in her nightgown and into the street, leaving the door to the house and store wide open for burglars at night. It is even said that she once climbed out of our bedroom window (unlikely—they were so round and high up) and that she walked like an acrobat along the ledge of the steeply slanted roof… She was sent to a boarding school for debutantes in Brussels. The girls became fearful of her nightly pranks and she was sent home with the recommendation that my parents restrain themselves in their fighting, for they were literally "driving their daughter up a wall… "

Evie[1] joined me at the University's Statler and helped with finding and looking up texts in Marie Bonaparte, Maryse Choisy, and Norbert Wiener for these exercises. She did splendidly—never an error! I wished she could accept the fact that she is a

---

[1] This is my friend from Antwerp with whom I lived in the village of New York City at 51 West 11th St., in the apartment she found for us in 1941.

superiorly endowed, capable woman. She looks most attractive and refreshingly youthful at this stage in our lives. She's as slender and outstandingly curvaceous as ever. I love her truly and know that being alone mostly now, as I am, is not good for her. Thanksgiving was the day on which I saw her as I would remember her. We were alone on the entire Schoelkopf athletic field. Hundreds of rows of empty benches encircled us like a giant's pair of outstretched arms. The field was carpeted by pale green, roofing the demoniacal accelerator-cyclotron which lay 50 feet beneath the ground. There were four lanes for running... I left her and went on a trot... half-way through I looked up to see her far in the distance, tall and ethereal seeming still, though wrapped in a heavy princess-style blue winter coat. She stood like a birch tree swaying in the wind. I imagined her green eyes were laughing but contained a hint of worry. Her small hat was rolled up at the edges like a boy's. Half running, half walking I barely completed the last lap. Felt so well afterward. We then went on a good two hours walk to end at the bus station when she left. She said in parting that I was "a true friend—really." I was happy. We helped each other and she reassured me about my sanity at the time—what with all that digging into the past...

Alone on Campus at Cornell, for some ungodly reason kept encountering and fell into the presence of couples who ripped destructively away at each other—not responding pregnant women who ate away while their husbands angrily expressed themselves to say they felt cannibalistically consumed by them. Was it the time of year? The campus emptied of footloose non-expectant students? The lack of harmony I ran into at the deli, at the restaurant, precipitated the remembrance of a woman beaten in a hotel room in Anchorage, Alaska, where I had stayed not that long ago.

With all the puzzling over dropping out of the Atheneum for a breath of fresh air and freedom and which resulted in the worst oppression of all, I was led again to those early adolescent years which insisted on a further hearing again.

"The Party at the Ringers'" came up. The Ringers were cousins on my mother's side. They had recently arrived as refugees from Germany and had opened a restaurant and German type of cabaret. This particular family party was attended by great dignitaries, for there were visitors from England. The occasion? Uncle Harold's sweet wife was being visited by her famous brothers, one of which, the Ophthalmologist was attending in person.

My father has died recently. I stayed away from the large crowd and the honor table. The notable uncle chooses me and comes over to talk to me. He has told my sister Sara that he found me attractive and that I had lively and intelligent eyes. She told me this as though it were a secret which no one must know about... The fellow spoke softly and only in English and I had to pay close attention. He was small and cross-eyed it seemed behind glasses. But his was a fascinating presence indefinably for me at the time. I had began to round out and my sisters said I'd become a nicer person by then. While going over more of the above and wanting to summarize the hither and forth cadence of these waves of events that now want to surface, Cayuga Lake beckons in the distance between slate roofed buildings nearby the library room where I've almost become a constant till late at night.

Waiting for the snows. Thinking of Sara, ten years older than I, in the end epitomizing masochism in women. Used to sleep with my arm around her waist on the fourth floor of our house on Pelikaan Street. The Zoo—enormous and highly guarded had beautifully kept flowering grounds. Many ferociously wild animals had been caught in what was then the Belgian Congo and other parts of Africa. They lived a few paces from us, and we could hear them at night, the lions, leopards, elephants. Enormous snakes were shedding their skins just next door to our bedrooms. Only the trains (heard all day long coming to rest in the station situated on an elevation across the road from our house) separated us from the Zoological gardens spread out beyond the Central Station's tracks. Piercing the roaring sounds from Africa, I could hear the crystal clear carillons from the Cathedral near the Steen on the river Scheldt. I woke up once on a warm spring night to look straight into the eyes of an eagle, an enormously winged animal. He stood perched in the nearest round window to our bedroom, apparently yawning… I pushed my body in fright against Sara, and wet warmly. No one believed I'd seen an eagle, the largest ever. How did dearest Sara ever stand for all of this? How was it she managed to love the child I was to the point where she came to consider me her own? She seems to have squandered all her energies on correcting our parents' mistakes, rather than stay with her outstanding ability in music. She practiced some eight hrs/day… Her husband forbade piano playing in their flat when they were married. He said it "enervated" him, and interfered with her household duties.

Despite appearances to the contrary did I too aspire to subjugation by a man? Father, Mother, I could have loved enough to abdicate totally . . . Has this, as with Sara, been a buried need in me, as it seems to deeply inhabit many a woman? In Sara's life the trend has remained infinitely entwined within her very existence. Between her and her husband Fred there is a textbook dependence of a sadomasochistic nature.

Is it the unconscious wish for subjugation in me that leads to inescapable attractions like what I felt for a manly figure as Henry's had been? A good Gestalt Therapist named Elizabeth Mintz, said at our last encounter group, the one of our community of professional healers: "Women who have been rejected by their fathers have a knack later in life for attaching themselves to rejecting men... " That stayed with me. It rang true. One thing my father did which to me was a torturous event: before he'd give me a penny when I went by his store where he would happily show off my type of 'idiot savant' facility with arithmetic to his Dutch friends, he would ask: "And who do you love best? Is it your mother or your father?" I can't for the life of me remember how I wound my way around this one. Probably told him time and again I loved them both best. His fun way of relating to me in that manner might have been a learned Dutch mannerism of putting a child on the spot.

Now, Uncle Fred, Sara's husband—well, there's worse than Fred. Here at least was a man who had learned his religion well and was able to hold himself at a distance from the fanatics who according to him misinterpret protocol unlike the deeply religious Saint, as my mother's father was. It would be offensive to the Good Lord to call attention to one's manner of dress by being out of tune with the times and with the others. Of course not! Humility and cleanliness... His life's aim had been to become a singing, sunny elegy to the infinite wisdom and love of the Great One. By Fred's lights the laws of extreme cleanliness were likewise not kept as intended by some of the fanatics. His knowledge of scripture I often found relevant and enlightening. His delivery though was not that pleasing. He was way too tense, stumbled over his words in French and unlike my sister, his wife, he did not express himself with that musical facility of gracious gliding in her gestures and which she possessed in all she did. I've kept asking myself why the hell does this delicate, fair, blue-eyed man, the Saintly Elder keep appearing in this work of digging down deep. What is the meaning of him in my world now? I only know that my mother (as well as my father, who in his own way highly respected him)—that she worshipped him, entirely, unlike all other men.

What irritated my father about me to the point where he called me unlovingly "Josell Punim", was what he considered was my tendency to have a permanent expression of victimization, whining, crying, belligerent, wetting when I should not have, and difficult to manage. I reminded him he said of his youngest brother Coba of Amsterdam who was said to have had similar problems to mine in his younger years. I burst into my analyst's study in Geneva once, crying desperately. He got up, gave me a napkin and said "So there you are... The running fountain... You're illustrating what we've talked about in your relationship with your father... " I had pushed Doddi, a surgery resident and my love companion, to the brink of irrationality by threatening the previous night to leave this time for good. In his flat I had found a strong-box ready to be shipped off and which contained some three to four hundred (Yes! That many) love letters from as many different women he had been with, indicating physical affairs... Finally, on impulse, he pushed me against the wall and went straight for my face with his fist. I thought he'd knocked my front teeth out of their sockets, but it was the inside of my lip which was deeply cut and the wretchedly sharp spur of my nose which got knocked askew... How different from the softness, the roundness, the almost Cushing-like moonfaced appearance when I was 18 years old and met Claude.

From later interactions with Claude I conclude I do not

know how far he has come. Remember the previous accidental encounter in Paris? He seemed hurt on seeing me, still angry. Was he? During our first interaction in his home, I was still strongly physically attracted to him, as strongly as previously. Because of my loneliness and the longing to see my son in safe hands near me, it threw me back to my first fixation on him. From a later interaction I retain the memory of his kindness toward my children, his infinite patience and extraordinary sensitivity when he saw my worry about my daughter, who climbed wildly into trees after his two boys; also his sweetness in putting himself out for both children. I also retain a rather bad aftertaste (now most understandable) of his wife's impatience to see us leave. I remember her discontent and rebelliousness by that time; the fact that she called Claude's letters and poems from 20 years earlier addressed to me, which Henry, my husband had sent expressly to her attention "disgusting!". I am certain now she did not mean the letters were disgusting but rather the sending of the packet of these touching mementos... Had other girls from the past pursued him? I remember above all his explanation to me of his surprise at receiving a telephone call from Henry. He thought Henry could not have been right about my Welsh mathematician, (whom Henry called a "nobody—the kind he wouldn't even greet in England, no more than the grocer boy"). Claude said he knew Henry must have been wrong, for "to be working for the kind of company he was working for, you simply couldn't be just run of the mill... you would not be paid the kind of good money these people get if you weren't at least well educated and pretty smart!" When Claude compared what he knew the Welshman's training had been to that required to become an airline pilot, he realized it didn't mean what Henry had tried to tell him on the phone. Following a short halt,

Claude continued, snapping his fingers, "I knew right then, he couldn't be right in what he said." He added, looking at me in great earnest, trying to meet my eyes, "Henry asked me if I loved you… I told him, NO."

During my first weekend stay at his house in Mass, I walked with Claude to his office… He took me along past Harvard's enormous library and quoted the astonishing number of books accumulated by this great institution. "Why!" he exclaimed, swallowing, his Adam's apple pointed with pride, fascinatingly moving up and down, while he smacked his tongue against his palate as he had always done, "This must be just about the best and largest library in existence." He spoke to me of some of the people we had both known and been associated with. "Why, just about all of them made the top in their respective fields… "

We walked across Harvard Square. I said I liked the quiet stone buildings and the statues which looked comfortably settled in that area. He was pensive. I had forgotten these were his familiar undergraduate places too, but he said only, "Just about all of the greatest of today have taught here at one time or another… "

In his small and impersonal-looking office, (where he said he spent as little time as possible) I noticed a book in French by Jean Piaget, which I wanted to look at and possibly borrow… After all he had let me borrow the Teddy Grace records and even parceled them up lovingly and strongly for me. He took the Piaget book, looked at the index and said it was his only copy. He seemed truly sorry about this. At least I could carry Teddy Grace's singing away with me for a while.

When I finally approved of some of the popular music we heard play on the radio when we were in Provincetown, he found the common denominator (he always did) to the tunes I liked more than the others: "It's always the same composers", he said with puzzlement. They were, it seems, always pieces composed by Gershwin or Cole Porter... When we walked past the library, he seemed much interested in remembering the exact number of books housed in the building's hold. I told him in truth "I can't stand libraries any more. I'm sick of the entire scene... "

Little did I know then that once again some 14 years later I would happily dwell in peace and eagerness among similar walls on the Cornell campus... My message to him, I now realize, was "Nothing has quite turned out as well as I once hoped it would... " His essential message to me: "I'm a great success now... Everything has turned out well, if not better than I once dreamed it would". To me it meant: *Je suis assis sur mes lauriers.* I'm sitting on my laurels or rather rocking content in my hammock overlooking the Mystic River ... "

The second time I went to see them, "He didn't love me anymore", (perhaps he never really had, in the way I had hoped he still would). I wondered if he had not become something of a gadget worshipper, as though gadgets had some intrinsic value. He had also become fascinated with theories of probabilities as they applied to finance, especially the stock market. All the psychology and physiology books in his enormous home library had been displaced by books relating to the financial field, which seemed amusing to me. But when I insisted on receiving tips from him, (after all Barney O. said he'd multiplied by 60 what he owned!) he refused to give me any. He feared the responsibility if he were wrong, and I were to lose money because of his advice. I insisted on taking both the gamble and the full responsibility. He tried to explain to me that morally he would still feel responsible and then wondered if I was having financial difficulties. I extracted some hints as to what he himself had done in terms of investments and let it go at that. Every one of these was in reality a great money making scoop for its time, and had I had the money… If only my mother--totally absorbed by then in stock market transactions, a new interest which she shared with her friend Harry Winston, the jeweler. (The latter's son kept wondering who it was his father phoned that often in central New York where I lived… My mother had availed herself daily of his office phone to call me)—if only she had followed the advice so painstakingly given by him…

Would Norbert Wiener consider Claude's new interest and success as derived from Mephistophelean Alchemy? Must one be an anointed priest of capitalism to be invested with the power to alchemize gold out of one's brain substance? Who's to say? And who's to say it may only be performed to anoint for the sake of another, never for oneself directly. Does history really say so? For once, Norbert Wiener might not have been on the mark here.

* * *

"Circumpolar Trek"

Bringing everything up again to find greater finality now that Evie went home and arrived safely in Manhattan. At lunch at the Rathskeller during the noon hour when most of the faculty parade in and out, with very few women at that—I was staring at the beautifully chiseled and sensitive Oriental face of a scientist. He responded to my gaze suddenly by staring back at me. I was taken by surprise and aghast I thought of a young Asian; I still do not know which of the racially distinct groups of Eskimos he belonged to. Two years ago in Anchorage I was walking down the deserted main street that runs along the bay, surrounded by the abandoned structures from the last Good Friday earthquake when I saw him, sauntering toward me from the opposite direction. It was about the middle of the afternoon in early January, a time when day is fairly indistinguishable from the night at those latitudes. He came very close as he passed me in that cold, milky white hazed light, and swayed under the influence of too much liquor in his young body. I saw him very close by and he was young and strong. Our eyes met. His gaze was the coldest, darkest, and saddest I had ever seen—it pursued me for hours… The highest suicide rate among young men in America is to be found among the Alaskan Native.

I had come to Anchorage—No, I had literally flown in driven by ill-augurs as in painfully vivid premonitions. My nose said, despite repeated negations by them on the phone, that the children had landed alone in this misty, snowy environment and were not being looked after by an adult. There I found my daughter not in the best of health and she seemed relieved to have me there. My son had been enrolled overnight two years beyond his 9th Grade standing in a local high school having promised his father he would stay. He might have sacrificed his future—anything to try to please his father. I was, thank heavens, careful not to stay overnight in the house with them. When he came home a week or so later Henry was much surprised to see me. His new wife as I suspected had left—possibly the day the children arrived. Henry said that now that our son was to stay I could too if I wanted to. "There's plenty of work for a psychiatrist here," and he took me at once to the State Hospital for an application and interview. I asked for financial equality in responsibilities. While we ate out with the children he asked me to come up with a detailed accounting proposal, and I worked on this intently. But when I presented him with a few neat sheets of figures he said he didn't understand why I wanted to do this. Both children quietly said "Dad, now, you asked her to draw up an account… " He showed me the door.

When near him I still found him magnetic—at the time I was already many years into single hood. Away from him while I was staying up there I went to court to ask for help with all the accounting. I'd become fearful about my safety. Thank heavens for the manager of the hotel where I stayed in town. He originated from a hamlet less than 5 Miles from where I lived. After many attempts we succeeded in getting the drunken louts out of a nearby room at night. I had heard sounds reminiscent of the bleating of an injured sheep. These emanated from what might have been a highly retarded young woman. I heard them as cries for help as I felt the repercussions of flesh pounding flesh.

My son resumed his schooling in England and my daughter—I believe she came home with me that time. Within a year or two Henry was to be transferred out of Alaska.

To Maria:

This elegant introduction to the most aesthetic and recondite of the sciences may aid an esoteric girl in understanding the etiology of an elliptical admirer.

C.

Photocopy of Inscription by Claude to
"What is Mathematics" 1943.
by R. Courant & H. Robbins

CHAPTER 12

Free Association Five: Game Playing Machines

I understand a game-playing machine may be used to secure the automatic performance of any function, that is, if the performance of such is subject to a clear-cut, objective criterion of merit. In checkers and chess, this merit consists of victory over the opponent, of winning the game according to the accepted rules.

"Otherwise," says Norbert Wiener, "the game assumes the formlessness of the croquet game in Alice in Wonderland, where the balls were hedgehogs and kept unrolling themselves, the mallets were flamingoes, the arches cardboard soldiers who kept marching about the field, and the umpire the Queen of Hearts, who kept changing rules and sending the players to the Headsman... Under these circumstances, to win has no meaning... a successful policy cannot be learned... "

I am not able to work tonight. I feel deeply disappointed with my daughter. A very cold cloud has passed over us. There have been many in the past! Gradually they buried warm feelings. I learned that one must not see when it comes to children; one must over-look. It is difficult: their lack of consideration, their total immersion in themselves, seems to go on forever. There is no joy now in the giving; it has become begrudging. Despite years of putting children ahead of every other personal consideration, it is unlikely this was always done without reproach, or without some tacit, implicit, holding back.

T.D.: Unlikely? Most unlikely! And you know it, sot!
U.D.: It's still very good with the boy.
T.D.: Yeah, especially as he's not around that much lately.
U.D.: I panic when he's coming. I panic when he's leaving again.

The week that passed consisted entirely of work at the office. One interesting first dream was brought in by a very ill 19 year old girl, who called herself Ms. During a good deal of the session she mumbled, whispering in a near inaudible and incomprehensible muttering, which came forth from between clenched teeth. For a minute or so I pursued N. Wiener's ideas about the stages of communication with the deaf. He attributes the pitiful animal sounds they emit to their inability to hear their own sounds. With Miss Ms. I began to feel she didn't want to hear herself, though she pathetically complained that other people said they couldn't understand her and that she feared reaching the stage of being unable to live with others… She is a suicidal child who now spends part of her nights as a go-go dancer—a mute go-go dancer who keeps her bikini on and performs gestured poetry to the music in which she sees constellations of Mercury and

Uranus. She was a student at the University this semester but became enamored with one of her professors, and would not leave him alone. Once when she was hitchhiking, he gave her a ride but she would not tell him where she wanted to be driven to… Finally in exasperation, he stopped his car in front of his own home, and then committed his main error: he took her to bed… a man's reflexive answer to irreducible situations. During lovemaking he apparently kept screaming at her: "Why don't you treat me as a human being? Why won't you talk to me?" A few days later she returned to his home, where he locked all entrances to her. She smashed through the picture window in his living room, and proceeded to cut herself with large chunks of the shattered glass. Ambulance sirens screaming, red police-car lights flashing, she was taken off to the State Hospital from which her parents, who flew in from New York, "rescued" her the next day. She could not have hurt herself that much if now, a mere few weeks later, she can dance with the bare minimum of cover. She has dropped out of school and has come to see me. She has quite a 'Beziehungswahn' (delusional ideas often of an obsessive nature) going with the Professor: he's constantly on her mind, and supposedly knows what she feels, all her comings and goings. She says she can hear him say things even though he's not exactly around. I am praying she will take the medication I prescribed and strongly advocated. It won't necessarily change the content of the delusions, but she won't be so deeply upset by her hallucinations, and it would cut the cycle of alienation furthering alienation. She has taken "some" of the samples I gave her, but mutters that the medication has made all her food tasteless. I promised her this side effect would eventually wear off. She doesn't seem to restrain herself on all the other "stuff" she experiments with—the frequent use of marijuana, occasional mescaline, and whatnot. I stressed that the most important business on hand "right now" is to regain her sanity. I told her pointedly she had a sickness of the mind and that she must, like a diabetic in need of insulin (we all seem to clutch at the same old analogy), treat herself at once, that the miracle drugs presently available would speed the process.

"I lost the prescription… "

"Here is another one… "

Mouth barely open… whispers… mutterings… Very long, thick blond hair matted over her face. Eyes hidden behind large glasses. Tears streaming… One out of every ten whispers I must ask, "What did you say?" in a whisper myself. Occasionally I decipher one. I referred her for testing. For the first time in the twelve years that we have worked together, after all the years of co-therapy and referral of patients, Abraham the psychologist refuses to test someone. He has sent me a letter about her; he has given her two trial sessions. He said he just couldn't put up with the sullenness. Did he perceive a willful provocativeness, an unwitting negativeness in her behavior? I did explain to him, though, that when she was sixteen her parents had tied her down to her bed with string around her arms and legs and cut her hair off. "Well, you can't win 'em all", he said.

She has a straight A average and seems highly gifted mentally. I feel she can be helped. These late adolescent schizophrenic reactions are of a very different nature and are at times totally reversible. They seem all too easy to mishandle; I will help her grow out of it, and not allow her to get stuck in it for years. I told her openly this sickness might destroy the joy of life for her in the next five years, leaving her with panic at the mere memory of all the suffering experienced here and now. She touches me deeply. I thought, well, if you want to be an eccentric, so do I, and I dashed for my knitting-crocheting bag. I crocheted, and to my ragged nerves' content I heard a clear voice, fully audible, and when occasionally I looked up to show her I was following her meaning, I saw her face uncovered and she told me a most significant dream. Oddly enough, through the dream, an awareness of the struggle between two of the three phases of communication in cybernetics terms appears. I took note of the inside-outside dichotomy underlined in the dream. Here is a proof of the righteousness of her refusal to let the outside world "in," (or is it in letting herself "out" to the world?) The negativism is expressed at the door, perhaps as much in as out. My Swiss professors of psychiatry pointed to the somatic position of what they called "the typical schizophrenic" who would stand on the threshold of the door, as immobilized between two wards (the day room and the bedroom) unable to leave the in-between space.

U.D.: Too much theory. Is there possibly some identification with this girl and my own guilt-laden escape from reality at her age?

My analyst C. Baudouin indicated that I had become hypertrophied in the direction of intellect at the expense of emotional-instinctual needs. I, too, at her age might have waited around for a Prof. on whom I had a crush. Who hasn't at one time or another? But I would never have smashed in like that. What if she'd been under the influence of whatever? That's plausible, and she may not be a schizophrenic, but she might indeed have a rotten set of parents—that is, by the sound of what she perceives is her truth. The girl's first dream, as much as I caught of it, is as follows:

In an insane asylum—Four characters—Sort of designed like a restaurant—People come in and go out and when they come back on the inside—to the other people, it's exactly the same as before they left. There are 4 characters: 1.An old lady—whimpering. 2. A young woman with black hair. Not sure who the others were. I am one of them. There are men there. Not sure. A man is running the place.

One of her poems called the "Pulse Poem" has some deeply touching lines:

"The tears have made us beggar mortals
for a touch of grace"

Reading her poems made me aware of the related psychodynamic antecedents; she's the one who fell out of grace—with her father, that is. Her younger brother (at first a minor figure in the family constellation) usurped her place. The father (a quiet, youngish-looking man) was her strongest love object. At the height of her adolescent crisis she attempted to break away from the dependency. Instead of helping her, her father helped her mother who tied her down to the bed. A castration scene occurred there (cutting off hair with arms and legs tied). One never reads enough of one's patient's written communications.

T.D.: Too much expostulation, too much theory. Where are we?

U.D.: In Ithaca, in a different room, just one floor beneath the one I was staying in last time I was here. (Last week?) I must plunge in again and go on with this writing about unfinished situations. I do not intend to work on mothering and my relationship with the children unless I have to. My son is coming home either for the Christmas holidays, or for New Year's. I am truly glad the boy is coming home. He has done art work as well as the sciences, and I am certain this is good for him. It will be wonderful to have him around again, and I won't even think of his leaving till I have to. Oddly, when he leaves, Clara, my patient, calls for an appointment. She has done so in the past, to ask for help with her void when mine is the deepest.

Once again all that analysis: like an experimental cadaver—oneself on the slab—pulling guts out into the open for an undetermined period of time. The exposure leads to cleansing, a sort of purification by a filtering process, and with luck to a much greater objectivity. Freed from the mind boggling childhood contaminants, the muck of shame, the mud of guilt, the monster of hate, a good period usually follows. A need ensues to live up to the best that has been brought out into the open.

T.D.: Too much theory again. What the hell am I after?

U.D.: I'm sick of all that digging.

T.D.: Who's avoiding? You've said at least a hundred times that the end is in sight. Where is it? This Claude dependency business. Avoidance, denial; what the hell is it in the end?

U.D.: Who says there is an end at that? Who's avoiding?

T.D.: If you want to get this thing written up one day, you'd better finish it. What sort of an idiot is it that wants to go around her whole life feeling she's made the biggest mistake of all, and behaved irresponsibly at that?

U.D.: I don't feel that way anymore. There's just a piece somewhere that I've got to dig up…

Having a lovely brunch: Scrambled eggs, bacon, Tab to drink. An apple for later. Last night "the tea spilled over again"…

The ruddy puking which follows indiscriminate food intake when I write continues. Anything non-essential is perceived as surcharge that must be gotten rid of. I don't feel too comfortable in my new room on the University Campus. I find it is cold near the window. The sky is of a luminous grey and has a touch of silver. We are far away from the sea, though Cayuga Lake is nearby and just below us. I can see the perpendicular rain falling around the street lantern. The branches of the tall tree outside my window still have buds on them and now the pearls of rain, frozen, miniscule icicles, stay glued to them. The highest branches of the tree reach to the fourth floor where I stayed previously. The wet pavements dampen the sounds of the cars on the road. On the silenced T.V. screen I can see skiers gliding gracefully in zigzags across the snow covered hills of Mount Snow in Vermont. I am thinking of my son… I am thinking too of the cottage at a nearby ski resort where I spent an overnight and began to write of the experience with Carlos… A French Canadian ski instructor came to spend a few hours with me in that cottage. Gad! he smelled so strongly of urine. He was otherwise kind, rather inarticulate, and at times stuttered. The delicately small fellow was inebriated beyond repair; in a fit of uncoordination, his fist came down powerfully on my face. For a few days my nose was askance, and now I have a small spur on the other side of the one that used to come into my field of vision. Forget it! At this stage, what difference does it make? Middle age masks. A crawling, wanton, delicate smoothness from vagina upward. Robbed of elasticity we carry an air of resemblance.

At Willard-Straight Hall I am seated at a large round solid wooden dining table in the side dining-hall, and I can see the back of the Olin Tower, made of stone. How grey and strangely carved these stones are! What odd shapes, and there seem to be so many of them from here. From my room, at a distance, the tower usually looks to be of an even deep brown color. That of an elongated pyramid seemingly made of four large solid slabs. From nearby, how different the structure looks! It is divided into so very many sections, each of variegated hues. There are delicate, almost transparent vines glued to the small cloister-like window panes. The time clock, accompanied now by clearly resounding chimes, shows 12:30 p.m. Students are quiet, apparently preoccupied. Final examinations are coming up. Three tables across from mine there is a girl with a red handkerchief on her wet, naturally fair and wavy hair. She wears a striped overall like farmers (and now skiers) do. She's eating and studying, her back to one of the large windows, which allows the light to trickle in to the side of her, on her books. She's intent on her work, and gives an air of being well organized. Milky fog has now settled thickly just beyond the sternly Anglican looking building which houses the post office. From above the lace-fringed and lingering fog, the hills are emerging, now that it has stopped raining. I feel much held up having to copy my handwritten notes; new impressions keep intruding.

Here in the dining room the only loud sounds one occasionally hears are from the non-students. Highly boring stuff... It leads me to what is really on my mind today. I AM STILL NOT FINISHED WITH CLAUDE. It's better, but it's not resolved yet. Events still cause him to emerge—so much need to evoke him to strangers, which must stop, of course. I want to stop the turnstile in my dream of him from going around. I would like to find that finally the Manichean character has ultimately stayed in the background, in the disintegration of the darkness—*WERSCHWUNDEN, PARTI, FINI.*

It is almost night. The seventh floor of the Olin Library has come brilliantly alive, surrounded by a heavily pillared balcony I had not previously noticed. The entire structure is an elongated, dotted rectangle, an immense pagoda! It floats surrounded by eerie, white crepuscular veils. The dancing lights of its seventh and uppermost deck are like a gay ribbon, which sails toward the darkened Olin Tower, a lighthouse—a bastion carried toward the steaming cold waters of Cayuga Lake.

T.D.: What the hell does this game-playing theory of learning machines that play checkers and chess have to do with us?

U.D.: Well, this is specifically what was going on between Claude and I. He was my creator!

T.D.: Your creator! That's a new one! Meaning what sort of dependency shit again?

U.D.: I hate all that name calling. Claude never swore. It wasn't till I met Henry that all of a sudden everything became bloody… With Claude I could have moved in the game with him "as if" a creature of his creation. That's what I mean—for alternatively, I could move only one other way and that was to become his "Queen of Hearts". Within the context of Alice in Wonderland she made up the rules as she went along, and sent all of her people…

T.D.: Including herself?

U.D.: To the henchman. If I had followed him as his creation, the game would have become uninteresting to him. He played with me admittedly:

> *"With love and kisses,*
> *With curses and hisses"*

That last inscription was the most personal one of all those he wrote in the many books he gave me. What matters is that he wrote that one on the very day, or perhaps a few days after he had said, "Baby, I think we ought to get married. What do you think?"

T.D.: Well, then—what the hell did you think?

U.D.: I think I was afraid. He wrote this in the Key Book to

Finnegan's Wake.

T.D.: Most appropriately named for the occasion. There's your key, you idiot!, That's the key…

U.D.: What about the one other book's inscription?

T.D.: He gave another copy of that same "What is Mathematics?" to his analyst. He was just asking the two of you to understand him, to recognize his greatness. Except for his science tutors, who else ever had?

U.D.: And who gave me any? Remember, I was the martyred one, victimized by everyone. The only way to get some recognition at home was to let them bully me day and night, and then play the smart-assed clown with the sharp tongue. That made them sit up and take notice.

T.D.: Are we back to the self-pitying whining? We're talking about Claude. Remember?

U.D.: To play a matching game with him that kept his interest, I had to learn his ways. His dedication to "What is Mathematics?"

> *"To Maria: This elegant introduction
> to the most aesthetic and recondite of
> the sciences may aid an esoteric girl in
> understanding the etiology of an elliptical
> admirer."*

But I could not play by his rational rules, for that would have made me completely predictable to him. I wanted to play *Le Jeu de Dames* (Checkers is called Ladies' Game in French) as we played it on the Continent. With me he either wouldn't or couldn't at the time—his mother, perceived by him as unloving, and the competitive academic and business cultures from which he sprang, saw to that. Eventually he managed to play *Le Jeu de*

Dames with a—come be truthful—by far more compatible, and loving, and closer replica of himself.

The clock on Olin Tower has just been lit. It's five o'clock in the evening. I'm hungry—I hope I can eat at the Rathskeller tonight. In "God and Golem, Inc.," Wiener says of the playing machine designers and their theoreticians: "One such master becomes aware that some of the supposedly human functions of his slaves may be transferred to machines... "

T.D.: I perceived that it was the pain of personal involvement, the learned process of pain, which taught Claude a pattern of avoidance in human interactions. Remember the expression, "Proud as Lucifer"?

U.D.: Gads! Wiener calls such people Mephistopheles! He says that all authorities insist that: "... not only is sorcery a sin leading to hell but it is a personal peril in this life. It is a two edged sword... "

I'm anticipating still; I know already what will follow. I think Wiener means it as Alphonse Daudet intended it in an allegorical story I remember from way back. In his book "Letters from my Windmill" (and A. Daudet really lived in a windmill) he wrote the story about a man born with pure gold in his brain. He finds out about it one day when as a young man he hurts his head. Instead of having the usual blood, serum, and derivatives, he finds out there is pure gold there at his disposal. Wiener continues his own exorcisms.

T.D.: Don't forget, he wrote these books I believe are great about himself and his times after he had had some analysis— (with Karl Deutsch? The same man who avoided telling Freud of the cancer that was consuming his throat?). Wiener's books are of the Graphotherapy group, too.

U.D.: As far as I'm concerned the *graphotherapy* ones are the most informative written today. There just isn't time for semi truths any longer. Here comes the *pièce de résistance*:

"In addition to the motive which the gadget worshiper finds for his admiration of the machine in its freedom from human limitations of speed and accuracy, there is one motive which is harder to establish in any concrete case, but which must play a very considerable role nevertheless. It is the desire to avoid the personal responsibility for a dangerous or disastrous decision by placing the responsibility elsewhere… "

Claude never wanted to take the responsibility for a decision that involved another: Me!

T.D.: Did you for you? For him? For the two of you?

U.D.: After all, I was many years younger than he. Besides, I was the woman and I was playing *Le Jeu de Dames*. My specialty was checkers, not chess.

The formulation of human purposes means involvement with humans. This is the very act avoided carefully by those afflicted with the pain at the fearful responsibility of possible error. The latter probably motivates the love of gadgetry in the first place… Wiener stresses that since the discovery of the atomic bomb a great deal of recognition has been given to the technocrats, the "know-hows" in America. The need to first "know-what" has become a secondary consideration. He illustrates this point by saying (and here, wretchedly here, was where my fascination with his reflections began) in *Cybernetics and Society*:

"Some years ago, a prominent American engineer bought an expensive player-piano. It became clear after a week or two that this purchase did not correspond to any particular interest in the music played by the piano but rather to the overwhelming interest in the piano mechanism. For this gentleman, the player-piano was not a means of producing music, but a means of giving some inventor the chance of showing how skillful he was at overcoming certain difficulties in the production of music. This is an estimable attitude in a second year high school student. How estimable it is in one of those on whom the whole cultural future of the country depends, I leave to the reader."

T.D.: He sounds pompous here. So he doesn't like Claude's attitude. Too bad! If that's what Claude wants to do with his money, that's his own business!

U.D.: O.K.! But I didn't like it either. Wiener goes on to say: "In the myths and fairy tales that we read as children we learned a few of the simpler and more obvious truths of life, such as that when a djinni is found in a bottle, it had better be left there…"

T.D.: That makes sense.

U.D.: Why couldn't one take it out, and then put it back in again later? At least have a look, I'd say.

T.D.: Jack and Jill went up the hill… Jack fell down and broke his crown… and all the King's men… couldn't put it together again.

U.D.: The end of this exorcism of Claude's Mephistopheles is in sight.

T.D.: You've been saying that for ages now. You're boring us to death!

U.D.: Boring? That's the aim. Just a few more turns, we're boring in and down. Fritz Perls has been an inspiration, although I'm not too certain he would have considered this *graphotherapy* as a valid replacement for other therapies.

T.D.: I'm almost certain Karen Horney would have; she said as much in "Self-Analysis", which is certainly a worthwhile attempt in psychoanalysis, but oh how difficult to read! As a matter of fact, though he was nearly seventy years old, Fritz attempted the same. The Graphotherapy that comes through "In and Out of the Garbage Pail" set the stage for others.

U.D.: Claude was kind to me. What with my stream of pranks with other men, and in school, he always extended his hand to draw us together again. He forgave so many times, I have lost count and he never bore a grudge. I hope I don't sound like the delusional patient in the asylum in Brussels who said to me:

"The King of all Belgians (Leopold III at the time)is such a gentleman!"

"Why?"

"He never made a pass at me, like some other men did... "

T.D.: Are you saying Claude didn't really care?

U.D.: Who cares?

T.D.: You do. You still do.

U.D.: So what? I, too, believe in trying to understand the here and now in its totality, holistically within the context of our experiential selves, but I don't want to compartmentalize. The NOW, of course, comprises our total past. I would have talked to an encounter group about Claude; I would have talked of him till I talked him and all others into the ground!!! They might have helped me find the void which in periods of loneliness I filled with him. Those who have managed to touch us deeply, and thus have combined to change the direction of our destiny, need more than (mere) acceptance; they must be understood within the totality of their own existence. Objectivity demands knowledge of their priorities, as compared to the primary values in our own life, i.e. *Their trends must be gotten hold of within the context of their own life, then we can let them go where they belong.*

Had Fritz Perls received this help, I believe he might have been more at peace with himself and with his wife and children. His relations with women never received enough objective input. That was a shame. But he nevertheless succeeded in helping me as well as many others, of that I am certain. We follow an inescapable system of priorities.

T.D.: Who says it is inescapable? Anyhow, like what?

U.D.: The children come first. I've seen too many children who felt unloved. Not just the unwanted ones either. Too many who, when it counted, were never able to receive the unquestioning love they needed.

T.D.: Well, one can find good substitutes—as long as it's done with their interest in mind.

U.D.: Within my frame of reference the caring of the children had to come first. It meant not having other things… men, interesting friendships, good professional exchanges, so much. But there was no other way for me. When I whined and complained about the children's omnivorous need of me, Dr. Ellis said, just like that: "Get rid of them!" He did some strong reality testing there. The idea of boarding schools came to me then—as much in their interest as in mine. Who ever has everything going for them at the same time? No one that I know of. During chosen moments in their life they do, but it does not prevent the child in us from crying out, "I want it all!" The hunger for more is inevitable as long as hope remains. If I had introduced myself in my present situation during a Marathon Gestalt Therapy Encounter, with the need to exorcize Claude, to comprehend within the fiber of me what happened in the past, to liberate myself for however many years there are to come, how could I ever have arrived at the point I reached here? I've had to go through this (self analysis) in my own way. In a group it's easy to find other people's problems which seem more in need of solution than your own. *'Noblesse oblige.'* A "Blitzkrieg Insight" (Karen Horney's term)—the kind one can receive during an encounter group still leaves you with the work to be done. Trying to write a book about the menopausal changes in women has made me very conscious of my own situation. My patient Clara stirred me even more—She helped me to I realize I had reached a new stage, and that indeed it was high time to take stock. Four or five years after one's analysis, it is time to look back again in one form or another. After 20 years, why, it's an "absolute indication!" as we say in medicine, i.e. if you do not intervene the chances are minimal—even nil—that the patient will do well at all. In order to bring this about I have needed the help of a man who, though a genius, has the naiveté, the touching clumsiness of my own father (as I remember him). I have read all of N. Wiener's non-technical writings. I love his directness. He has the artfulness of a jeweler, and the acute need of the histologist to cover details with the same thoroughness as the larger picture. This invites impatience with his writings. But when I need to know the meticulous details of whatever subject, locale, or person that was delved into by his studies, it is to him I turn. Last night I became engrossed in Wiener's last non-technical text, "God and Golem,Inc.". It contains many ideas, positions, I felt I must retain in the context of my own experiment. In his preface he expresses the belief that only HERESY can lead to a genuine breakthrough in any field of endeavor. He pays homage to the sacred, the holy, an unusual tribute to what is considered the sublime aspect of life, which is always keeping the "dibbuk" in mind.

There is presently an unveiling I feel I must undertake. What struck home in his chapter on the theories which underline game-playing machines was the almost similar indifference he expresses towards both checkers and chess. Thank heavens he debunked chess while simultaneously elevating the game of checkers!

When I previously mentioned a first and last encounter in Antwerp with a notable uncle from London, I had not come close to this hurt, this feeling of non-recognition by the family. I always had to fit into the same mold: "The youngest of the four—difficult lately—has some looks, ergo (tortured ergo!) no brains! I kept on describing "*The family gathering at the Ringers*", but never quite came to grips with a feeling that there was something at least for which I should have received recognition and never did. While reading Wiener it came to me. I WAS UNBEATABLE AT CHECKERS! No one in the family ever beat me at it. For years, during the long rainy winter months we spent each Saturday playing the game, and I always won. I never cheated. At cards and other games, I clowned around, much to everyone's irritation, but checkers was a dead serious game to me. Why didn't anyone ever say, "Marieke is best at checkers; of the whole family she is the best checker player? Was it a sin then to play checkers on the Sabbath? Was it so for girls too? Why did no one ever take notice?

My father did, the night he died. I was teaching him how to play that very evening. He had already told me the previous week he did not like to come home anymore. I must have made it my business to improve the ambience at home for him. That was the very night before my sister Fanny was to be married. I was teaching and playing with him at the same time. Fanneke came to watch us play and she began to help him so that he would not loose to me easily. She removed one of my pieces as though he had won it. I began to put up a fuss when the game took an unexpected turn. When he showed his disapproval of my loud protesting conduct, I was on the verge of tears. Luckily I calmed down and said to him, "Isn't it the same with You? Don't you get upset too, when mother comes into the store and interferes with YOUR business?" He burst out laughing and said with pleasure that this was correct, and that this was an argument that showed I could reason well. He gave me a kiss and sent me off to bed, for he didn't feel well, and the smells in the flat from all the baking bothered him.

The next thing I knew was the frightening screams. When I came running out, everyone was in his bedroom. He was choking and blue already, gasping for breath. Fanny held him in her arms... I ran down the four flights of our new apartment building into the dark of night on Pelikaan Street in search of a physician, without having a notion as to where to go. When I ran back, realizing I did not know what I was doing, they had all made up their minds that he was dead. A physician who turned up later also said that he was dead. It must have been past midnight by then, on the 30th of December, in 1937. My mother had already draped all the mirrors, all the reflecting surfaces of the furniture, the silverware, the lights, in the flat. White bed-sheets, white tablecloths were placed on everything, as in an abandoned house. Candles sprang up to throw large quivering shadows onto the walls. She wailed and howled... Her moaning filled the covered night with, "Max, Max, what have you done now? She called him affectionately by his nickname, Max, instead of his full name of Emmanuel, and blamed him for dying. What had he done? What had he done?

Fanny believed she had held him in the wrong position, that was, upward with his head crouched in her arms, instead of letting his head rest flat against the sheet, without a pillow... I felt I should have let him win the game that first time. The game remained unfinished, and the board and checker pieces remained on the table in the room once so forbiddingly ornate, now with draped mirrors and walls which crept with howling sorrows and spiraled shadows thrown by weeping white candles. Except for the Sabbath on which day grownups venerated the Lord, and my cousin Sabrina and I played checkers, I lost interest in the game. On the morning of his funeral he was taken to Putte, in Holland, for burial and for the first time in its history the Diamond Bourse suspended all trading activities. The diamond merchants who were not following the procession on foot down Pelikaan Street came out and stood in front of the Bourse while we were driven by, far behind the men... On rainy cold days, and there were many at first, the coldness of the ground in which he lay sent shivers of guilt through me. I felt I had abandoned him, and had an impulse to join him to keep him warm. With the first personal experience of death in our family came the first awareness of the meaning of the death wish. Instead of sitting in chairs like everyone else, I would stretch out on the hard wooden floors. Eventually, not too long after that, a vague suicidal attempt, in the act of waiting for what? Mysteriously, waiting began. It began like a pervasive feeling preempting everything else, and invaded and contaminated every deed with ill-defined promises.

I am thinking of Putte, where all my people are buried. There is the section for the Coheenen (the Priestly sect) also the cordoned-off section where the Saint, my mother's father, lies buried. I wonder how far away the Saint's wife is located, my aloof, tall, thin, maternal grandmother, the only grandmother I ever and only passingly knew. On my first visit to Claude and his wife and his children, I played with his youngest son, though I remembered little about chess, and I let him teach me. After some time when I saw him flustered with explaining the rules of the game, I thought it had lasted long enough and helped him win. I was glad he enjoyed himself. We announced happily to Claude that he had won. Thereupon Claude called his wife, and scratching the thick hair behind his right ear in his customary manner when he was puzzled, said, "Can you believe that? Maria lost to him! I laughed at first, then when I saw he had taken the game playing seriously, I felt annoyed and walked away. It really irked me though. I reminded him he had never won at *Le Jeu de Dames* (checkers) with me, though I recognized he had magnanimously given in to playing (unexpectedly) continental checkers, at which time my moves halted his good game. This was usually my technique; I played dumb, and then took people by surprise and cleaned up the board. Still he rarely, if ever, played checkers with me again. He preferred chess, in which I lost interest quickly while playing with him. I learned the game too late in life compared to checkers, where I could see the whole game evolve after only a short while with a player. When I played chess with him he played very slowly, and always dealt in his head with much more than the mere playing. The logistics of the game absorbed him as much, if not more so, than winning and in addition, he became upset when he lost. I feel Norbert Wiener is saying something about the Mephistopheles in my dream of Claude. I really want him to tell me that Claude is the fellow in his touching Sunday-best suit, able to smile sweetly at life and love it just as we loved each other sometimes, not always in sadness and pain during those difficult years of slowly growing up on our own.

T.D.: You say that. What is it you're really after? Aren't you still in search of the demoniacal side of him?

U.D.: Everyone has a moon-side to them. There is always a reverse to every side, the hidden dark aspect. True, I have always suspected his shadow, that "otherness" when the switch was turned off and he withdrew defensively into a shell that insulated his soul from that of others. I remember Claude and me on 8th Street, at the café where we usually ate dinner. Close to us, in the back of the long, rectangular dining room, there was a large round table around which some 10 or 12 University students, all boys, were seated. They were possibly celebrating a graduation. One boy had spoken up, and the others were attacking him. He became excited, flustered, and raised his voice. Claude said, "He'd better keep quiet, for they'll just chop his head off. It is better not to stick your neck out when you do not have to. Others are only too eager to get you for it… " These might not have been his exact words, but I was struck by the fact that he suspected that the world at large was a nasty, hostile, cannibalistic place. He felt that any individual outstanding and different in any respect would be dealt with mercilessly by the others. To me it also meant not taking risks, and having to be absolutely certain before one struck. I suspected for the first time that he could be shrewd and was most capable of fencing his way around. My perception of him as a co-sufferer, a co-victim of mainly inner difficulties changed. I had fought the realistic recognition of this aspect of him for a long time. He had belonged too long to a different and unique class, apart from the rest of mankind that had made me run, licking wounds, to America and into his consoling arms! This fear of men—of the world in and out of Sin—has obviously been suppressed for a very long time. Was this Mephistopheles his other side, which finally came forth with my own awakening to a less unreal and schizoid world? Was the dichotomized nature in the dream mine rather than his? Weren't we both proud as Lucifer? Years later in California I enticed his close friend Barney O. to a motel bed. As he left me untouched (he was being faithful to his wife) and upset, he said, "You and Claude are very similar people really. I did not suspect this before… " At a time like that he could only have meant our adventurous, playful sensuality. Or did he mean we were really very similar?

Landed at the "Chef Italia" after feeling lightheaded with hunger and rushing down the hill. Pouring, truly pouring, rain! I'm just becoming aware of real weather now that I am car-less. Went across the street to the University Delicatessen. I asked for a hot chocolate and enjoyed its warm, sweet fumes even more than the drink itself. Then I sat in the back room, feeling much better after supper. Quietly I got my Norbert Wiener out again, and fell on sorcery, black masses, and mummery condemned as Sin. To wit: "… what is more natural than that some soul, damned but ingenious, should have hit upon the idea of laying his hold on the magic Host and using its powers for his personal advantage… The magic of the Host is intrinsically good, its perversion to other ends… is a deadly sin."

He keeps comparing laying one's hand on the magic Host and using its powers for one's personal gain and using the magic of modern automation to further personal profit. For some reason he considers both a deadly sin, whether one believes in God and his greater glory or not. For some ungodly reason I was not enjoying the hot chocolate any longer. I went from succulence to truculence; I felt enervated… A studious looking boy sat in front of me, eating. He had a young but already very large long-haired dog who came to sniff between my legs. I have nothing to give him but the remnants of what I took along from the restaurant… I find myself thinking of the phobias I suddenly developed at the Central Islip State Hospital while I studied bacteriology for the Medical boards. That 40-room spook mansion on the C.I.S.H. grounds, where I was alone for about 7 months. The house faced a not too distant building which housed the 600 maximally "dangerous" female patients I was tending then. At times their screams filled the night.

T.D.: What the hell brought this on?

U.D.: Well, the fact that I talk so much about Claude and that I have been alone again for so long.

T.D.: Not true! Bill just called to ask if I would join him and put a deposit on a ski excursion to Chamonix, France…

U.D.: But I don't want to go with Bill. He is vibrant and dances and skis with exceptional grace, but when he drinks…

T.D.: Besides, and it's beside the point, the only one I really long for again now is my son.

U.D.: Well then, longing for him, many lone walks, some sadness, the waiting; the typical female waiting from early adolescence onward.

T.D.: Am I trying to say I'm going berserk again? Same thing as at Central Islip? Longing for children, displacement unto Claude… Are you back at that? These are delaying tactics.

U.D.: Not at all! OK—These are all sorts of delaying tactics. Disgust, absolute nausea with this digging—

T.D.: Stay with it and resolve the Claude, the scientist first lover—Science first, once and for all. Please stay on.

U.D.: I believe it's coming through, but why this excitement at the University Deli? Wasn't Mephistopheles, his jade eyes blazing with intensity, inescapably beckoning again? Through Wiener's writings I saw the ruddy mechanical piano gadgeteer rearing its head again. He calls that type "a gadget worshiper".

From Wiener I can accept that machines multiply and

reproduce, that they have a memory comparable to, if not much better than man's, that they can learn, that they reproduce replicas possibly by a mechanism like that of the transmission of genetic knowledge through the nucleic acids, and that the science of genetics can learn as much from machines as machines can learn from human physiology. God knows if he's not right in all he says.

T.D.: Well, I've certainly gained some years and am wiser now than the recalcitrant youngster who heard the same from Claude. You felt so uncomfortable with the same knowledge which he was trying to impart to you nearly thirty years ahead of his time.

U.D.: That's not it. The intuition of Mephistopheles on the turnstile, the painting I made of him…

T.D.: Don't be silly, you old idiot! You're probably worse than ever in your irrationality, despite all the years of experience you proudly claim to people at this stage as your "calling card". Read on and be done with it, once and for all.

U.D.: I'm too excited. The chocolate is giving me a hard time.

T.D.: Get rid of it and go on with this business!

U.D.: I'm excited as though I am on the brink of a breakthrough, and now of all things, as always since early adolescence, and all throughout my adult years, I'm getting a bad headache. I must stop for awhile.

T.D.: Get on with it, at least with the sentence from Wiener.

U.D.: A sentence?…

"… the use of great powers for base purposes will constitute the full moral equivalent of Sorcery and Simony… Power and the search thereof can assume many a garb… Mephistopheles…

Of their devotees many regard with impatience the limitations of man and woman—their undependability—unpredictability."

T.D.:He's talking about the regimented Russians, you idiot!

U.D.: Did I find Mephistopheles in Goethe's poem "The Sorcerer's Apprentice"? No, just allusions. I'm calmer. I believe I've been exorcized.

T.D.: How? You're a jilted lover.

U.D.: No! That's not it. The essential points from Wiener I must remember now with respect to the Claude-Mephistopheles imagery are the following: His need to avoid personal involvement and his need to avoid the rejections by others which he regarded as all-destructive. This encouraged a certain autism, a solipsism of feelings early in life in one so gifted. His earliest avoidance motivation? The beloved—her hurtful games of unpredictability and rejection?

T.D.: Too simple.

U.D.: Not really. Hypersensitivity goes hand in hand with hyper-intelligence. The controls are set higher in every respect.

T.D.: Every respect? Now what does that mean? That's a useless message.

U.D.: It's not informative enough?

T.D.: Double talk, *nichts, rien.*

U.D.: I still say they perceive more intensely whatever message they receive, and therefore 'Bad Mama' has a greater impact. 'Good Mama', too. Rosen says the same in his "Direct Analysis." Harold Searles says it too, when he refers to the inanimate world in which the baby lives. He says that the inanimate world can be perceived as sweet happiness in dependence, and it can leave a longing which many of us glimpse again later in life. Our attachment to a piece of wood, the sky, the stars… Machines and Computers are the inanimate world more securely remembered later on. The inanimate world of machines for instance is perceived as kind and good versus the animal world. Insatiability might result from feelings of having been poorly, not sufficiently loved. LOOK, Maria, LOOK, MARIEKE, LOOK! Don Juanism (whose?) will do as a last victory over early feelings of rejection.

T.D.: If he lies comfortably in his hammock near the Mystic River and has refused offers to outdo Mephistopheles, this might be due to wisdom he has gained over time. The greatest wisdom under the circumstances. Why the hell do you doubt this, bitter Maria?

U.D.: They say he's the greatest, the most wonderful father imaginable. A few more comments and I'm done.

I hear winds howling. I'm going to take a walk to Willard Straight Hall. Perhaps they'll play the Carlos song: "Longfellow's Serenade". A hymn of love, the agony and ecstasy over the dying and resurgent God. It is snowing heavily now. The Olin Tower clock shows quarter past two in the morning; and as usual, I find it difficult to let go. I have spent some time today reading Rosen on Rosen, about his direct psychoanalytic therapy with psychotics. The verbal expression of visual representations in dream states is of course intriguing. He is touching, and sounds good and real. There are indications presently that psychopharmacology will help greatly with the sorting out job that absolutely needs to be done on psychosis.

I have been working, attempting to put this section of Free Association together. It demands a new frame of mind. There seems at present much 'Einstellung'(a term derived from Gestalt Psychology—not Gestalt Therapy—meaning mental after-images of an interfering nature) from previous explorations. A nostalgia for introspection remains. It has only been one day since I just about resolved, had greater insight into, lived out the dream of Mephistopheles-Claude.

Let is snow, let it snow all night! People around these parts know their way around the slippery, white cotton. To the students here at Cornell University, it must announce the forthcoming exams and then their liberation for more than a month. There seems to be a holiday spirit as of today, Chanukah began yesterday, Christmas is forthcoming. My daughter received her ticket to Alaska and our son ought to be on his way later today to Anchorage. They are to visit their father. I saw a poem of ecstasy on the TV today. A young Russian gymnast by the name of Olga Korbut, an Olympic gold medal winner—Perfect! Then I saw a Canadian by the name of Crankshaw, on ice skates. He was as graceful, maybe more so, than Nureyev. True greatness is indisputable; only the sick at heart can avoid recognizing it.

I am thinking of the state of self-centeredness brought about by emotional illness. What Albert Ellis says of those afflicted by sickness of the mind and soul I found to be true. It also holds for all of us when we're exceptionally upset for any period of time. He calls them (us) "the worst whiners… they whine and whine and cry at the drop of a hat… they're sickeningly, easily the greatest bores on earth… " Above all, though they smart and hurt, they carry the heavy carapace of shallowness, an anesthesia towards other people's feelings, and a callousness towards any infringement by the impinging outer world. The latter has sublime joy to offer. What a shame to have to lose a single day… CARPE DIEM!

With pounding heart, mouth parchment dry, I reread a good part of the "Free Associations". All this material as a result of the dream: Claude as Mephistopheles! I nearly collapsed with the sadness of it all, then felt shocked into a state of sleep.

Dreamed (a whiff remains) of CLOTHES: delightfully warm and colorful, unobtrusive in their fashionable lines…

These pages must be filed chronologically as they came about. The imagery has a particular systole, followed by its own diastole, a pulsing quality which should not be tampered with.

Why then and what did he, Claude, hang on to? Had I contaminated him in the end? Was he as convinced in reality as I was that there was something not right in what we did? How puritanical was he? Possibly as much as I was, though he tried to convince himself and me of the opposite. Though he called me his shining light, I might have been the shadow of his past. Who then left whom? Does it matter now? Still, the truth was that I left. The abandonment took place as a result of my inability to share in taking the risk with him. Risks terrorized and mistakes were destructive. One way to diminish the risk of hurt is to stay away from people. Machines do not talk back; they feel no power, no joy in destroying the dreams of men and women.

Bad human reasoning and error will multiply of themselves, but a computer error may correct itself. The essence of Claude's communications to me while I visited him in his home that last time consisted of "Look!, I, and all of my friends, have reached the highest rung of the ladder… " The strongest points I made about myself: "Nothing has turned out as I thought it would. My second marriage is giving me a lot of grief, my children are far away and motherhood is now getting messed up too. I have no money, and I don't care for the present". There was one sour note in his message of success (a passing stage in his life at the time?): he expressed the belief that "Nothing new had been created for many years. Not in music either—nothing new that was worthwhile." How could he say a thing like that? Even in Jazz music I had heard a band in California that played a sort of Arabic-Oriental beat, and extremely well at that! He asked who they were, and as usual I couldn't remember the name. How could he say that about science? I told him I didn't feel that way at all in my field. We were on the verge of breakthroughs. (We'd mistakenly felt that way for over half a century!) I asked what he had done lately in science that was new. His wife exclaimed, "Ouch! That is one below the belt." I certainly had not meant it that way. He was fascinated with the acquisition of wealth and applied his knowledge from other fields to speculation in the field of finance. It seemed odd, inasmuch as to me it implied taking great risks. But he told me emphatically that he did not think this was true, for he considered it a gamble only if you did not know what you were doing. At the same time he seemed to be showing strong rebellion against men in his field by not getting involved beyond the required essentials. I thought he was saying, "I won't, not a ruddy thing anymore…". And there I felt somehow that he was more than right and finally deserved his peace of mind. He also appeared to spend a lot of time training his children to think scientifically, and was probably highly successful in this. In his new "hobby" (finances) he was like a Faustian disciple, making gold out of brain matter. Is this Faust or Mephistopheles? It depends on the perspective. He has gone from suffering angel, masterminding eccentric machinery as an independent demon, to the wonder boy of Alphonse Daudet's "Letters From My Windmill", who discovers he has gold in his brain which at first he can produce at will,(with what gigantic concentration and effort—not ever more than passingly spoken of?) only to find eventually it has diminished to less than a trickle. Will there be some left in the end for his own salvation? Wiener seemed to believe that to apply one's godly endowments to one's own advantage was of the nature of sorcery, Mephistophelian... Who is to say?

This morning I left the Cornell Campus, possibly for the last time as a resident typist of my own notes, a *"bouquinist"* dreamer. While still on College Avenue, I returned once more to the record store where months earlier I had looked for some of the blues records Claude and I used to love. I found there instead a worthwhile collection of originals of Brel's sung poetry. I asked in parting whether they had by any chance found any of the records of Teddy Grace singing the blues? A conscientious student looked up my request from three months earlier. He checked the catalogues again with as little success as his predecessor. The fellow was tall and very well built, probably in his mid-twenties, and appeared to be sharp minded and sensitive. He wore an Indian headband round his long, fine reddish-blond frizzy hair. As I left, I said with a sigh, "Well, perhaps they'll reprint her original Decca records or else I'll ask my old-time friend who has the originals to lend them to me again."

He suggested in seriousness as he bade me good-bye: "You might have to learn to appreciate some of the newer blues singers instead... " I was startled, for I realized that unknowingly he had responded with his feelings to my total situation. He had made the main point very clear to me, and I thanked him. Let the past rest resolved—let others say Amen.

Twenty-five Years Later: Women's Sequential Stages

Now, it is again 25 years later. I have lost my daughter. She died recently from an atrociously sudden death after struggling for 10 years to keep her dignity intact against the ravages of a severe and seemingly unending war with her artistic temperament and moods. Of her great art as a friend from Antwerp expressed his regrets: "There won't be anymore!"

Claude too, has died, after having slipped away over the span of long years from an incapacitating brain disease which devastatingly attacked his memory.

My own menopausal upheavals are behind me. I believe the writings which saw me through are presently as helpful as they were 25 years ago, when I wanted to impress on others the help one receives through graphotherapy.

During her life's journey the modern woman has lately been met by greater opportunities around the time of her middle years. This did not come about as clearly, nor at all as frequently in the past. One admires the choices a woman of today has in view of being able to live through *sequential stages* in her life. We believe this has contributed to greater contentment for her and has advanced the cause of a greater society. The educated woman of our time expects better health throughout an increasingly prolonged life-span. While during the years of nesting, marriage, and motherhood she may have had to interrupt her studies, even her profession, today, she may realistically expect to resume her career either where she left off, or consider new endeavors when she joins or rejoins the out-of-home workforce. The sequence of stages by which women seem able to live nowadays has led their near middle aged spouses/companions to wonder WHAT NOW?

A passenger on a plane to California, seated next to me, a few days ago, in December of '03 had just been to Washington as part of his University's Professorial Program. He wanted to know why his wife had gone to work full time when their children were in elementary school, then insisted on staying home almost full-time when they were in high school. She told him, he said with some puzzlement, those were the dangerous years, when they needed her home more, and now that both their children were College bound, she thought she would look around and see what she might have to learn anew to get back to the work she had originally prepared for when she herself was in College. This same man's sister-in-law, in her late 30's and childless, had gone back to school to study medicine, had done very well, and was now able to join her husband in medical missionary work, the two of them now volunteering together every six months to serve in medically under-developed parts of the world.

Twenty-five years ago, when I taught my students at our local University about Psychoanalysis through the Women's Studies Dept as part of the Medical Clinical Campus programs, I had them practice with guided free-associative writing, in order that they might learn what graphotherapy could offer as a means of self-analysis. Their self-revealing essays astounded me not only because of the beauty of the writing, but also by what I considered their unrealistic expectations about the future. They thought they could have it all: a full career, the husband of their dreams, an ideal house filled with many children. How in heaven's name did they think this would come about? At least in this day and age, they can realistically expect to reach many of their original goals as they follow the dictates of the changes experienced during the sequential stages in their lives.

When menopausal changes set in, when peri-menopausal upheavals tug at women, their spouses, mainly influenced, it would seem, by her changes and *her* renewed aspirations for self-expression, tend to change accordingly. From close observation by sociologists and therapists, it would appear that under normal circumstances she is the earlier and original instigator. As he follows the dictates of her changes he too undergoes a type of metamorphosis, and may become the more gentle and supportive of the two.

Claude & Maria, 1944. Provincetown, Mass.

To Maria
With love and kisses
With curses and hisses
Claude
Provincetown, Sept 9, 1944

Claude's Inscription to "The Key to Finnegan's Wake"

WWII and its Secrets

When Claude died, I read many of the admiring and often humorous eulogies which were published about him in the scientific press. Some time afterward I came across the more personal remembrances written about the work he did while employed during WWII. Ultimately, I came to realize how deeply he had felt oppressed by the secrecy demanded of him at the time. He detested the work, as I was well made aware of, but in addition, there was the secrecy factor about what his assignments were about. It placed a pall on his social relations and certainly affected his most intimate relationships: Ours, his and mine, that is, became painfully distorted by the demands for silence that weighed heavily on him. It insidiously gnawed at the trust and faith in one another that we were both thirsting for at that very time in our lives.

We never spoke of this for he was not at liberty to share these burdens with me. Not long ago, I came upon a more extensive and thorough biography of Claude which mentioned, in passing, an important mathematician named Hermann W., who had assigned and supervised some of Claude's secret work during WWII.

This at once evoked a remembrance of our first escapade together: a trip to Provincetown, Mass, in the summertime. We traveled by bus from New York City. It was to be his first vacation in a wretchedly long while. I was as thrilled as he was, but also much troubled by what unconventional liberties I knew

I was taking for love's sake. During a small excursion we found ourselves in a crowd near the harbor, on the main pedestrian thoroughfare that led to the idyllic flat he'd found for us on a nearby wharf. Unexpectedly, we ran into a French student from the Sorbonne University in Exile, which we were both attending at the time in Manhattan. She was a Miss W., a most pleasant young woman, who said eagerly in French to me that she would like to join us. She wanted to introduce us to her father; they had just arrived by boat on the Cape. Claude and I came upon them as we pushed our bicycles along, one of my arms around his waist, his around mine, as was our custom.

Both she and I couldn't help but notice the about face suddenly taken by her father Dr Hermann W., nor the haunted look in his eyes as he looked at Claude and I and his daughter and then immediately turned away from us. Claude seemed to follow his example as he abruptly turned away from Dr. W. and his daughter.

I felt uneasy, wondering about what I'd seen. I was not certain, either, that I wanted Miss W. or anyone else at the school to know I'd gone away with Claude.

Claude denied to me he knew Miss W.'s father and even denied that it had been rude to leave them behind so suddenly. The episode created both sadness and havoc between us. He insisted on going that same afternoon to the telegraph office. He emerged from there with a long telegram addressed to me, the content of which was written entirely in code. I couldn't decipher a single word of it without his timidly transmitted translation, word by word, poetic meaning by poetic meaning. It was a cryptogram, he said tentatively. I'd never heard of one before.

This too became oddly troublesome for me and it finally

made me insist that we must stay more distant from one another during the time left to us of that day. We quarreled that night. I had never seen him, or any other man, cry. His sobs were heartfelt. They were deeply wrenching.

This was but one episode—among many others—which left me wounded in the end by guilt. It added to what the murderously uprooting, burning fields of Europe's World War II, had brought about. I finally understood that in addition to the unending worldwide repercussions of that war, there was the personal injury, inflicted on as great a man as Claude, and on me, his friend who though unable to share in his burdens, remained enamored of him for life.

Conducting self-analysis using Graphotherapy: Principles and Application

In the dialogues held throughout the preceding Free Associations a moral repositioning was achieved in the end. One's persona and one's defensible convictions are placed as though on one side of a delicate scale. On the opposite side there are packets of previously unanalyzed material. None of the singing joy experienced during moments of exuberance, nor the ecstasy of healthy group interaction in our immediate Antwerp circle asked to be viewed here. Where does the delight of feeling so well in one's sturdy skin appear? Why did I have to keep digging to find out where I stood in comparison to others in elementary school? Clearly I did not care then. The realization of its importance came later, when I was alone, away from the group. In an esoteric, idiomatically babbling subset of a minority group as ours was, socialization into a larger group is preceded by competitive comparisons within the group itself. This leads eventually to a desire to keep up, not to be left out, or behind. The climbing out of a subset into the light of day involves an optimal effort against an intense ambivalence of conviction, against a clinging suspicion that change is SINFUL, versus a will toward growth, whereby change is GODLY.

In the Free Associations the material did not give way to sudden conscious insights. Knowledge came through a slowly unfolding process, through a step-by-step unveiling which preceded the all important understanding of others within their own selves. I found the unconscious expresses itself through writing with a certain cadence of reoccurring allusions. One hears minor themes at first and they bear an odd resemblance. One realizes finally that they were introductions to a major theme—another way of believing—a new way of feeling, of seeing, of listening. When the contradictory facets of one's personality mosaic form an understandable totality at last, it is wonderful to learn that one will not die a complete idiot! The main problem of resolving an existential message received through a dream about an obsessive first love became one consisting in reality of variegated smaller problems (strikingly numerous stones of different shapes and hues.) The mosaic puzzle then needs to be reunified into a much larger insight about the self. Every realistic breakthrough implies the death of an illusion. Giving up the love of this strongest first attachment implied reliving the abandonment through death of the father. Lack of recognition and giving due recognition, the guilt and pain of abandonment and of abandoning—one reflecting the other. In retrospect, when Mephistopheles emerges on the revolving stage of the dream as Lucifer, illuminating, though shrouded in darkness, as unscrupulous and destructive, though annihilated by guilt, forbidding though forbidden, the gliding stage in the dream revealed my duality far more strikingly than Claude's. Revelation of the tension of opposites in the nature of one's unconscious emerged as function of the character traits which were projected unto the beloved in the dream.

From the numerous examples of self-analysis through free-associative writing, it would seem quite clear that to be successful, this type of self-exam still demands involvement and time for the *working through* of what has emerged. One is reminded of Freud's admonition to a young American analyzand to please get to the labor of "*ein bisschen durcharbeiten Herr Doctor!*" The latter wrote about his analysis with Freud in which he described his disorientation and the obstacles to understanding what Freud meant till he was well ready to receive its meaning.

In order to learn and practice short duration techniques which help to induce relaxation before one begins to write by expressing oneself in a self-searching manner there is a world of relaxation exercises to choose from. One might want to consult a more recently written text of 2002, fetchingly named "The Writing Cure" (Ed. S. Lepore). In its "Seasons of Life" appendix one may find an illustration of six consecutive writing periods with step by step exercises to facilitate the induction of relaxation before one begins to write.

At the University from 1981 onward, my students were encouraged throughout the semester to experiment with *Graphotherapy*. Their course in the Women's Study Department consisted of an introduction to the fundamentals of Psychoanalysis. Through expressing themselves by writing free-associatively they had an immediate experience about its relevance and alleviating nature.

I found it helpful in the Classroom to begin *Graphotherapy exercises by encouraging them to take deep and then deeper breaths— to feel the breath from deep within one's self as it passes through one's mouth, gently as it flows over one's lips when you breathe out. When given the quiet time to do so—over a span of about an hour one is advised to visualize as Edith Wharton did in "The Fullness of Life" where she wrote she "sometimes thought a woman's nature is like a great house full of rooms ", where one is advised now to open doors to them, to begin say with the hallway, say in one's parent's home : to open the door to the entrance hallway—the hall through which all must pass—through the great passageway—To eventually direct oneself to one's parents' room. To write about what one is reminded of. What sort of feeling do you experience in this atmosphere? And lastly, turn the knob and open the door which might lead to your very own corner. Write and make certain you remember to leave the censorship behind. It is fine to sound childish. Just write what you are reminded of, and if you can, what it feels like. Express yourself through writing, and try to remember what it was like for you, you who may one day reach the soul who will forever inhabit you.*

ACKNOWLEDGMENTS

In the original writing of this book, which remained for very long in silent gestation, I received substantial assistance from Mrs. Marguerite Leighton, an editor and English teacher, who was unique in her light touch and in her implied respect for people's freedom and personal follies. With great luck, 25 years later, she helped me again with gentle suggestions and modifications to ungrammatical accentuations – what with the same old tongue twisting phrases which had managed to reappear in this text! How can I thank her enough?

I also want to express my sincere gratitude for the understanding, thoughtful, and imaginative staff of the New Media Resource Center of Binghamton University's Computer Center. They rescued the old, and by far larger, manuscript from oblivion by diligently scanning it into a new and workable form, as well as bringing truly ancient photographs back for viewing.

I must also thank the staff of Binghamton University's Publishing Department for offering to print this text. I did not think I had the time to wait the required period at this late stage in my life when one cannot trust one's powers to last unaffected in both one's capabilities of recollection and physical endurance. I am deeply appreciative to Professor Ken Lindsay and his inspirational wife Christine, for reading many parts of this book. Ken, The Prof., for many years Chairman of the Art Department of Binghamton University, was highly supportive by his practiced wisdom and by extending as much as day-to-day encouragement.

I also want to thank my son Rex, for being the Prince of can-do, and for keeping me healthier through his meticulous medical advice while far away. He has succeeded time and again to help by his exceptional largesse of spirit and warm and generous heart.

But my first and last debts are to my daughter Ariele, on whom I relied for her artist's illustrations, help, and encouragement during the early versions of this work. She gave me her fine editorial advice and assisted me with her poetic sense of a direct language in English. I often felt she had given me my life back as only one's lively and intense relationship with one's daughter can. If only I could have saved her still young life for her!

ABOUT THE AUTHOR

Maria Moulton-Barrett, M.D. has practiced Medicine through the application of Psychiatry and Psychoanalysis for some 50 years (!). She was trained in Psychoanalysis as a student of Karen Horney in New York City at the New School (then named The New School for Social Research), where she studied with the Gestalt Psychologists Max Wertheimer and Wolfgang Koehler, and with the anthropologist Claude Lévy-Strauss. She was in training analysis with Dr Charles Baudouin while she studied for her medical degree, in Geneva, Switzerland.

She interned at French Hospital and worked at the L.I. Home, in N.Y. as a psychiatrist and then proceeded to work for years for the New York State Mental Hygiene Department's State Hospital system. In 1965 she was finally able to establish, until recently, a private practice in psychiatry in Binghamton, NY, a Central NY community, usually referred to as part of Upstate New York.

She was able to contribute to the training in Psychiatry of Syracuse University's medical students. At Binghamton University's Women's Study Department she offered undergraduates an immediate experience in the practice of Psychoanalysis. She taught them certain aspects of its history and application by writing through Graphotherapy, finding that this type of writing is on the whole an original contribution to ways of exploring the unconscious in search of one's truer self.

Printed in the United States
By Bookmasters